pokpok

ANDY RICKER
with JJ Goode

Food and Stories from the Streets,
Homes, and Roadside Restaurants
of Thailand

PHOTOGRAPHY BY
Austin Bush

TEN SPEED PRESS
Berkeley

contents

foreword
by David Thompson

"One more plate of *laap*—please, Andy," was my plea. I needed more. I had just finished a plate of this Northern Thai dish of chopped meat (pork, in this instance) mixed with spices and herbs. I have eaten *laap* many times before—it is a regional classic. However, this rendition was irresistible. The minced pork was rich and smoky, the spices bitter and tangy, the herbs enticingly aromatic. The combination of all these flavors left a wonderful taste that lingered long after I'd finished my last bite. I simply just had to order a second plate.

I confess I was surprised by how good it was; really, it had no right to be so delicious. After all, I was sitting in Portland, Oregon—a far, far cry from Chiang Mai, the Northern Thai city that is this dish's home.

I guess I shouldn't have been astonished. Andy may have opened his first Pok Pok restaurant in Portland, but the food he cooks has deep roots in Thailand. It might seem strange that this six-foot-tall Vermonter is cooking Northern Thai food so well, until you understand Andy's love for the Thais, their cuisine, and in particular the hazy mountainous province of Chiang Mai. Andy makes regular visits to Thailand, where he trawls the markets—watching, asking questions, and collecting recipes. He chats engagingly with local cooks, who share with him tips and techniques—but he is also a keen observer, and gets ideas and knowledge from furtively watching other, unsuspecting cooks. Either way, by whatever means, Andy gets the goods.

Whenever Andy comes to Thailand, I see him in Bangkok, where I live, and occasionally we travel together up-country. Accompanying Andy as he pursues his culinary quarry can be exhausting. He moves quickly from shop to shop, market to market, or village to village with nary a regard for his fellow travelers. He walks past the stalls that don't pass muster, refusing to stop, while those of us in his wake bleat plaintively, wanting to eat, looking longingly at dishes he dismisses and leaves untouched. Mr. Ricker demands the best and thus he commands my respect, even if I do often end up hungry, tired, and sulky.

Andy has turned his not being Thai into an advantage. He is not limited by an inherent belief, as many Thais are, that his mother's is the best and the only way to cook. His approach is much broader and more encompassing; he casts his culinary net wider, across all of Northern Thailand and its verdant and fertile fields.

Andy first backpacked through Asia and landed in Thailand in 1987, around the time I was making those same laps. I am surprised I didn't run into him. Although, given the similarity of our quests, our mutual love for Thailand, and our crazy partying ways, it's quite possible we did. . . .

Andy's moment of culinary epiphany came over a mushroom. Mine was over a serpent head fish, clearly demonstrating that we can't choose our moments. The objects of our inspiration—some fungi and a fish, respectively—might seem silly, but in the end, they prompted both of us to change the course of our lives, including how we eat and cook.

I still recall that sour orange curry of serpent head fish, tart with tamarind leaves, plump with flavor. The seasoning, tastes, and textures of that curry transformed my understanding of Thai food. From then on I was hooked.

I moved to Bangkok to learn about the city's remarkable cuisine, regal past, and sophisticated tastes, opening a few swank restaurants in the process. Meanwhile, Andy was researching up-country, eating his way through the north of Thailand. Later he opened the first Pok Pok restaurant in Portland on a maxed-out credit card, a mortgage, and with little capital. In the decade since then, he has established himself as an important voice in Thai cooking and an emissary of Northern Thai food internationally.

I remember working with Andy in both New York City and Portland and being amazed at his rather informal approach to cooking, kitchens, and restaurants. His very first restaurant was built out of his kitchen and partially demolished house, the food served through a window onto his porch and into the backyard—much like some small countryside restaurant in Thailand. You see, I come from the dainty world of fine dining, where certain things—such as grilling over charcoal in smoky forty-four-gallon drums, backyard coconut pressing, drinking beer on the job out of glass jars, fermenting mustard greens on the roof, and more beer drinking—were simply not done (unfortunately). But the casual appearance of Andy's restaurants belies the rigorous, ambitious cooking that happens in his kitchens. He is obsessed with making the very best food he can. I admire the canny way he doctors his lime juice

to approximate the taste of lime juice in Thailand, the resourceful way he finds and secures Thai produce, and his faithful adherence to Thai recipes, techniques, and tastes. The restaurants may not look terribly fancy, but inside, Andy and his Pok Pok crew are complete perfectionists, constantly adjusting and tinkering with their recipes to ensure everything is right.

Andy has almost singlehandedly created a market for regional Thai cuisine in the United States. Such food was practically unknown in the US before Pok Pok, but now, many of the dishes he cooks are the objects of cultlike devotion. For proof of his swashbuckling success, simply observe the lines that wind down the street outside of the Pok Pok restaurants. People clamor for his food—a style of cooking that they didn't know existed before 2005. One excellent example is that delectable pork *laap*, which was as lip-smackingly good as any version I have found in Thailand.

While eagerly waiting for my second plate, I looked across our table—with its now-empty plates of grilled sausages, noodle salads, soups, curries, and chili dips— to the other tables of equally replete and happy diners. I couldn't help but wonder, what would this damned skillful cook do next?

Well, you're now holding Andy's latest project: the *Pok Pok* cookbook. In it, Andy chronicles Chiang Mai's wide-ranging culinary repertoire—including my longed-for pork *laap*, a sour orange curry quite similar to the one that first enthralled me so many years ago, and many other Northern dishes. This book is the product of years and years of research, practice, and experience, and clearly demonstrates why Andy and Pok Pok are so successful: great food; honest, practical advice and guidance; and a sincere desire to please without compromising the integrity of the cuisine. It's a winning recipe.

introduction

I'm staying with my friend Sunny in the village of Ban Pa Du. One night, we decide to take his pickup truck to the city of Chiang Mai to scout out a restaurant specializing in the blackish jumble of minced meat called *laap meuang*. But on the way there, I spot an open-air restaurant with a ton of motorcycles parked out front, people milling around, and no signs written in English—all the hallmarks of a place worthy of a stop. I ask Sunny what it's all about. "Ah, very old-style food," he says. By the time I finish chiding him for never having told me about this place, we've pulled over.

It's a typical roadside spot—a dusty lot scattered with tables and benches crudely nailed together, plastic stools sunk into the dirt, and a roof fashioned from teak tree leaves. Soft light comes from bare bulbs. It's hot, so we start pounding Leo beers, a kind of Miller High Life equivalent, poured into ice-filled glasses. Our food starts coming out. After a few bites, Sunny and I look at each other as if to say, *Holy shit, this is good*. We're eating pig brain mixed with curry paste and lime leaf, then wrapped in banana leaf; charred, chewy hunks of pig teat; and sour sausage—essentially pork mixed with rice and left to ferment in the heavy heat. It's awesome.

I start chatting with the guy who runs the place with his family. I learn that their day of prepping, pounding, and frying begins at 5 a.m. The food is all made in a rudimentary outdoor kitchen—a couple grills and outdoor stoves. They open for business in the midafternoon, serve food until midnight, then get up and do it all again. Seven days a week. He tells me that he's been doing this, in the same dirt patch, for eleven years. He's forty-five years old, tops. And I can tell by the way his young daughter is charming the crowd that she'll probably end up doing the same.

This is the Thailand I know. I've been traveling there for almost two decades, and I've fallen for the country, the people, and food that bears no resemblance to the pick-a-protein rainbow curries or sweet piles of *phat thai* that I'd wolfed down in restaurants in the US.

So seven years back, I decided to open a takeout-only shack in Portland, Oregon, devoted to the revelatory grub I'd found on the streets of Bangkok, markets in Loei, and homes in Chiang Mai. Friends warned me that no one would want to eat lemongrass-stuffed game hens and bowls of *khao soi*, Chiang Mai's famous curried noodle dish, even though I modified the rotisseries just as they do in Thailand and pressed the coconut milk myself. But I figured at least a few people would, and that would be enough for me. Today I run four restaurants in Portland and two in New York City, all serving food you'd be hard-pressed to find outside of Southeast Asia.

* * *

I remember the moment everything changed.

More than a decade before Pok Pok was even a glimmer in my eye, I'd been living in New Zealand and

1

Australia, doing odd jobs—I picked pumpkins and packed kiwis, I DJed, I painted houses, I cooked at restaurants—when I decided to backpack up through Singapore and Malaysia. I ended up on a stunning group of islands on the east coast in Southern Thailand. I ate well. I loved the food. But my experience was similar to that of most tourists—I was eating better versions of the stuff I'd had back home. Eventually, I wound up in Portland. It wasn't until four years after my first trip that I returned to Thailand and had my revelation.

I was staying in Chiang Mai with my friend Chris and his wife, Lakhana, a village woman steeped in the local culture. They took me to a restaurant that specialized in Northern Thai food. I didn't even know there was such a thing as Northern Thai food. It was a sweltering April. At that time of year, Thais forage for *het thawp*, a slightly bitter puffball-like mushroom, which came to us floating in a soupy, herbaceous "curry." I dipped my spoon and tasted. It was like seeing an entirely new color. It was nothing like anything I had eaten before. It was unbelievably good.

From then on, my eyes were open. On every street corner, I saw people eating dishes I'd never even heard of. There was *yen ta fo*, noodles and fish cakes floating in soup tinted pink from fermented bean curd. There was *kuaytiaw reua*, or boat noodles, so named because the bowls of dark, murky broth, fragrant with cinnamon and star anise, were once sold from the vessels floating in the canals and rivers of Central Thailand. There were simple relishes—*naam phrik* and *lon*—that served as fiery or funky dips for boiled vegetables, otherworldly herbs, and crunchy curls of pork crackling.

Occasionally, I found a dish whose name I recognized, but what I got when I ordered it was something almost unrecognizable. Hunched on a way-too-small plastic stool in Chiang Mai, I ordered *laap*, expecting the pleasant, lime-spiked chopped-meat salad I'd eaten all my life in Portland and New York City and LA. Instead, the stuff that arrived was fragrant, bitter, black—and wonderful. At the time, I could barely keep track of what I was eating. All I knew was that if this is what Thais eat, then I wanted to eat it, too.

Back in the States, my obsession with Thailand made me hard to hire, because every winter, I'd have to quit my job and go back. That's when I decided to take up house painting full-time, after spending much of my working life in restaurants. It gave me the flexibility to spend months at a time in Thailand. I took language lessons. My eating became more systematic. I'd taste something, get obsessed with it, and eat it everywhere I could. So much of the food there is cooked outdoors, in plain sight, so I watched the food being made. I talked my way into the homes of friends, and friends of

friends. I'd hang out with street vendors, picking their brains over glasses of rice whiskey. Gradually, I learned to cook the dishes I loved most, to tweak them and tweak them until they tasted just like they did at my favorite spots. *Someday I'll open a restaurant*, I thought. *Americans need to know this food.*

At this point, I'd been painting houses for eight years straight. When I'd go to work, I'd just stare at the unpainted walls. I could barely bring myself to pick up a brush. I wanted to open a restaurant, but at this rate, I never would. Then I thought about my friend Ethan.

Ethan is a friend from Vermont, where I grew up. He lives in Austin, Texas, and we called the four-room shack where he lived at the time the Vermont Embassy, because that's where everyone from Vermont crashed when they came to town, sometimes twenty of us at a time. Once I was down there visiting and noticed a leak under his bathroom sink. I called him in and suggested a few stop-gap repairs. He took one look, and yanked the leaky pipe out of the wall. I was shocked. We could've stopped the leak. But he said something I'll never forget: "Now it's completely broken. Now, it'll have to get fixed the right way."

When I got back to Portland, I started applying the Ethan Method of getting things done. I knocked down walls, smashed windows, and threw everything into the backyard. I made my home unlivable. That way, I had to fix it up. I spent three years doing just that. Then I took out another mortgage. My plan was to use the proceeds to open a restaurant.

I ultimately decided I'd serve a limited menu of simple dishes I wished I could find in the States, and go from there. I knew one thing for sure: I wouldn't call the place a Thai restaurant. If I did, people would show up expecting *phat thai* and cashew chicken.

The property that caught my eye, on a particularly unsightly stretch of SE Division Street, was owned by an elderly Japanese couple—probably the thriftiest people I've ever encountered. The house and shack hadn't seen any major improvement since about 1935. There was an ancient, cracked deep fryer. There was an antique gas stove, the kind with cast-iron legs that looked like it should be burning wood in some pioneer's farmhouse. I don't even know how they found it. Yet there was an exhaust hood in the basement. And there was a stainless steel triple-sink—the kind you'd get for $39.99 at Home Depot. I would have an operational—barely, but still—kitchen, and under the city's regulations, it would be grandfathered in as a commercial restaurant. I could start cooking immediately.

So I got to work on the glamorous chef stuff—you know, plumbing the shack, adding electrical service, and tackling a three-day-long jack-hammering project to break through an eighteen-inch concrete slab. I finally opened the takeout-only shack with a dinky eight-item menu—including rotisserie chickens, a few papaya salad permutations, pork *sateh*, and *khao soi*—and one employee—my buddy Ike from Vietnam. I named it Pok Pok, after the sound a pestle makes when it strikes a clay mortar as you make papaya salad. I told a few friends to come by and hoped for the best. Within six months, there was a line snaking down the driveway to Division Street. I couldn't believe it. Customers embraced the food with so much fervor that you'd think I was serving cupcakes.

Now, I'd worked in enough restaurants to know that a busy restaurant doesn't mean a profitable one. Sure enough, a year later, despite the success of the shack, I was broke. More than broke. I had maxed out about six credit cards in the process of building out the rest of the house into a proper restaurant. I fielded menacing calls from creditors. I'd broken every rule there is about opening a restaurant: I'd set up shop in an undeveloped neighborhood. I'd put up my house as collateral. I wrote checks blindly. My mom had to loan me seven thousand dollars that she couldn't afford so I could make my first payroll. All this to serve food not many Portlanders had ever heard of.

Finally I opened the sit-down version of Pok Pok. In the winter. I had to sell my house, moving from one cheap rental to another, even living for a while in what would later become Pok Pok's upstairs dining room. Equipment started breaking; employees weren't making money and were losing faith. When it seemed like the jig was up, *The Oregonian* named Pok Pok "Restaurant of the Year." Business tripled. By the end of the year, I was debt-free and Pok Pok was packed every day.

* * *

I've accidentally spent the last ten years preparing to write this book. It is, I suppose, the Pok Pok cookbook. It's a collection of recipes from the restaurant, but it also includes food that reflects some of my fondest memories and moments of discovery before and since that day in November, 2005, when the shack's window first opened.

One thing that it's definitely *not* is a Thai cookbook, in part because Pok Pok is not an exclusively Thai restaurant but also because Thailand is a vast, diverse country that even after two decades of eating and exploring I still have much to learn about. The range of recipes in this book is severely constrained by my knowledge, experience, and ability. I've included recipes from all over Thailand and other countries to which my early travels took me, though many come from Northern

Thailand, where my first revelation occurred and where I've had many since.

After people eat at Pok Pok, they often assume I have an army of Thai women in my kitchen pounding pastes and simmering sauces that they've made since they were girls. Me, the big white guy? I probably just taste whatever they've made and give it the thumbs up. No such luck.

I've researched every one of the dishes we serve at the restaurant. I've tried and failed and tried and failed to make them come close to my favorite versions in Thailand. And I've at last deciphered a recipe, a way to replicate real-deal Thai flavor using ingredients available in the West. But more important, I've figured out a way to communicate the techniques and flavors to my new cooks, who at first think papaya salad is something you'd find in the deli cold case next to the cubed watermelon. Because not so long ago, I was like them (and if I may be so bold, like you): someone who loves Thai food but doesn't know how to cook it.

My hopes for this book are simple: to show you how to cook some of the dishes that made me fall for Thai food and to provide a sense of place—context for a country, culture, and cuisine that can be so inscrutable to an outsider, which I once was and in many ways still am.

This book is a tribute to the cooks of Thailand. Which leads me to disclaimer number one: I'm not a chef. I didn't invent this stuff. The food at my restaurants is not my take on Thai food. It isn't inspired by Thai ingredients. I'm not riffing or playfully reinterpreting. There are American chefs who have successfully managed to apply their creativity to the flavors and ingredients of Thailand. Not me. I'm a proud copycat. The recipes in this book are my best approximations of some of my favorite versions of my favorite Thai dishes, which have been created, cooked, and perfected by Thai people.

Disclaimer number two: I am not a trained scholar of Thai food or culture. My knowledge is largely anecdotal, gleaned from twenty years of observing, eating, cooking, wandering, and wondering. There are aspects of Thai life and food that I may never understand. I still learn something new on every trip I take. The more I learn, the more I understand how much I don't know. I heartily recommend that anyone interested in a scholarly English-language paean look up David Thompson, the Australian-born chef of Nahm in Bangkok and the author of several excellent cookbooks, including the incredibly informative tome *Thai Food*. He has learned to read long-defunct Thai script, unearthed long-forgotten recipes, and generally devoted his life's work to the study of Thai history and culture as seen through its cuisine. If this book joins his on your shelf, I'd be thrilled and honored.

I do realize some of you won't cook through every last dish in this book. Some of my favorite cookbooks have sauce-splattered, dog-eared pages. Others are pristine. So another of my goals in writing it is to provide a glimpse of Thai life and culture. I hope the book helps illuminate why the food is the way it is, not from a preponderance of historical facts, but from the ingredients and techniques used to make it, and from observations about where and how it's eaten, from me and from the mouths of some of the characters who have taught me what I know.

These characters, I should mention, are getting older and their knowledge is being threatened with extinction. Many members of the younger generation of Thais no longer want to take over their parents' food stalls or learn the secrets of their grandmothers' bamboo shoot salads. They want to go to college, move to Bangkok, or leave the country. And like kids just about everywhere nowadays, they're eager to eat at KFC. These changes aren't bad or good. They reflect a changing economy that has created new opportunities for young Thais. It is what it is. Many of this book's recipes embody traditions that are rapidly disappearing. Even if you don't cook through the recipe for Northern Thai *laap*, at least it will be on paper. At least there will be a record in English of its existence.

how to use this book

To begin, let me acknowledge my two seemingly conflicting tasks: dispensing with the myths that keep people from making Thai food at home in the first place but also recognizing the effort it entails. You shouldn't be dissuaded by nonsense, but you should know exactly what you're getting into.

First up, two big myths. One: Thai food is too laborious for home cooks. I've eaten too much mind-blowingly good food cooked in ramshackle kitchens with single-burner stoves for this to hold any weight with me. And the casualness of much of the preparation is liberating. When I hire a new cook, I immediately explain that he's not at a high-minded fine-dining place where they serve deep-fried hummingbird with truffle tincture on a tree bark platter. So he should stop thinking like a twenty-year-old culinary student aspiring to a job at Noma or Per Se and start thinking like a forty-five-year-old rice field worker who just opened a food stall. He won't use a $150 knife; he'll have a $4 stainless steel blade. He won't cut carrots into brunoise or slice cucumbers into fettuccine—he'll cut them up into crude bite-size chunks. Cooking this food is relatively straightforward. The hardest part is finding the ingredients.

Two: You can't cook Thai food in the US, because you can't get any of the ingredients. As you might have guessed, I ran into this roadblock when I set about reproducing Northern Thai *laap* in Portland. A lot of ingredients in Thailand, like young tamarind leaves and banana blossoms, are either nearly impossible to find here or dramatically inferior to their Thai counterparts. And since trying to make banana blossom salad without banana blossoms would be like building a brick house without the bricks, I developed a revolutionary

approach: I just don't make banana blossom salad. The recipes in this book embody that same logic—they're dishes you can make with ingredients available in the US without sacrificing the flavor you'd get in Thailand.

Next up, what you're getting into. This isn't *How to Cook Asian Food in Three Easy Steps*. Some recipes are simple, not because I've dumbed them down, but because the recipe in question happens to be simple. Some recipes will take work. You can't just pop over to the corner store for water spinach, galangal, and fresh noodles as you can for broccoli raab, ginger, and spaghetti. You can't just whiz curry paste ingredients in a food processor and expect a truly great result.

With this in mind, I've intentionally limited the number of recipes to about seventy. When I first endeavored to learn about a cuisine with entirely unfamiliar ingredients and techniques, I was overwhelmed by the vastness of what I didn't know. Poring over encyclopedic volumes and then trying to cook, felt like taking Physics 101 and then trying to build a space shuttle. By focusing my efforts, I'll have the room to provide the knowledge and tools you need to make faithful reproductions. If I'm going to ask you to make food that's unlike anything you've ever cooked, the least I can do is guide you through the process.

To that end, I chose to write recipes packed with the details you'll need to successfully make this food, even though that makes the recipes look long. For the more complicated recipes, I've included a plan that makes it clear when certain components or steps can be done days, even weeks or months in advance. I will urge, coax, coerce, and threaten until you make the extra effort it takes to do this food justice. I will be a bit of a dictator, but a benevolent one. That's why some recipes that call for a particularly onerous step or hard-to-find ingredient offer another option—but only if that option truly serves the final product.

INGREDIENTS AND SUBSTITUTIONS

My recipes aim to recreate particular dishes with particular flavors. Some dishes can be replicated at home with concessions to convenience. Some can't. I've provided substitutions only when the result won't suffer. When an ingredient is available in the US, I ask you to buy it. To help, see Ingredients (page 11) and Mail-Order Sources (page 21). When it isn't, I've developed a bunch of hacks—useful tricks for accessing true Thai flavor. This is why, for instance, every recipe that calls for limes recommends taking the extra step to find Key limes, which ape the fragrant, fruity, slightly sweet Thai limes, or calibrating the juice of typical limes with a squeeze of Meyer lemon juice.

Again, many ingredients are not easy to find. My suggestion, then, is to go to the market with a few dishes, not just one, in mind. That way, you're prepared when the fresh ingredient you're after isn't there.

You might wonder whether you can, say, omit the Chinese celery in Yam Khai Dao (Fried egg salad), page 51, or serve the chile sauce meant for a deep-fried whole fish over a simple pan-fried fillet. My hope is that after you cook through this book, after you get comfortable with the ingredients and techniques, you'll be able to make your own calls about which substitutions and shortcuts work and which don't. While this book's primary goal is to help you replicate specific dishes, I wouldn't be upset if it simply helped you make great food at home.

THE LIMITS OF RECIPES

Any cookbook worth its cover price acknowledges that recipes are by nature imperfect. This is especially true for a cookbook like this one, where the recipes rely on less-than-familiar ingredients and techniques. There will be a major learning curve, no question. So here's a caveat before you begin cooking: the dishes in this book might not come out perfectly on your first go. My goal in writing the recipes was to make sure that your first attempt turns out close to perfect at best and really tasty

at worst. My hope is that you cook these dishes more than once, knowing that the results will improve with each attempt.

This next piece of advice may sound obvious, but I've certainly been guilty of not following it myself, so it bears repeating: before you start cooking, read the recipe first. That way you'll know what can or must be done ahead and what to expect as you cook.

SEASONING TO TASTE

One Thai bird chile is eviscerating hot while the next is surprisingly mild. One brand of soy sauce is saltier than another. Recipes can only attempt to account for this. They can guide you toward a desired result, they can get you close. But only you can take the final few steps it takes to get there, so most cookbook authors tell you to season—with salt or lemon—to taste. In Thai cooking, seasoning to taste is particularly important. For vendor fare that's made to order, customers typically request more heat, less sweetness, more tartness, and so on. Most noodle dishes come with things like chile powder, vinegar-soaked chiles, fish sauce, and sugar so diners can tweak the flavor themselves.

If I were new to Thai cooking, and you told me to season Som Tam Lao (Lao/Isaan-style papaya salad), page 40, to taste, I'd probably dump in three times the palm sugar. The dish would taste decent, sure, but it would no longer taste like Lao/Isaan-style papaya salad, which is defined as much by its ingredients as by its flavor profile—sour, salty, and funky, not sweet. The point of these recipes is to take you to a specific place, perhaps somewhere you've never been before. To help, each recipe has a brief description of the proper flavor profile (listed from the most prominent flavors to the least), so at that inevitable point in the recipe process when you must season to taste, you'll at least have some idea of your goal. The stories, I hope, provide some context that will guide you as well. For instance, something that might taste too intense to be eaten by the spoonful might be just right when eaten with sticky rice. It also helps to get to know your raw ingredients, especially ones with which you might not be familiar. So sniff, bite, chew. That way, you'll know how they can affect the final product.

You'll notice that many recipes that ask you to pound a bunch of ingredients into a paste have you make more of this paste than you'll ultimately use. That's intentional. Not only does it avoid the absurdly precise measurements you'd need to come up with exactly the right amount of paste, but it also means you'll have extra in case you think a curry needs more punch.

FORGET WHAT YOU KNOW

A key to successfully cooking unfamiliar food is deny-ing some of your culinary instincts. Western cooks tend to want to brown meat before stewing, cook the meat until it's falling-apart tender, and reduce thin broths to intensely flavored liquids. That's all good when you're making Daniel Boulud's braised shortribs, but not if you're making *jin hoom*. Same goes for the temperature at which food is served. Many recipes in this book are best served not steaming hot but just above room temperature—or, as I like to think of it, at room tem-perature if that room is in steamy Bangkok.

HIGH HEAT, COOKING TIMES, & CO.

I won't travel too far down this rabbit hole. I think it goes without saying that your stove and mine have different definitions of "high" and "low" heat. And that the time estimates each recipe provides for frying paste, cooking meat, and pounding chiles to a powder are approximate—dependent on stoves, pans, and individ-ual cooks. Treat them as guidelines. Pay closer attention to the descriptions of what things should look, smell, and taste like. Understand that though my goal in writ-ing these recipes was to give you great results on your first cook-through, each dish will get better the more times you cook it.

MEASUREMENTS: VOLUME AND WEIGHT

I've used volume for liquid ingredients, but also for those that are grated, minced, in powder form, or otherwise fine enough for volume to be an accurate measure. I've included weight for most solid ingredients. A good digi-tal scale costs twenty dollars. Splurge. Calling for "2 small shallots" or a "medium daikon radish" just won't do (one person's small is another's large). Nor will "1/4 cup thinly sliced lemongrass," whose impact in a dish will depend on the thinness of those slices and the cook's tendency to pack those slices into the cup measure. It may sound fussy to call for "3 grams of garlic," but it is simply more precise—and looks less insane than the imperial equiva-lent of "0.1 ounces," which is why I included gram mea-surements for weights under 1 ounce. And since many of the ingredients, techniques, and foods in this book will be unfamiliar to most cooks, precision is especially important. The instincts you'd typically rely on to make up for a lack of precision don't apply. The good news: Digital scales are inexpensive. Weighing ingredients is really easy. So is toggling between grams and ounces. Once you start, you'll be hooked.

That said, I did ultimately give in to entreaties from scale-less friends, and in many recipes I've provided volume equivalents for the weight measures. (I still urge you to buy a scale and treat the weight measures as gospel and the other measures as guidance.) I drew the line, however, at ingredients that are to be pounded to a paste. For those, precision is key. (Dried chiles are the only exception; since they're too light to accurately reg-ister on some scales, I've indicated the number of chiles as well as their weight.)

BUILDING A PANTRY

At first glance, many of the recipes in this book might seem intimidating. A relatively simple stir-fry calls for Thai oyster sauce, thin soy sauce, and yellow bean sauce. A salad recipe asks you to make toasted–sticky rice powder and toasted-chile powder. A curry requires you to make a special shrimp paste, pound a curry paste, and fry shallots. Recreating true Thai flavor in the West takes work, no question, but at the same time, cooking this food is not as difficult as it appears to be.

To the problem of lists full of seemingly strange ingredients, one big shopping trip is the solution. Once you build up even a modest pantry, cooking this food becomes infinitely less onerous. Dried or preserved ingredients such as palm sugar, dried chiles, dried shrimp, and bottled sauces last indefinitely in your cup-board or fridge. Many fresh ingredients such as chiles, galangal, and kaffir lime leaves can be purchased frozen and keep frozen for months.

With the challenge of recipes within recipes, some perspective helps. Thai cooking relies on a pantry that's different from our Western one. A cook in Thailand has certain staple ingredients on hand—such as chile powder, toasted–sticky rice powder, and pork stock—or they can easily find high-quality versions at the mar-ket. In the US, some of these must be made at home, because store-bought versions aren't up to snuff. Yet no one's saying you have to make toasted-chile powder every time you cook. Take the time to make it once and you're set for a while. Other ingredients, such as tama-rind water and palm sugar simple syrup, last for a week. Still others can be prepared a day or so in advance. I've indicated whenever possible how long ingredients like these can keep.

To further help with the task of making this food, I've identified recipes in this book that become signifi-cantly less daunting once you break them into several tasks to be performed over a few weeks or days. Each of these recipes includes a game plan meant to ease your mind and get you cooking.

EQUIPMENT

If you want to cook everything in this book, you'll have to buy some special equipment. There's no way to make great sticky rice without a sticky rice steamer. It costs twelve dollars. There's no better vessel for stir-frying than a wok. Buy one. To make great *som tam*, you need a large, deep clay mortar; to pound curry pastes, you'll need a medium-size granite mortar. Each recipe explains exactly what equipment is necessary to make the recipe. Here are two lists (neither include a large pot, blender, spice grinder, and other things a well-equipped kitchen has)—one for those looking to cook the most dishes with the least equipment and another for those cooks determined to make every recipe in this book. Aside from the digital scale and charcoal grill, which are available virtually anywhere, you'll find them all in Thai and other Asian markets or online (see Mail-Order Sources, page 21).

AT THE LEAST

* **Digital scale**
* **Flat-bottomed wok**
* **Wok spatula**
* **Medium Thai granite mortar (the opening about 6 inches in diameter) and pestle**
* **Large Thai clay mortar (the opening about 8 inches in diameter)**
* **Wooden pestle**
* **Electric rice cooker**
* **Sticky rice steamer set (both the woven basket and pot-bellied pot)**
* **Long-handled noodle strainer**

A STEP BEYOND

The above nine plus:

* **Charcoal grill**
* *Tao* **(Thai-style charcoal stove)**
* **Wide aluminum Chinese steamer**
* **Clay pot**
* *Laap* **knife or other heavy cleaver**
* **Thick wood chopping block (not bamboo)**
* **Papaya shredder (look for the Kiwi brand)**

MAKING A MEAL

Making the recipes in this book into a larger meal deserves a little elaboration. The dishes that follow (even the non-Thai ones) fall into three general Thai categories: *aahaan kap khao*, the proper meal; *aahaan jaan diaw*, the one-plate meal; and *khong waan*, sweets.

AAHAAN KAP KHAO: Dishes to eat with rice as part of a shared meal

The proper meal comprises a number of dishes that everyone shares along with plenty of rice. These meals, taken in homes and restaurants alike, strike a balance between sweetness and tartness, saltiness and bitterness, mildness and heat (not necessarily within each dish, but in the meal as a whole) that is particular to the place where they're eaten and the people eating them.

The meal is different from how we typically eat at restaurants in the US. We order appetizers that we occasionally share, but then it's every diner for himself. One person orders the steak, another the pasta. We even do this at Thai restaurants, where someone orders the green curry, another, the red. That's one reason the idea of a communal, balanced meal can be a difficult sell at Pok Pok. Yet this notion of a balanced meal should seem entirely familiar: Every year, we gather for family-style dinners of turkey, salty stuffing, sugary sweet potatoes, and tangy cranberry sauce. Everyone makes his own meal from the same dishes in the center of the table.

For our purposes, however, you need only pick a few dishes that complement each other. In general, avoid serving multiple dishes with similar flavors or making a meal of all meat or several super-rich dishes. In other words, use your head. To get you started, I provide serving suggestions for each dish, selected with flavor profiles and balance in mind. My serving suggestions also take into consideration the effort required to make each recipe—though it bears repeating that many of the meals you'll make take time and planning.

Most of the recipes in this book that fall into the category of *aahaan kap khao* make relatively small portions, because again, they're not supposed to be the centerpiece to a meal. Yet I understand that if you're cooking for a bunch of people, you might want to make larger portions. To that end, I've indicated whenever a recipe can be easily doubled (that is, without significant changes in cooking process). For the especially complicated dishes in this book—Laap Meuang (page 106) and Yam Jin Kai (page 158), for example—and dishes that would be awkward to make in small portions—Kaeng Hung Leh (page 170), for instance—I've gone ahead and provided a recipe for a more substantial portion that you can serve with rice and another simple dish or two.

AAHAAN JAAN DIAW: The One-Plate Meal

The one-plate meal is what it sounds like it is: dishes that by themselves make a meal or at least a hearty snack. I devoted an entire chapter to these dishes (page 183), which you can turn to when you're not up for making the multiple dishes that constitute *aahaan kap khao*.

KHONG WAAN: Sweets

Notably not synonymous with dessert, this category includes an expansive roster of snacks that happen to be sweet. The handful of examples in this book barely scratches the surface. But the genre has become one of my favorites among those in the Thai culinary catalog.

HOW TO EAT THIS FOOD

Look, you can eat Thai food with a spatula for all I care. But there are a few things worth saying about how Thais eat. Spoiler: chill with the chopsticks.

Before the nineteenth century, when Thais began to adopt Western utensils like spoons and forks, they ate seated on the floor and with their hands. Even now, in sticky-rice country (Northern and Northeastern Thailand), people often forgo silverware, instead grabbing a small clump of rice and using it to snatch up food. Still, it's common to find a fork and spoon at the Thai table, especially when the rice is jasmine. Generally speaking, Thais use the spoon to eat and the fork to occasionally deliver food from plate to spoon. The spoon is a much more efficient implement for scooping up the many saucy or soupy dishes. Eat this way enough and using a fork on a curry begins to seem as awkward as drinking wine out of a beer mug: it works, but not well.

Knives don't typically appear at the table—meat and vegetables are typically served in bite-size pieces. Nor do chopsticks, unless you're eating noodles. Chopsticks are a Chinese-born implement for a Chinese-born foodstuff.

> ### A QUICK NOTE ABOUT TRANSLITERATIONS
>
> In general, the Thai words in this book have been transliterated (rendered in phonetically similar words in the Latin alphabet) according to the Royal Thai General System of Transcription (RTGS). One quirk of this system worth mentioning here, because it clashes with a quirk of the English language: Some words are transliterated with the letters "ph" (such as *phat* and *kaphrao*). This "ph" does not indicate an "f" sound, but rather an aspirated "p" sound.

ingredients

When you set out to cook the food of a country thousands of miles away, you're not going to find every ingredient at the Stop & Shop. To make the recipes in this book, you're going to have to make trips to your local Asian market. Sometimes you're going to have to search the aisles, or the Internet.

Yet there's good news, too. You'll be surprised by what you can find—and where you'll spot it. Your local Whole Foods may offer not just Thai chiles and lemongrass but also fresh turmeric root. Your local farmers' market may sell cilantro with the roots on. Your local Mexican market might sell the herb *culantro*, which happens to be the same as the Thai herb *phak chii farang*, which is used in many Northern Thai dishes.

And once you build up a pantry of not-so-perishable staples, your trips will become less frequent, because so many Thai dishes share a similar roster of ingredients. For those ingredients that are virtually impossible to find in the US, I've provided hacks, the same ones I use at my restaurants, for those readers willing to go the extra mile—for instance, adding a squeeze of Meyer lemon to lime juice in order to ape the flavor and aroma of the limes cooks use in Thailand; using easy-to-find Mexican puya chiles as a stand-in for a nearly-impossible-to-find dried Thai chile. For some ingredients—citrusy, almost soapy galangal; sharp and fragrant fresh Thai chiles—there are no substitutes. You've got to find them. I want to help.

Here's a rundown of the least familiar ingredients and those familiar ingredients that take a slightly different form in Thailand. It includes where to look, what to look for, and how to cheat. Keep in mind that labeling varies widely, as do the transliterations (see A Quick Note about Transliterations, page 9).

For the ingredient glossary, I've chosen brevity as my guiding principle: you'll find no history of the chile or tasting notes of kaffir lime leaf, no advice on choosing between a wilted bunch of cilantro and a healthy one (hint: use your eyes)—just what you need to know to cook the recipes in this book. I've included storage advice for fresh ingredients only when that advice defies common kitchen sense. In general, buy fresh ingredients as close as possible to the time you plan to use them.

Banana leaf (*bai yok*)
Available fresh and frozen in many Asian and Latin markets.

Bean sprouts (*thua ngok*)
Look for bean sprouts in the refrigerated section of Asian markets, where they're often sold from bins or in bags. For the purposes of this book, you want to use mung bean sprouts, which have slender yellow tops, not soybean sprouts, which have bulbous yellow tops.

"Betel" or wild pepper leaves (*bai chapluu*)
Available fresh in many Thai markets, where it's frequently labeled "betel leaves," and Vietnamese markets, where it's called *lá lốp* or *lá lốt*. They last longer than most herbs in the fridge: pick the leaves and store them

sandwiched by paper towels and in a resealable plastic bag for up to two weeks.

Blood (*leuat*)

A few recipes in this book call for raw pork blood and steamed blood.

Your best bet for **raw blood** is the freezer case at Korean and Chinese markets or butcher shops. You may find fresh blood at retailers who make blood sausage or butcher shops that deal closely with small farms and allow special orders. Defrosted, the blood will have either a liquid or gelatinous texture.

Steamed blood is sold in butcher cases or the refrigerated sections at Chinese and other Asian markets. It is sometimes labeled "blood cake."

Chiles (*phrik*)

These are the most commonly used chiles in this book.

Dried puya chiles (sometimes spelled "pulla"): It might seem strange to call for a Mexican chile in a Thai cookbook, but they mimic the size and flavor of *phrik kaeng*, a medium-size dried chile used in Thailand. They're available in Mexican and Latin markets, the "Latin foods" section of some supermarkets, and online.

In many recipes, I ask you to pound these chiles to a powder in a mortar. Though the chiles have been dried, their moisture content varies, and those that contain more moisture (that are supple rather than brittle) are more difficult to pulverize. So some batches will take longer than others.

Dried Thai chiles: The dried version of fresh Thai chiles, these are narrow, 2- to 3-inch-long red chiles. Look for bags that specify "from Thailand" or "grown in Thailand." They're readily available online as well as in Southeast Asian–focused grocery stores. If all else fails, the dried chiles available in virtually every Asian market will do.

Some recipes call for toasted or fried dried Thai chiles. You can toast or fry the chiles (see box at right) up to 1 week in advance if you store them in airtight containers at room temperature.

Fresh Thai chiles (often labeled "bird," "bird's eye," and occasionally "finger" chile in English): You'll find these fiery, narrow, approximately 2-inch-long chiles at Asian markets and many big-city grocery stores like Whole Foods. Because their heat level can vary significantly, always taste them (carefully) before you use them. Ripe red chiles and unripe green chiles have different flavors and fragrances, so each recipe suggests the ideal color.

Frozen fresh Thai chiles are fine (in my experience, they actually tend to have a more consistent heat level). In fact, you can freeze any fresh Thai chiles you don't use within a few days. They defrost quickly at room temperature.

Hungarian wax, goat horn, and Anaheim chiles: In this book, I use these chiles to stand in for types of moderately spicy, flavorful green chiles that you can't find in the US. As always, the heat levels of chiles vary widely, so when it applies, I've asked you to supplement these chiles with smaller, hotter ones. You'll find Anaheims in supermarkets large and small, and Hungarian wax and goat horns at farmers' markets in warmer months. The long (5- to 6-inch) unnamed green chiles sold in Asian markets in the US will also likely do the trick.

TOASTED DRIED THAI CHILES

Put the chiles in a dry wok or pan, set the pan over high heat to get the wok hot, then decrease the heat to low. Cook, stirring and tossing them almost constantly, until they're very fragrant and a very dark brown color (nearly black) that's several shades darker than they were when you started, 15 to 20 minutes.

FRIED DRIED THAI CHILES

Put the chiles in a wok or pan, add enough vegetable oil to coat the chiles well, and set the pan over medium-low heat. Cook, stirring and tossing almost constantly, until the chiles are a deep, dark brown color (but not black), about 7 to 10 minutes. Keep in mind that the residual heat of the oil will continue cooking the chiles. Use a slotted spoon to transfer the chiles to a paper towel to drain.

Chinese broccoli (*gai lan* in Chinese)

Almost every Asian market plus some farmers' markets carry this vegetable, which is sometimes called Chinese kale. If you can, buy the smaller, slim-stemmed variety ("baby" Chinese broccoli), sometimes called *gai lan* "tips" or *gai lan miew*.

Chinese celery (*keun chai*)

This variety is leafier and has much thinner stems than the celery common in the US. Look for it in Asian markets.

Cilantro (*phak chii*)

Whenever recipes call for chopped cilantro, use both the leaves and thin stems. Those of you willing to go the extra mile will seek out at Latin markets what's called *cilantro macho*, which looks like cilantro going to seed. The smaller, feathery leaves resemble the *phak chii doi* (mountain coriander) common in Thailand.

Cilantro root (*rak phak chii*)

In the US, bunches of cilantro are typically sold without the roots attached. When you see roots-on bunches at farmers' markets and Asian (particularly Thai) markets, buy them (or ask a farmers' market vendor if you can place a special order). Rinse the roots under running water, rubbing with your fingers, before you use them. Clean them thoroughly but don't bother peeling them for the recipes in this book. If you don't use them within several days, thinly slice and freeze them.

Coconut milk and cream (*kati* and *hua kati*)

There is no substitute for the freshly pressed coconut milk and cream used in Thailand (and which we make at Pok Pok), but as home cooks, we're stuck with the boxed and canned stuff. In my experience, boxed is best, not least because it's typically 100 percent coconut milk or cream. Look for the terms "Tetra Pak" or "UHT" on the box. If the fat in the box has solidified and separated from the liquid, empty the contents into a saucepan and gently warm over low heat, stirring occasionally, until it's all liquid. For recipes that require "cracking" coconut cream (heating the cream in order to separate the water from the fat), using a boxed variety is close to essential. If you can't find it, be aware that the cream might take longer to crack (or might not crack at all). I have, however, had good luck with cracking the Savoy brand canned product. Regardless of the packaging, make sure you buy only the unsweetened kind.

Dried shrimp (*kung haeng*)

Most Asian grocery stores stock dried shrimp loose or in bags. The shrimp come in different sizes. Look for medium-size (sometimes you'll just see the letter "M" on the bag) for the purposes of this book.

Fermented fish sauce (*naam plaa raa*)

Also spelled *nahm pla raak, naam ba laa*, or a similar phonetic spelling; also *mắm nêm* in Vietnamese. Look for the Pantainorasingh (Thai) or Phú Quốc (Vietnamese) brands. Make sure there's no sugar in the ingredients list. If you buy a Vietnamese brand, for instance, avoid the "*pha sắn*" variety, which is meant to be eaten as a condiment and has sugar added.

Fish sauce (*naam plaa*)

Use Squid, Tiparos, or another Thai brand unless directed otherwise.

Galangal (*kha*)

This knobby rhizome looks like pale-skinned ginger. Find it fresh in Thai grocery stores and in the freezer section of many Asian stores.

Garlic chives (*kuay chai*)

Look for these (which are flat like blades of grass and not to be confused with the chives with yellowish buds at the tips) at Asian markets.

Green onions (*ton hom*)

Use the white and green parts of the green onions (aka scallions) unless otherwise noted.

Green papaya (*malakaw*)

This is unripe papaya, eaten when its pale-green flesh is still crisp and slightly tart. Look for the firm, green-skinned fruit in Asian markets.

Kaffir lime leaf (*bai makhrut*)

Look for these fresh (they're typically found in the refrigerated aisle) or frozen in Thai, and some Asian or Indian, grocery stores. Do not use dried leaves. If you don't use them within a couple of days, freeze the fresh leaves. Don't worry about defrosting them; it usually takes less than a minute for the leaves to defrost once you remove them from the freezer.

Kaffir lime (*luuk makhrut*)

The fruit, used primarily for its bumpy, incredibly fragrant skin, is sold fresh and frozen. If you don't use the fresh fruit within a day or so, freeze it.

Lemongrass (*takhrai*)

Fresh lemongrass has become fairly common in big-city markets, Asian and not. Do note that the flavor begins to deteriorate after a few days in the fridge. Many recipes call for the soft, tender heart of the stalk. To access it, cut off about 1/2 inch from the bottom and about 5 inches from the top of the stalk, reserving scraps for stock. Peel off the tough, fibrous layers until you reach the soft, pale yellow heart. When you slice, start from the fatter end and keep going until you feel serious resistance, at which point you can peel off another layer and keep slicing. The size and freshness of the lemongrass will affect the yield of thinly sliced tender parts, though figure about 1 tablespoon for every large, fresh stalk.

Lime (*manao*)

The limes you find in Thailand are closer in size and flavor to Key limes. The recipes all work with regular lime juice, but I urge you to look for Key limes, which are available in many major supermarkets, or to add a squeeze of Meyer lemon to regular lime juice. The goal is a more fragrant and less bitter juice. Choose limes with smooth, shiny (not dull, rugged) skin. These have thinner skins and contain more juice.

kabocha squash

cha-om

daikon radish

Thai apple eggplant

chayote

long Asian eggplant

Chinese broccoli

long beans

khanaeng (Thai Brussels sprouts)

young jackfruit

king oyster mushrooms

cherry tomatoes

yu choy

oyster mushrooms

water spinach

cucumbers

young ginger

white turmeric

krachai (wild ginger)

galangal

mature ginger

yellow turmeric

orange chile

skyward-facing chile

Thai garlic

Thai shallots

phrik khii nuu

red Thai chile

Chinese garlic

shallots

kaffir lime

kaffir lime leaves

lemongrass

green Thai chile

phrik num

dill

mint

betel leaf

banana leaf

lemon basil

Vietnamese
mint

cilantro
with roots

Thai
basil

hot basil

pandan
leaf

sawtooth
herb

Chinese
celery

green onion

garlic chives

durian

durian flesh

bataeng laai (a fragrant Thai melon)

green papaya

lime

guava

mango

Rice vermicelli noodles (*khanom jiin*): In this book, these dried noodles stand in for the fresh *khanom jiin* (page 231) sold in Thailand, which require no cooking, and are not available in the West. Look for Thai brands, such as Cock and Butterfly, or Vietnamese brands, such as Three Ladies. And look for the Vietnamese words "*bún gà*" on the package.

Thin, flat rice noodles (*sen lek*): Two dishes in this book call for thin, flat rice noodles, and each requires a slightly different type. If you can find only one and not the other, using them interchangeably is not end of the world. For Kuaytiaw Reua (page 204), buy flat, thin noodles (often labeled "*bánh phở*") that resemble linguine in shape. For Phat Thai (page 221), buy flat, slightly wider noodles (often labeled "*phat thai*") that resemble fettuccine in shape.

Both types come in semi-dried and fully dried form. Semi-dried noodles are slightly pliable and kept in the refrigerated sections of Chinese and Southeast Asian markets. Fully dried noodles are brittle and kept on shelves. Before you use these noodles for either recipe, soak them in lukewarm water until they're fully pliable (though not completely soft), about 15 minutes for semi-dried and 25 minutes for fully dried noodles.

thin fresh wheat noodles (for *ba mii tom yam*)

thin fresh wheat noodles (for *khao soi*)

semidried thin rice noodles (for *phat thai*)

fresh wide rice noodles

glass noodles

khanom jiin (cooked, in bundles, as it's sold in Thailand)

rice vermicelli

Long beans (*thua fak yao*)

You'll find these in almost every Asian market that sells produce. They're occasionally called yard-long or snake beans, but you won't need a label to identify them, since they look like very long green beans. If you have a choice, choose the thinner, darker variety, which is the one preferred by most Thai cooks. In a pinch, you can substitute haricot vert or green beans.

Noodles (*kuaytiaw*)

The recipes in this book call for five different types of noodles. Shopping for noodles is complicated by particularly ambiguous and mercurial labeling, so pay close attention to the shape of the noodle and refer to the photo at right.

Glass noodles (*wun sen*; also called mung bean, bean thread, or cellophane noodles): Look for the *dried* version in bags at Asian markets.

Wide rice noodles (*sen yai* in Thai; *chow fun* in Cantonese): Look for *fresh* wide (about 1½ inches across), flat rice noodles in the refrigerated section of Chinese and Southeast Asian markets or, even better, at shops dedicated to making and selling fresh noodles. I don't recommend substituting rehydrated or boiled dried noodles. Precut noodles are often too narrow, so if you can, I recommend buying rice noodle sheets and slicing them yourself. You might have to unfold the sheets to slice them properly.

These noodles are already fully cooked. If you're lucky enough to find freshly made noodles or sheets, use them the same day you buy them. (To figure out if they're freshly made or not, taste them: if they're fully supple and delicious, they're freshly made; if they're starchy and slightly brittle, they've been hanging around for a few days.) Most likely, they will have stiffened and stuck together by the time you buy them. That's fine. Before you use fresh rice noodles or sheets, carefully peel them apart (it's fine if they break, but try to keep them as intact as you can). If they're too brittle or clumpy, you have two options: briefly microwave the noodles just until you can separate them, or dunk them in boiling water for a few seconds to soften them (remember, these noodles are already cooked). Drain them, of course, before using.

Thin fresh wheat noodles (*ba mii*): Look for these uncooked yellow noodles (sometimes called "wonton noodles") in the refrigerated sections of Chinese and other Asian markets. For Ba Mii Tom Yam Muu Haeng (page 207), look for thin, round noodles similar in shape and size to spaghetti. For Khao Soi Kai (page 214), look for thin, flat ones that resemble fresh linguine.

Oyster sauce (*naam man hoi*)

Use Maekrua or another Thai brand with a mellow sweetness rather than just intense saltiness.

Palm sugar (*naam taan beuk* or *naam taan piip*)

There are two main varieties of palm sugar: the harder kind (*naam taan beuk*) sold in disk form and the softer kind (*naam taan piip*) sold in jars or bags. While you'll occasionally spot the softer kind in the US, it's often hardened from improper storage. In this book I only call for palm sugar in disk form. There are a few recipes that use the softer kind, and those recipes include a simple method for recreating it in the microwave. If you don't have a microwave, put the palm sugar in a mortar, sprinkle in some hot water (each recipe will provide the amount), and pound to a smooth paste.

Look for brands that sell 100 percent palm sugar from Thailand, such as Golden Chef or Cock.

Pandan leaf (*bai toey*)

Fresh leaves (sometimes called pandanus) of the screwpine tree are hard but not impossible to come by in the US, but you're more likely to find these long leaves in bags in the freezer section of Asian grocery stores.

Pickled mustard greens (*phak dong*)

Look for Cock or other Thai brands sold in bags on shelves (not necessarily in the refrigerated section). Avoid mustard greens that are khaki gray or neon yellow for obvious reasons. Before using them, drain the mustard greens, soak them in water for 10 minutes, and drain again.

Pickled or salted gouramy fish (*plaa raa*)

Also called *pla raak*, *pa laa*, *ba laa*, or a similar phonetic transliteration from Thai; *mắm cá sặc* in Vietnamese. Look for the Pantainorasingh brand or another brand that sells whole or fillets of fish (not "creamy" or "cream style").

Rice (*khao*)

The recipes in this book call for two types of rice: **jasmine** and **sticky** (also called "glutinous" or "sweet"). For the purposes of this book, only buy rice grown in Thailand. For more about rice, see chapter 1.

Salted radish (*chaai pua*)

Also called preserved radish. Look for a Thai brand sold in a bag, either shredded or whole (not minced). My recipes call for the preshredded version; if you can only find whole, cut them crosswise into ⅛-inch-thick slices, then lay those flat and cut them into very thin strips.

Sawtooth herb (*phak chii farang*)

Also called saw-leaf herb, known as *culantro* and *recao* (in Latin markets) and *ngò gai* (in Vietnamese ones), the herb has long, narrow leaves with serrated edges. Its flavor resembles a more intense, slightly sharper and more bitter version of cilantro.

Seasoning sauce (*maggi*)

Yes, it's called "seasoning sauce." Use Golden Mountain, Healthy Boy, or another Thai brand.

Sesame oil (*naman ngaa*)

This light-brown oil is made from roasted sesame seeds. Look for Asian brands that are 100 percent sesame oil, or at least the highest percentage you can find.

Shallots (*hom daeng*)

For shallots that are to be pounded into pastes for stir-fries, curries, and so on, my preference is for the small, round shallots sold at Asian markets, which have a more appropriate size and flavor and lower water content than torpedo-shaped French shallots. For shallots that aren't to be pounded (for example, those sliced for salads or simmered in soups), you can get away with using the larger French shallots or even red pearl onions.

Shrimp paste (*kapi*)

For our purposes, there are two kinds of shrimp paste.

The first is **kapi** (also spelled *gapi*), which is dark, pungent, and not actually made from shrimp but rather from *khoei*, a tiny crustacean. It's just the thing for most Central Thai dishes and readily available here. Look for Thai brands such as Twin Chicken and Pantainorasingh. Do not buy shrimp paste that contains soybean oil.

The second is **kapi kung,** a more mellow kind that's preferred by the Northern cooks I know and something you have to recreate using two store-bought products (see page 274).

Soy sauce (*si ew*)

Thais use three types of soy sauce. **Thin soy sauce** is salty without a particularly intense flavor. **Black soy sauce** has a strong, molasses-like character and tastes slightly sweet, though markedly more so than thin soy sauce. **Sweet soy sauce** is syrupy and very sweet, as sugary as Aunt Jemima pancake syrup, compared to the molasses-like sweetness of black soy. For all three types, look for Thai brands such as Kwong Hung Seng (look for the dragonfly on the label), Healthy Boy, or Maekrua.

Tamarind pulp (*makham*)

Sometimes called "paste" or even just "tamarind." Look for seedless pulp from Vietnamese or Thai brands, such as Cock. For many recipes in this book, you'll have to make a simple extract (see page 275).

Thai basil (*bai horapha*)

Look for this licorice-scented variety, sometimes called "sweet basil," in Thai and other Asian markets and at farmers' markets. (Keep an eye out for purple stems, even if the herb is just labeled "basil.")

Tomatoes (*makheua thet*)

Tomatoes in Thailand tend to be significantly more tart and crunchy than the sweet, soft, juicy tomatoes we covet. So if you want to go the extra mile, buy firmer, slightly under-ripe tomatoes.

Vietnamese mint (*rau răm* in Vietnamese, *phak phai* in Thai)

Look for this herb in Southeast Asian markets, where it also goes by "Vietnamese coriander" and "laksa leaf."

Wild ginger (*krachai*)

Also spelled *grachai* or *kachai* and sometimes referred to in English as finger root, lesser galangal, or Chinese keys. You'll likely find it frozen in the US. But washed well, frozen *krachai* works well for the recipes in this book. Do not use canned, jarred, or shredded *krachai*.

Yellow bean sauce (*tao jiaw*)

Use Kwong Hung Seng (look for the dragonfly on the label) or another Thai brand.

Yellow turmeric root (*khamin*)

Find it fresh in Indian and some Thai grocery stores (and even certain Whole Foods locations) and in the freezer section of many Asian and Indian stores.

Yu choy (*phak kat*)

Similar in appearance to Chinese broccoli, this Asian green has a slightly different flavor and can typically be identified by its tiny yellow flowers.

BOTTLED SEASONINGS AND SAUCES

My short advice on choosing the right bottled sauces is to go to an Asian food-focused store and look for Thai writing, a Thai brand, or "Product of Thailand" written somewhere on the bottle. Using, for instance, Japanese soy sauce for Thai recipes won't give you the right flavor. To provide a little more guidance, and to steer you clear of "Thai Kitchen" brand and its ilk, see the individual entries for a few brands to look for.

mail-order sources

If you don't live close to good Asian markets or you're having trouble finding a particular ingredient, spend some time on the sites below: you'll be shocked by what you can get shipped to your door.

Importfood.com

Find just about all the equipment you'll need for this book: carbon steel wok, sticky rice steamer, clay pot, *tao* (Thai-style charcoal stove), clay and granite Thai mortars, wide Chinese steamers, noodle basket, and thick wood chopping block.

Fresh ingredients: Pandan leaves, betel leaves, green papaya, galangal, yellow turmeric root, kaffir limes and leaves, fresh Thai chiles, and more.

Pantry ingredients: Boxed coconut milk and cream, tempura flour, rice flour, dried *phat thai* noodles, bottled sauces, and more.

Kalustyans.com

Pantry staples such as palm sugar and shrimp paste; spices such as fresh whole mace (here, called "mace blades") and dried Indonesian long pepper (here, called *pippali*); and dried chiles such as Thai and puya.

Templeofthai.com

Find just about all the equipment you'll need for this book: carbon steel wok, sticky rice steamer, clay pot, *tao* (Thai-style charcoal stove), clay and granite Thai mortars, noodle basket, multiple sizes of Chinese steamers, papaya shredder, and more.

Fresh ingredients: Galangal, yellow turmeric root, kaffir limes and leaves, fresh Thai chiles, and more.

Pantry ingredients: Sticky rice, dried Thai chiles, tamarind pulp, shrimp paste, salted radish, pickled mustard greens, palm sugar, and bottled products, including tough-to-find items like *naam plaa raa* and *plaa raa*.

Wokshop.com/store

Find most of the equipment you'll need for this book: woks and wok spatulas galore, sticky rice steamer, granite Thai mortar, wide Chinese steamers, mandolines, and spider skimmers.

thai regional rundown

"We're ordering Thai," a friend says. "What do you want?" I bet most of you wouldn't need to look at a menu. I know I wouldn't. I'm sure papaya salad's on offer along with spring rolls and *tom yam* soup. There's surely a range of proteins, tofu included, offered in chile-basil sauce or floating in one of several pastel-colored curries, green or red or yellow. And, of course, there's *phat thai, phat khii mao,* and *phat si ew,* noodle dishes now as familiar to most of us as spaghetti with meatballs and penne à la vodka.

"Thai food" has come to refer to a certain circumscribed canon of dishes. Yet it's meant to represent a geographically and culturally diverse country that for most of its existence was a gaggle of peoples of many religions, languages, and cultures, all loosely linked by landmass and nominally by government purview and political borders. In other words, Thai food is so much more than those menus would lead you to believe.

Thai food isn't unique in this respect. Chinese food, too, has become a monolith in the American consciousness. China—that massive country of almost 1.5 billion people scattered throughout more than two dozen provinces, each with its own world of gastronomy— has a cuisine effectively distilled to orange beef, fried rice, lo mein, and General Tso's chicken. Even Italian food, which is surely more familiar than those eccentric Eastern cuisines full of preserved fish and alien vegetables, is often reduced to an unchanging menu— Puglia, Liguria, Sicily be damned. We can all agree that saying, "Let's go out for Italian" is as absurd as saying, "Let's go out for American food." Absurd and entirely understandable.

People expect me to look down my nose at American Thai food. I can't. I don't know whose brilliant mind first winnowed the infinite Thai repertoire to a couple dozen dishes, but he or she was incredibly shrewd. Of all the incredible Asian cuisines to challenge Chinese and Japanese for supremacy in the US, from Malaysian and Singaporean to Vietnamese and Korean, Thai food has won out precisely because the items on that ubiquitous menu appeal to our palates. And now we can all revel in the knowledge that there's so much more of the country's cuisine left to try.

* * *

Like cooks everywhere, before cars, planes, and trains enabled large-scale cross-pollination of foods and cultures across the country of Thailand, Thai cooks were limited to the stuff in their proverbial backyards. It should go without saying that people who lived far from the coasts had no access to ocean fish, and that people who lived far from the coconut trees of the south of Thailand weren't making coconut curries. Those who lived near jungles and forests ate wild birds and swine, reptiles and insects.

Dense forests and mountains made low-tech travel from region to region next to impossible. This topography separated communities that today we'd consider neighbors, but back then were virtually unknown to one another. Even after the country unified in the fourteenth century, its borders contained many different ethnic groups who spoke many different languages, political borders having little relation to de facto ethno-linguistic ones. Kings had official dominion over cities that in reality were too far away to influence, let alone control.

Over the centuries, the various kingdoms, cultures, and nomadic peoples of Thailand gradually coalesced, blurring the regional distinctions. It's easy to find restaurants serving food from Isaan in Chiang Mai or vendors hawking fiery Southern curries in Bangkok. Cooks in the North employ shrimp paste, and people dine on ocean fish and coconut shoots, all relatively recent entrants to the local pantry. But even as regional cooking evolved with the introduction of new ingredients and techniques, many local flavor profiles, techniques,

and ways of eating persisted. Cooks incorporated novelty while retaining regional identity.

Today the country comprises four major regions, whose food I've summarized in this section. My regional rundown is by no means comprehensive. Dividing the country into vast swaths requires generalization, since recipes, truths, and traditions change from city to city, village to village, household to household. For an in-depth look at the regions and the food, I suggest you spend a few weekends with David Thompson's *Thai Food*.

Still, this should give you a sense of the four basic cuisines of Thailand and if nothing else, drive home how different they are.

NORTHERN THAILAND

AT A GLANCE
Filled with rivers, mountains, and (in the past, at least) forests, with a comparatively cool climate and a historical abundance of food. Its distinct cuisine reflects the temperate climate, mix of ethnicities (including Lao, Burmese, Shan, and the Jin Haw of Southern China, plus indigenous tribes such as the Hmong, Karen, and others) and strong foreign influence. Its major city, Chiang Mai, was under Burmese control until the late eighteenth century, independent until the late nineteenth, and remote for decades after.

THE RICE Sticky

FLAVOR PROFILE AND EMBLEMATIC SEASONINGS
Marked by generous use of dried spices, frequent appearance of fresh turmeric, and prevalent bitterness from leaves, shoots, spices like *makhwen*, and, occasionally, beef bile. Cooks tend to use tamarind instead of lime. Northern cooks historically used *tua nao* (fermented soy beans dried in disks) rather than fish sauce and shrimp paste, but today you see all three. All else equal, Northern is the mildest in heat level of the four regions.

ICONIC DISHES
Simple boiled (rather than fried) curries like Jin Hoom (page 154) and Kaeng Khanun (page 166); relishes like Naam Phrik Num (page 174); grilled meats; and Laap Meuang (page 106), a dish so different from the *laap* of Isaan that they might as well be from separate countries.

Chiang Mai

Bangkok

NORTHEASTERN THAILAND (AKA ISAAN)

AT A GLANCE
Infertile soil, a manic climate—prone to monsoons and also to scorching heat and drought—and, until relatively recently, virtual isolation from the rest of Thailand. Bordering Laos and Cambodia (and populated by ethnic Lao and Khmer peoples), the land is flat with numerous rivers and lakes and mountains to the south and west.

THE RICE Sticky

FLAVOR PROFILE AND EMBLEMATIC SEASONINGS
Historical scarcity of food gave rise to a peasant cuisine—simple, pungent, and fiery, probably so because, as David Thompson writes, a small amount of food manages to flavor a large amount of filling rice. Fat and fuel (like trees) were traditionally in short supply, so cooks favored slow-grilling, boiling, and serving food raw or cured. The fundamental seasoning is *plaa raa*, essentially an unfiltered, unrefined fragrant sludge of fermented fish. Small dried red chiles (less humidity means chiles here can be dried easily) are used with abandon.

ICONIC DISHES
Som Tam Lao (page 40); Laap Isaan (pages 117 and 119); *plaa som* (fish that's fermented then fried); grilled skewered meat and offal with tart, spicy dipping sauce; and Kai Yaang (page 135).

CENTRAL THAILAND

AT A GLANCE
Defined by fertile soil and proximity to the Gulf of Thailand, to the coconut trees of the South, and to the modern locus of money and political power (the region includes the country's capital, Bangkok). The upshot is a wide variety of fruits and vegetables, lots of seafood such as fish, shrimp, crabs, and mollusks, and a sophisticated cuisine that reflects both foreign influence and local bounty. Ethnic Thais make up the vast majority here, with Chinese Thais as the largest minority.

THE RICE Jasmine

FLAVOR PROFILE AND EMBLEMATIC SEASONINGS
Sweetness from white and palm sugars, tartness from vinegar and fruits like lime and tamarind, saltiness from shrimp paste and fish sauce, and richness from coconut cream. Spicy, but not as fiery as Southern and Northeastern food.

ICONIC DISHES
Rich fried (rather than boiled) curries like green curry (Kaeng Khiaw Waan, page 161) and roasted duck curry; sweet-and-sour soups like *tom yam*; noodles and stir-fries like Phat Thai (page 221); and lots of bright salads.

SOUTHERN THAILAND

AT A GLANCE
A large Muslim population, lots of coastline, and the convergence of tropical temperature and fertile soil distinguish the region's cuisine, which sports abundant seafood, coconut, and fruits, as well as goat and mutton. Geographically, most of Southern Thailand is on the Isthmus of Kra, the trunk of the elephant-shaped country. It was once an early stop for merchants from India, the Middle East, and Europe. Today it's where tourists, foreign and domestic, go to hit the beach.

THE RICE Jasmine

FLAVOR PROFILE AND EMBLEMATIC SEASONINGS
The food of the South is perhaps the spiciest in Thailand, thanks to lots of fresh and dried bird (or "Thai") chiles. Spices abound, like fresh turmeric and also Middle Eastern spices like cumin and clove. Dried shrimp, shrimp paste, and fermented fish sauce provide salt and funk, and sour fruits like pineapple and tamarind provide balance. Coconuts grow like crazy in the South, so many dishes make use of coconut milk and cream.

ICONIC DISHES
Chicken and fish fried with turmeric and garlic; *kaeng massaman* (rich and sweet Muslim curries with potatoes); sour yellow coconut curries with fermented bamboo shoots; and a dry, fiercely spicy dish of curried fish or beef.

the mortar and pestle

I was on the train—diesel rail car, special express—from Isaan to Bangkok. It's a long trip. The train had no sleepers. You just sit up for eight hours. Riding with me were a bunch of men from Isaan, and we got to talking. They asked what I was doing in Isaan, which is not exactly a tourist destination. I told them I was there to eat. I asked if they knew how to cook. One guy piped up. "Yes," he said. "*Pok pok pok*"—the Thai onomatopoeia for the sound a pestle makes as it strikes the mortar.

This was almost a decade before I opened Pok Pok. But clearly, his response stuck with me. Notably, the guy didn't answer, "Sure, you should see my wok skills" or "Yeah, I make a mean curry." He immediately equated cooking, the making of food, with the use of a mortar and pestle. This spoke volumes about the significance of the tool in Thai cooking.

The mortar is an elemental tool. Using it is not a far cry from banging two rocks together. It provides a glimpse into a preindustrial world. Yet there is no modern tool that does the job as well. The food processor is more efficient, sure, but it is the tool of last resort: the resulting flavor and texture of curry pastes, sauces, dressings, and relishes never matches those produced by pounding, plus too much paste irrevocably gets stuck inside the processor.

THE TWO MORTARS

For the purposes of this book, there are two types of mortars, each specific to a type of preparation: a granite mortar, heavy and shallow, used mainly for pounding ingredients to pastes, and a clay mortar (in Thailand, it's also made from wood), deep and almost conical, used for making the category of dishes best exemplified by

papaya salad. The two are not interchangeable. Look for them at Thai-focused markets and other shops selling specialty cookware, or order them online. If you can, inspect them carefully for cracks before purchasing.

The mortar and pestle is easy and intuitive to use, but the technique deserves some elaboration. Caveat: Plenty of cooks do things differently. The following is simply the Pok Pok way.

The Granite Mortar

The Goal: Ingredients pounded in the granite mortar generally take four forms in this book, listed below.

- **The slightly wet-looking mixture of briefly pounded (bruised and broken into small pieces) ingredients for dishes like Phat Khanaeng (page 91) and Plaa Neung Manao (page 76).**
- **The coarse, fibrous pastes used as marinades for meats like flank steak (page 68) and pork neck (page 125).**
- **The fairly smooth pastes used for boiled curries like Jin Hoom (page 154) and stir-fried vegetables like Phat Fak Thawng (page 94).**
- **The smooth pastes used for fried curries like Kaeng Hung Leh (page 170) and Kaeng Khiaw Waan (page 161).**

The weight of the granite pestle and heft of the mortar are essential for properly pulverizing ingredients for pastes.

The Technique: For smoother, more complicated pastes, you'll cut fibrous ingredients, often against the grain, into manageable pieces before you pound. Counterintuitively, though, most ingredients are not cut into very small pieces, because they'd go flying when you try to pound them.

Set the mortar on a folded towel. This will help steady the mortar and lessen the impact of the pounding on your counter or table. It helps to place the mortar at a corner of the table directly above a leg, which transfers the force of pounding to the floor, sparing the table surface some impact and your ears loud banging. Pound the ingredients one type at a time, completely pulverizing one ingredient before adding the next, in the order listed in each recipe—in general, you'll start with the toughest, most fibrous ingredients (dried chiles, lemongrass, cilantro root), then move on to slightly less tough ingredients (galangal, turmeric), then to softer, wetter ingredients (garlic, shallots), and finally to very soft ingredients (shrimp paste).

You'll quickly get the hang of it, though some details are worth mentioning:

* Keep a relatively loose wrist as you pound, letting the weight of the pestle do most of the work.
* When you first add an ingredient to the mortar, add it to the center of the mortar and pound firmly to flatten and begin to break it down. After you do, *then* use the pestle to further crush and scrape it against the walls of the mortar until it's fully broken down to a paste.
* Stir powders and pastes occasionally with a spoon as you pound to make sure no large chunks are hiding out.
* As you incorporate the softer, wetter ingredients, the paste will become slick and it'll take more time to incorporate the new ingredients, so it's a good time to focus your energy on scraping and crushing the ingredients against the walls of the mortar.

The Clay or Wood Mortar

The Goal: To use the pestle to very lightly bruise the main ingredient (papaya, cucumber, what have you) just enough so that the dressing can permeate it, but not so much that the ingredient loses its shape or its crisp texture. The lightness of the wood or clay pestle is essential for this type of gentle bruising. The deepness makes it possible to stir while you bruise.

The Technique: Take the pestle in one hand and a large spoon in the other. As you pound with the pestle, do it lightly and come at the ingredients from a slight angle, not from directly above. As a guideline, the pestle should strike the side of the mortar at more or less the same time as it does the ingredients, blunting the blow and making that *pok* sound. Because the particulars of the method are subtle, it also helps to keep in mind what not to do. Do not pound in a straight-up-and-down motion. Do not aim for the center of the mortar. If you do, you enter into smashing territory. While you pound, use the spoon to toss the ingredients, scooping from the bottom of the mortar. As you scoop from below with the spoon and pound from above with the pestle, the effect is a slow tumbling, like clothes in a dryer.

KHAO

Rice

As long as I've known I would write a cookbook, I've known that the first chapter would be about rice. Of all the chile relishes and soups, stir-fries and salads, nothing is more integral to Thai food—to Thai culture, really—than this cereal grain.

The significance of rice is embedded in the Thai language. A good example, worn though it is, bears repeating: when you meet a friend on the street, you might say, "*Kin khao reu yang*?" or "Have you eaten rice yet?" More than just a greeting—a "What's up?" equivalent—the question doubles as an invitation. If you say that no, you haven't eaten rice yet, then you're accepting an offer to dine together. In other words, rice serves as shorthand for the entire meal.

That's because in Thai meals eaten centuries ago, rice was the main course. A family of four might sit on the floor in front of a spread that included a small bowl of fiery *naam phrik*, a plate of vegetables, a little meat (if the family was lucky), and a mound of rice—the variety would be one of hundreds. For our purposes, however, there are just two: jasmine and sticky. Until recently, a Thai meal without rice as the centerpiece would be unthinkable (unless, of course, you were eating noodles, a relatively modern import from China). Sometimes, rice is literally the centerpiece, a bowl or basket placed in the middle of the table. Everyone helps themselves. Today, however, you even see rice relegated to side dish in Thailand, where the rise of the middle class means people are more willing and able to indulge in a meal heavy on meat and fat and light on rice.

Still, rice for most Thais is absolutely integral to the meal. Its significance confounds Westerners, as it did me for a long, long time. In the US, rice is one of many possible side dishes, an optional accompaniment to the meal's focus—maybe a roast chicken or steak. To help understand how the plainest thing on the table could achieve such status, consider our familiar friend, the sandwich. Each sandwich is essentially distinguished by its filling—the ham sandwich, the Philly cheese steak, the BLT—just as the Thai meal is by the dishes on the table. The bread is implied. The bread defines the concept. Without bread, there is no sandwich. Same goes for rice.

Rice defines the repertoire of Thai food. That is, cooks over the centuries created dishes with rice in mind. This helps explain why the cuisine features the intense flavors that it does—a pittance of this and that had to be flavorful enough to season all that rice. Bear that in mind when you eat Thai food today and consider how strange it would be to eat, for instance, Kai Kaphrao Khai Dao (Stir-fried chicken with hot basil), page 189, without rice. This simple stir-fry of meat, chiles, and a shitload of hot basil is garlicky, fiery stuff. Tucking into a plateful of it alone would be as absurd as taking down a jarful of mustard. It just doesn't make sense. The dish needs rice. Eaten beside the other food, rice provides a mellow counterpoint, but also a distinctive character of its own—an aromatic, slightly nutty quality that doesn't so much complement the flavor of the food with which it's served as it does *complete* the flavor.

In the US, we tend to dump whatever we're eating onto rice, turning the rice into a wet mess. Don't do that. If it's sticky rice, use small clumps as edible eating implements. If you're eating jasmine rice, make spoonfuls that have both rice and some of the highly flavored food. Try to maintain the integrity of the rice as you eat.

THE ABSURDITY OF AUTHENTICITY

People often praise the food we serve at Pok Pok and my other restaurants as "authentic." I'm flattered, but that word and its cousin in compliment, "traditional," are banished from my restaurants. The words imply an absolute cuisine, that there is a one true Thai food out there, somewhere. I once had a cook at Pok Pok who was born and raised in Thailand and who'd look at some dish on my menu—one I'd eaten dozens of times, one I'd carefully calibrated to be just like the ones I'd had—and scoff, "Where are the tomatoes? That dish must have tomatoes." Same goes for other cuisines. Ask twenty Mexican cooks to make a tomatillo salsa and you'll get twenty different salsas.

Both terms are nonsensical designations—as if traditions are the same everywhere, as if they don't change, as if culinary ones don't evolve with particular speed. After all, some of the ingredients, techniques, and dishes we most closely associate with the food of Thailand are in fact relatively new to the cuisine.

To attempt to extricate foreign influence in search of something purely Thai would be difficult indeed. To neglect dishes with Chinese influence would be to lose a substantial portion of what we now think of as Thai food, including nearly every noodle dish and everything cooked in a blazing hot wok. And without Western influence, there wouldn't be bread or tomatoes.

Perhaps nothing defines Thai food for us Americans like the heat the chile provides. But the chile came to Thailand with Portuguese traders by way of the New World somewhere around the sixteenth century. That means the Thai people had been cooking for millennia before its arrival, employing the heat of peppercorns, galangal, and other sharply flavored herbs and spices.

And while, yes, the occasionally vigorous heat distinguishes Thai food from the cuisine of its neighbors, like Vietnam, the primacy of spiciness has been exaggerated. It's really just one element among many.

Plenty of Thai food is not spicy at all. When the food *is* spicy, heat is often an essential element. In the US, I've seen people order red curry and request that it be mild. In Thai, the category of dishes called *kaeng phet* is sometimes mistranslated as "red curry" but literally means "spicy curry." To order it mild is as absurd as ordering Kaeng Jeut Wun Sen ("Bland" soup, page 149) and saying "Can you make it spicy?"

Of course, I know what people mean when they reach for those dreaded words. They're communicating a noble desire to experience food as it exists in Thailand. As a traveler in Thailand, you often hear this question: "*Kin aahaan thai dai mai khrap?*" ("Do you know how to eat Thai food?") It seems difficult for Thais to believe that a foreigner might be willing to eat what they do. And understandably so. The flavor profiles are decidedly unfamiliar to newbies; the occasionally fiery and funky flavors are not for everyone. This is why vendors in Thailand often ply tourists with *phat thai* and banana pancakes. This is why Thais are so surprised and thrilled when I order Northern Thai food. They tell their friends and laugh with what I hope is delight. When I tell them I cook it, too, they practically lose their minds.

Even the take-out Thai food served throughout the US—ketchup-spiked *phat thai*, peanut sauce, rainbow curries—has itself become a cuisine, as real as anything. It's full of dishes that do exist in some form in Thailand but have been tweaked for the American palate, just as Khao Kha Muu (page 185) is Chinese food tweaked for the Thai palate. *Phat khii mao*, often translated as "drunken noodles," really means, essentially, stir-fry for drunk people, a dish that in Thailand is wickedly spicy, seasoned with hot basil, and originally might not have contained noodles at all. The American version is rarely that spicy, rarely has hot basil, almost always contains noodles. Inauthentic? Maybe. Tasty? Frequently.

Khao Hom Mali

JASMINE RICE

SPECIAL EQUIPMENT
- A fine-mesh strainer
- An electric rice cooker

Throughout Central and Southern Thailand, in a small pocket of Northern Thailand near Mae Hong Son, and in every last Thai restaurant in the States, you'll find steamed jasmine rice. For a long time, I thought that jasmine rice had, you know, some connection to the jasmine. Silly me. Its name in Thai (*khao hom mali* or, literally, "rice smell jasmine") seems to suggest that the rice itself smells of jasmine. But it turns out that my modest command of the language missed the nuance. In fact, the phrase is saying the rice is fragrant ("*hom*"), and the mention of jasmine just refers to the look of the raw grains, which supposedly resemble the pearl-like petals of the jasmine flower.

Not every plate of jasmine rice is created equal. At markets, you see different heaps of raw grains, each marked with a different price. These might be rices grown in different provinces, the prized grains of one area selling for twice that of the rest. Or they might be different crops of rice. At the pricey end of the spectrum is new-crop rice, sold shortly after it's harvested, when the moisture content is at its highest and it's at its most fragrant. This is special occasion rice. Most households and many restaurants, however, use rice that's been stored for a year or so, because its low, more consistent moisture content makes it easier to cook and the grains maintain their texture in the steamer for a long time. In the US, pretty much our only option is new-crop rice or new-crop that has aged. But that's just fine, as long as you make sure to buy rice grown in Thailand, which should be clearly indicated on the packaging.

DON'T BE A HERO

You might assume that I'm going to urge you to cook jasmine rice in a pot on the stove. Rice cookers sound like the easy way, and in cooking, easier tends to mean inferior, right? I'm happy, then, to report that my preferred cooking vessel for jasmine rice is an electric rice cooker. Just about every Thai person has one. So get yourself a good rice cooker (I like the Tiger brand). There's no need to buy one with more than one button. As you use it, make sure you keep the heating element and bottom of the rice pot clean and dry. Debris and moisture can interfere with the thermostat mechanism that makes the machine work so well.

{continued}

{Jasmine rice, continued}

MAKES ABOUT 6 CUPS COOKED RICE; THE RECIPE IS EASILY HALVED OR DOUBLED

2 cups uncooked jasmine rice from Thailand

2 cups water

Put the rice in a fine-mesh strainer set inside a large bowl. Fill the bowl with enough cool tap water to cover the rice by an inch or two. Use your hand to gently stir the rice, then lift the strainer from the bowl. The water in the bowl will be cloudy from the rice starch. Empty the water, set the strainer in the bowl again, and repeat the process until the water that covers the rice is, more or less, clear. You'll probably have to change the water two or three times. Drain the rice, gently shaking it occasionally, until it's fully dry to the touch, about 15 minutes.

Put the rice in a rice cooker in an even layer. Add the 2 cups of water, cover with the lid, press the button, and let the cooker do its thing.

Once it's done, let the rice sit in the rice cooker with the cover on for about 20 minutes. Don't skip this step. It allows some of the steam to dissipate and some to get reabsorbed into the rice. It keeps the rice from clumping and gives the grains a chance to cool slightly, so when you fluff the rice, the grains aren't so soft that they break.

Finally, fluff the rice: Use a spoon to gently rake the top few layers of rice to separate the grains, and gradually rake the next few layers and so on, working your way toward the bottom. Try your best not to break or smash the grains.

The rice keeps for several hours after fluffing in the rice cooker on its "Warm" setting. Store leftover cooked rice in a covered container in the fridge. Day-old rice is perfect for Khao Tom (page 196) and Khao Phat Muu (page 191).

Khao Niaw

SPECIAL EQUIPMENT

- **A fine-mesh strainer**
- **Cheesecloth or a clean mesh rice-steaming bag**
- **An inexpensive sticky rice steamer set (both the woven basket and pot-bellied pot)**

SERVES 6 TO 8, OR 4 ENTHUSIASTIC RICE EATERS; THE RECIPE IS EASILY DOUBLED

4 cups uncooked Thai sticky rice (also called "glutinous" or "sweet" rice)

Often the last thing people in the North and Northeast of Thailand do before bed is put raw grains of sticky rice in a pot, cover them with water, and leave them to soak. This is sticky rice country, and a day without sticky rice is almost unthinkable.

Also called glutinous rice, it has a different starch composition than varieties like jasmine. I'm not qualified to explain the world of amylopectin and amylose starches, so suffice it to say that the glossy cooked grains of sticky rice are particularly chewy and stick to one another in clumps, yet still remain distinct. It's a magical thing. Served in baskets, either one per person or as a mountainous mound to be passed around, the grains of sticky rice form moldable masses. Practiced diners snatch off a gumball-size piece, reflexively fashion it into a sort of spoon shape, and use it to grab a taste of whatever else is on the table. In these baskets or in bamboo tubes, workers carry this rice with them into the fields and forests, a portable, edible eating implement.

While you could argue that so-called "steamed jasmine rice" isn't steamed at all but rather boiled, sticky rice is actually steamed. In the Northeast, it typically goes into a bamboo basket; in the North, it's traditionally prepared in a clay pot with a perforated bottom, though today the pot is often aluminum. The basket or pot is set over a pot-bellied vessel filled with boiling water and the steam cooks the grains, already swollen from soaking, in just 15 minutes or so. The process is easy enough for uninitiated cooks. It just takes a little practice to get right.

Put the sticky rice in a large bowl and add enough tepid tap water to cover by an inch or two. Let it soak for at least 4 hours or up to 10 hours (as long as it's not very hot in your kitchen; if you're in a hurry, you can get away with soaking it in hot tap water for as little as 2 hours).

Pour off the soaking water. Put the rice in a fine-mesh strainer set inside a large bowl. Fill the bowl with enough cool tap water to cover the rice by an inch or two. Use your hand to gently stir the rice, then lift the strainer from the bowl. The water in the bowl will be cloudy from the rice starch. Empty the water, set the strainer in the bowl again, and repeat the process until the water is, more or less, clear. You'll probably have to change the water two or three times. Drain the rice.

Pour enough water into the sticky rice steamer pot to reach a depth of about 2 inches. Bring it to a boil over high heat. Either add the rice to the mesh bag and put the bag in the basket or line the woven steamer basket with two layers of damp cheesecloth and dump the rice onto the cheesecloth. Fold the bag or cheesecloth so it covers the rice, pat the bundle so the rice is in a more or less even layer, and cover with a pot lid or clean, damp kitchen cloth, tucking it around the bundle.

Decrease the heat slightly to maintain a steady but not furious boil and set the basket into the pot. Cook until the grains are fully tender but still chewy (almost springy) and definitely not mushy, about 15 minutes. (Larger batches of sticky rice take about 20 minutes, and the rice bundle should be flipped over once halfway through the steaming process.)

Transfer the rice to a small cooler or large bowl covered with a plate. Wait about 15 minutes before digging in. The sticky rice will stay warm for an hour or so.

You can successfully reheat leftover sticky rice; cover and microwave on low, then eat it right away.

SOM TAM
Papaya salad and family

My first attempt at making papaya salad did not go well. I was in Bangkok almost two decades ago, visiting my friends Chris and Lakhana. Lakhana gave birth to their third child the day I arrived, so I spent much of my trip shuttling their older kids around. One day I took them to Tae Kwon Do school, where the tykes were putting on a show of their skills. Because this is Thailand, where group activities and events always involve food somehow, the exhibition also featured a *som tam*-making contest. I was the lone Westerner in attendance and a conspicuous one at that—this was the first but definitely not the last time I was mistaken for Bruce Willis. Everyone clamored for me to participate.

So I sat my six-foot, two-inch ass on the floor beside a mortar and gave it a go. I started pounding and tossing, holding back on the sugar and, not wanting to appear the wimpy white guy, adding fresh Thai chiles by the handful. The first kid who tasted my version started leaping up and down in agony, his mouth on fire. Too sour and way too hot was the verdict.

After my epic failure, I set out to learn how to make it properly. The good news for anyone with the will is that the way is no secret. *Som tam* isn't often made behind closed doors. Everyone—from bar girls to taxi drivers to moneyed city kids—loves *som tam*, the dish that gave Pok Pok its name. Whether you're in a makeshift restaurant in Khon Kaen or waiting by a street cart in Bangkok, you'll hear its siren song—*pok pok, pok pok*—as the ingredients are pounded. When you hit up a vendor, the dish is made to order and all the ingredients are laid out for you to see. I got to know the mortar—a tall, deep wood or clay number, not the shallower granite one used for pounding curry pastes. I noted the order in which the ingredients were added and the surprising gentleness with which the cook applied the pestle.

Another thing I learned: papaya is not the defining feature of the dish, although the name is invariably translated as papaya salad. *Tam* refers, more or less, to the method used to make it. *Som* just means sour. The best-known iteration does have irregular shreds of unripe papaya as its main ingredient. But *som tam* takes many forms. Tam Taeng Kwaa (the word *som* is implied), page 45, is made with cucumber. Som Tam Phonlamai (page 43) is made with various fruits, green papaya being a minor part and 100 percent optional. I own a Thai cookbook that has recipes for more than one hundred variations, including ingredients like noodles or fried fish or pineapple, apples or ground meat or pork skins, just about anything you can think of.

That said, *som tam* does typically indicate papaya salad, though by no means does the presence of papaya end the story. Depending on your location or the establishment, you'll eat papaya salad seasoned according to the local palate with regionally beloved ingredients. The dish was likely born in Laos and then came to Isaan, the northeastern region of Thailand, whose people are ethnically Lao. My theory is that the dish readily spread throughout Thailand with the diaspora of Isaan workers, who left their traditionally poor homeland to find employment. The Isaan version is dramatically different from the version we're used to in the US, which at its best resembles the Central Thai rendition: sweetness, sourness, and heat exist in almost equal proportions, a flavor profile accomplished with palm sugar, lime juice, fresh chiles, and fish sauce. In Isaan, sweetness is virtually nonexistent. Instead, you're confronted with the gut-twisting heat of dried red chiles and the salty funk from preserved black crab and *naam plaa raa*, a particularly robust fermented fish sauce.

Yet just because these variations exist doesn't mean the flavors are prescribed. Papaya salad is, like many dishes in Thailand that are made to order, customizable. Before I spoke even a lick of Thai, I heard an unintelligible buzz coming from the crowds gathered around *som tam* vendors. When I finally did pick up the language, I realized that these customers weren't discussing the price of tea in China. They were explaining how they wanted their *som tam*—perhaps particularly sweet or tart, perhaps with extra tomatoes or carrots. I'd hear snatches of language, like *naam sii daeng daeng* (lots of chiles). I've even seen vendors offer finicky patrons a taste midprocess or stand back as a customer grabbed the pestle and started pounding himself. Once you become a regular, the woman with the mortar becomes just like your local barista, turning out your *som tam* just as you like it, without a word of guidance from you.

* * *

Here, then, are four variations: the Central Thai version, the Lao/Isaan version, *som tam* made with mixed fruit, and one made with cucumber that I once ate served over noodles.

The basic details are the same, though as always, they vary by cook. For our purposes, you'll pound chile, sugar, and sometimes garlic, not to a homogenous paste but to a chunky sludge so the flavors are released and still remain bright and separate. The more thoroughly you pound the chiles, the more their heat will coat your mouth when you take a bite. I prefer the little bursts of heat that chunks provide. I like to occasionally bite into a small hunk of chile or garlic.

When you add the main ingredient—be it green papaya, apple, or cucumber—you want to pound lightly with the goal of lightly bruising (not smashing or crushing) it, just enough so that the dressing can permeate but not so much that it sacrifices its texture.

I recommend making these four exactly as instructed before you start playing with the seasonings. Once you get a sense of the flavor profiles, my hope is that you'll be able to adjust ingredients to accommodate your preferences and new ingredients. Maybe the Central Thai version isn't fiery enough for you. Cool; add more chile. Perhaps you have green mango on hand instead of green papaya. Because it's more tart, up the sugar content.

SHREDDING PAPAYA

When shredding a papaya, the goal is irregular strips anywhere from 3 to 5 inches in length and 1/16 to 1/8 inch thick. You can accomplish this in many ways. Here are three.

One, use a mandoline. Easy.

Two, buy a cheap Kiwi brand papaya shredder and run it along the peeled flesh.

And finally, my favorite method and the trickiest to get right: Hold the peeled papaya lengthwise on its side in one hand, methodically hack at it with a large knife, making lengthwise grooves in the flesh every 1/16 to 1/8 inch. Once you've covered the upside with grooves, stand the papaya up on a cutting board and use the knife to shave off shreds. Repeat until you have the amount of shredded papaya you need.

Each method will yield strips of different thickness. The thinner the strips, the more lightly you should pound. You can shred the papaya a few hours before you plan to use it if you store it, covered, in the fridge to keep it crisp.

Som Tam Thai

CENTRAL THAI-STYLE PAPAYA SALAD

SPECIAL EQUIPMENT

- A papaya shredder (or mandoline or large knife)
- A Thai clay mortar
- A wooden pestle

This version of papaya salad, probably the most familiar to Westerners, sports the sweet, sour, salty, and hot flavors that have come to embody Thai food in the States. It is the reason we see papaya salad on virtually every Thai menu. This stuff is seriously good—right in a Westerner's wheelhouse—when the balance of flavors is right and the shredded papaya isn't bashed to death.

Flavor Profile NEARLY EQUAL PARTS SWEET, SOUR, SPICY, SALTY

Try It With Kai Yaang (Whole roasted young chicken), page 135, Plaa Phao Kleua (Grilled salt-crusted fish with chile dipping sauce), page 80, or Sii Khrong Muu Yaang (Thai-style pork ribs), page 128. Needs Khao Niaw (Sticky rice), page 33.

SERVES 2 TO 6 AS PART OF A MEAL; YOU CAN DOUBLE THE RECIPE IN A LARGE CLAY MORTAR

1 generous tablespoon medium-size dried shrimp, rinsed and patted dry

1 ounce palm sugar

1/4 teaspoon water

1 small lime (preferably a Key lime), halved through the stem

3 grams peeled garlic cloves (about 1 medium clove), halved lengthwise

3 grams fresh stemmed Thai chiles (about 2), preferably red

1 ounce long beans, ends trimmed, cut into 2-inch lengths (about 1/2 cup)

1 tablespoon lime juice (preferably from Key limes or spiked with a small squeeze of Meyer lemon juice)

1 tablespoon Thai fish sauce

1 tablespoon Naam Makham (Tamarind water), page 275

4 ounces peeled, shredded green papaya (about 1 1/2 cups, lightly packed)

3 ounces cherry tomatoes (about 6), halved, or quartered if very large

2 generous tablespoons coarsely chopped unsalted roasted peanuts

Wedge of white or green cabbage

DRY-FRY THE SHRIMP AND SOFTEN THE PALM SUGAR

Heat a small dry pan or wok over medium heat, add the dried shrimp, and cook, stirring frequently, until they're dry all the way through and slightly crispy, about 5 minutes. Set them aside to cool. They'll keep covered at room temperature for up to 1 week.

Put the palm sugar in a small microwavable bowl, sprinkle on the 1/4 teaspoon of water, cover the bowl with plastic wrap, and microwave on low just until the sugar has softened (not liquefied), 10 to 30 seconds. Pound the mixture in a mortar (or mash it in the bowl) until you have a smooth paste. Covered, it will keep soft for up to 2 days.

MAKE THE PAPAYA SALAD

Cut one of the lime halves lengthwise into thirds, then cut the thirds in half crosswise. Set aside 3 of the pieces (reserve the remaining lime for another purpose).

Combine the garlic, chiles, and 1 tablespoon of the softened palm sugar in a large clay mortar and pound just until you have a chunky sludge with medium pieces of chile and small but visible pieces of garlic, about 10 seconds.

Add the 3 lime wedges and pound very lightly, just to release the juice. Add the shrimp, pound lightly (don't smash or pulverize them), just to release their flavor, then add the long beans and pound lightly to bruise them (they should not break into pieces or totally flatten).

Add the lime juice, fish sauce, tamarind water, and papaya. Then use the pestle to barely bruise the papaya (lightly pounding at a slight angle, not directly up-and-down) for about 10 seconds, while simultaneously using a large spoon to scoop up from the bottom of the mortar, essentially tossing the papaya, palm sugar mixture, and the other ingredients as you pound. Do not smash the papaya. It should remain crisp.

Add the tomatoes and pound lightly, just to release their juice. Add the peanuts and mix briefly with the spoon. Transfer the papaya salad to a plate, liquid and all, and serve with the wedge of cabbage on the side.

Som Tam Lao

LAO/ISAAN-STYLE PAPAYA SALAD

The papaya salad favored in Isaan, the Northeastern region of Thailand, is not for the timid. (It's often called *som tam lao*, because Laos is the likely birthplace of papaya salad and because neighbors Laos and Isaan share so much, culinary and otherwise.) The ominous dried red chiles lurking among the tangle of papaya would give many an adventurous eater pause—that is, if the dismembered, blackish crustacean hasn't distracted the eye. Yet for a certain diner, the sweat-inducing, sea-funky version will supplant the Central Thai version as the one they forever crave with a heap of sticky rice.

Flavor Profile FIERY, FUNKY, SOUR, SALTY

Try It With Kai Yaang (Whole roasted young chicken), page 135, or either version of Laap Isaan (Isaan minced meat salad), pages 117 and 119. Needs Khao Niaw (Sticky rice), page 33.

SPECIAL EQUIPMENT

- A papaya shredder (or mandoline or large knife)
- A Thai clay mortar
- A wooden pestle

SERVES 4 TO 6 AS PART OF A MEAL; YOU CAN DOUBLE THE RECIPE IN A LARGE CLAY MORTAR

1 tablespoon medium-size dried shrimp, rinsed and patted dry

1 ounce palm sugar

1/4 teaspoon water

1 small lime (preferably a Key lime), halved through the stem

3 grams peeled garlic (about 1 medium clove), halved lengthwise

1 gram dried Thai chiles (about 4), soaked in hot water just until pliable, about 10 minutes, then drained

1/2 teaspoon crab paste (black in color; should not contain oil), preferably the Pantainorasingh brand (optional)

1 ounce long beans, ends trimmed, cut into 2-inch lengths (about 1/2 cup)

1 frozen whole Thai salted black crab, defrosted (see NOTE)

11/2 tablespoons naam plaa raa (fermented fish sauce)

1 tablespoon Thai fish sauce

11/2 tablespoons lime juice (preferably from Key limes or spiked with a small squeeze of Meyer lemon juice)

A scant tablespoon Naam Makham (Tamarind water), page 275

4 ounces peeled, shredded green papaya (about 11/2 cups, lightly packed)

2 ounces cherry tomatoes (about 4), halved, or quartered if very large

Wedge of white or green cabbage

NOTE: Salted black crab (puu khem, boo kem, or other phonetic transliterations; also called "paddy crab") are often found frozen in the US. Your best bet is Southeast Asian–focused grocery stores.

DRY-FRY THE SHRIMP AND SOFTEN THE PALM SUGAR

Heat a small dry pan or wok over medium heat, add the dried shrimp, and cook, stirring frequently, until they're dry all the way through and slightly crispy, about 5 minutes. Set them aside in a small bowl to cool. They'll keep covered at room temperature for up to 1 week.

Put the palm sugar in a small microwavable bowl, sprinkle on the 1/4 teaspoon of water, cover the bowl with plastic wrap, and microwave on low just until the sugar has softened (not liquefied), 10 to 30 seconds. Pound the mixture in a mortar (or mash it in the bowl) until you have a smooth paste. Covered, it will keep soft for up to 2 days.

MAKE THE PAPAYA SALAD

Cut one of the lime halves lengthwise into thirds, then cut the thirds in half crosswise. Set aside 3 of the pieces (reserve the remaining lime for another purpose).

{continued}

Combine the garlic, chiles, 1 teaspoon of the softened palm sugar, and the crab paste in a large clay mortar and pound just until you have a chunky sludge with small but visible pieces of garlic and slightly broken down chiles (do not turn the chiles into mush), 5 to 10 seconds.

Add the 3 lime wedges and pound very lightly and briefly, just to release the juice. Add the long beans and pound lightly to bruise them (they should not break into pieces or dramatically flatten).

Pry off and discard the top shell (technically, the "carapace") from the crab, scoop out and discard the gills, rinse the crab, and briefly shake it dry. Pull the crab into two pieces. Add the crab and the shrimp to the mortar, and pound lightly just to release their flavor (don't crush or pulverize the shrimp; the crab shell should crack but not break into pieces).

Add both fish sauces, the lime juice, the tamarind water, and the papaya. The next step is easy but subtle. You want to use the pestle to barely bruise the papaya (lightly pounding at a slight angle, not directly up-and-down) for about 10 seconds, while simultaneously using a large spoon to scoop up from the bottom of the mortar, essentially tossing the papaya, palm sugar mixture, and the other ingredients as you pound. Do not smash the papaya. It should remain crisp.

Add the tomatoes and pound lightly, just to release the juices. Mix briefly but well with the spoon. Spoon the contents of the mortar, liquid and all, in a low mound, and serve with the wedge of cabbage on the side.

Som Tam Phonlamai

THAI FRUIT SALAD

Just one of many examples of *som tam* that has nothing to do with green papaya (I do like to add some for this rendition, but you could certainly leave it out) and almost everything to do with the method of preparation: made in a clay mortar, the salad requires the same gentle pounding that aims to bruise but not smash the main ingredients, allowing some of the sweet-tart dressing to pervade. Use any fruit you want, even if it's just one or two kinds. Be sure to choose fruit that strikes a good balance between sweetness and tartness. If the fruit is very sweet, you'll want to scale back on the sugar and perhaps bump up the lime juice.

Flavor Profile SWEET, SPICY, TART, SLIGHTLY SALTY

Try It With Plaa Neung Si Ew (Steamed whole fish with soy sauce), page 79, or Kai Yaang (Whole roasted young chicken), page 135, and coconut rice (page 193).

SERVES 2 TO 6 AS PART OF A MEAL; YOU CAN DOUBLE THE RECIPE IN A LARGE CLAY MORTAR

1 generous tablespoon medium-size dried shrimp, rinsed and patted dry	1 tablespoon lime juice (preferably from Key limes or spiked with a small squeeze of Meyer lemon juice)	8 ounces mixed crunchy, sweet, and tart fruit (such apple, pear, pineapple, green mango, and persimmon), any inedible skin peeled, cut into irregular 1-inch chunks
1 ounce palm sugar	1 tablespoon Thai fish sauce	
1/4 teaspoon water	1 ounce peeled, shredded green papaya (about 1/2 cup, lightly packed)	8 to 10 grapes, halved
1 small lime (preferably a Key lime), halved through the stem	14 grams peeled carrot, cut into long (about 3-inch), thin (about 1/8-inch) strips (about 1/4 cup, lightly packed)	2 ounces cherry tomatoes (about 4), halved, or quartered if very large
3 grams fresh Thai chiles (about 2), preferably red		2 generous tablespoons coarsely chopped unsalted roasted peanuts

DRY-FRY THE SHRIMP AND SOFTEN THE PALM SUGAR

Heat a small dry pan or wok over medium heat, add the dried shrimp, and cook, stirring frequently, until they're dry all the way through and slightly crispy, about 5 minutes. Set them aside in a small bowl to cool. They'll keep covered at room temperature for up to 1 week.

Put the palm sugar in a small microwavable bowl, sprinkle on the 1/4 teaspoon of water, cover the bowl with plastic wrap, and microwave on low just until the sugar has softened (not liquefied), 10 to 30 seconds. Pound the mixture in a mortar (or mash it in the bowl) until you have a smooth paste. Covered, it will keep soft for up to 2 days.

MAKE THE SALAD

Cut one of the lime halves lengthwise into thirds, then cut the thirds in half crosswise. Set aside 2 of the pieces (reserve the remaining lime for another purpose).

Combine the chiles and 1 heaping teaspoon (or less if the fruit is very sweet) of the softened palm sugar in a large clay mortar and pound just until you have a chunky sludge with medium pieces of chile, 5 to 10 seconds.

Add the 2 lime wedges and pound very lightly and briefly, just to release the juice, then add the shrimp and pound lightly just to release their flavor (don't smash or pulverize them).

{continued}

{Thai fruit salad, continued}

Add the lime juice, fish sauce, papaya, and carrot. The next step is easy but subtle. You want to use the pestle to barely bruise the papaya (lightly pounding at a slight angle, not directly up-and-down) for about 10 seconds, while simultaneously using a large spoon to scoop up from the bottom of the mortar, essentially tossing the papaya, palm sugar mixture, and the other ingredients as you pound. Do not smash the papaya. It should remain crisp.

Add the fruit, including the grapes, and pound the same way you did the papaya, barely bruising the fruit and definitely not smashing it.

Add the tomatoes and pound lightly, just to release the juice. Taste the salad and if necessary, season with additional lime juice and fish sauce to achieve a salad that's, in descending order of prominence, sweet from the fruit, spicy, sour, and a little salty.

Finally, add the peanuts and mix well with the spoon. Transfer to a plate, liquid and all, in a low mound, and serve.

Tam Taeng Kwaa

THAI CUCUMBER SALAD

SPECIAL EQUIPMENT

• A Thai clay mortar
• A wooden pestle

The first time I had *som tam* made from cucumber, I was in Si Sa Ket, a small town in Isaan. I'd just seen the ruins of an old temple and I was on my way back to my hotel in God knows where. The motorcycle taxi I'd hired to take me to the ruins had dropped me off at a sort of crossroads. I was waiting there for a bus. Nearby was a general store where a bunch of people were hanging out, so I sidled over and greeted them in rudimentary Thai. They were making lunch, and I asked them what they were eating. They seemed excited to see a foreigner who wasn't part of a tour group and offered me a plate of food. Instead of everyone grabbing from a mound of sticky rice, as I'd expected, we all had our own bowls with a few skeins of *khanom jiin*, noodles made from fermented rice. One of my new friends spooned the *som tam* over the top. In the typical Isaan fashion, it was fiery, just faintly sweet, and intensely funky from the fermented fish sauce called *naam plaa raa*. Not only did it drive home for me that green papaya has no monopoly on *som tam*, but it showed me that even in sticky-rice country, you could eat *som tam* however the heck you wanted. As I began to say my goodbyes, a few of them semi-jokingly suggested that I stay and marry their daughters. "I'm too old!" I told them. It didn't seem to matter. My theory is that they were just thrilled that I happily ate *plaa raa*.

Flavor Profile FIERY, SOUR, SALTY, BARELY SWEET

Try It With Sii Khrong Muu Yaang (Thai-style pork ribs), page 128, or other grilled meat. If you're not serving it over rice noodles, eat it with Khao Niaw (Sticky rice), page 33.

{continued}

{Thai cucumber salad, continued}

SERVES 2 TO 6 AS PART OF A MEAL; YOU CAN DOUBLE THE RECIPE IN A LARGE CLAY MORTAR

1 tablespoon medium-size dried shrimp, rinsed and patted dry

1 ounce palm sugar

1/4 teaspoon water

1 small lime (preferably a Key lime), halved through the stem

3 grams peeled garlic (about 1 medium clove), halved lengthwise

1 gram dried Thai chiles (about 4), soaked in lukewarm water just until pliable, about 10 minutes, then drained

1 ounce long beans, ends trimmed, cut into 2-inch lengths (about 1/2 cup)

7 ounces Persian, English, or Japanese cucumbers (or any firm variety without large seeds and thick, bitter skin)

1 tablespoon Thai fish sauce

1 tablespoon naam plaa raa (fermented fish sauce)

1 tablespoon lime juice (preferably from Key limes or spiked with a small squeeze of Meyer lemon juice)

2 ounces cherry tomatoes (about 4), halved, or quartered if very large

2 generous tablespoons coarsely chopped unsalted roasted peanuts

2 ounces Vietnamese or Thai dried rice vermicelli, prepared according to the instructions on page 231 (optional)

DRY-FRY THE SHRIMP AND SOFTEN THE PALM SUGAR

Heat a small dry pan or wok over medium heat, add the dried shrimp, and cook, stirring frequently, until they're dry all the way through and slightly crispy, about 5 minutes. Set them aside in a small bowl to cool. They'll keep covered at room temperature for up to 1 week.

Put the palm sugar in a small microwavable bowl, sprinkle on the 1/4 teaspoon of water, cover the bowl with plastic wrap, and microwave on low just until the sugar has softened (not liquefied), 10 to 30 seconds. Pound the mixture in a mortar (or mash it in the bowl) until you have a smooth paste. Covered, it will keep soft for up to 2 days.

MAKE THE SALAD

Cut one of the lime halves lengthwise into thirds, then cut the thirds in half crosswise. Set aside 3 of the pieces (reserve the remaining lime for another purpose).

Combine the garlic, chiles, and 1 heaping teaspoon of the softened palm sugar in a large clay mortar and pound just until you have a chunky sludge with small but visible pieces of garlic and slightly broken down chiles (do not turn the chiles into mush), 5 to 10 seconds.

Add the 3 lime wedges and pound very lightly and briefly, just to release the juice. Add the shrimp, pound lightly just to release their flavor (don't smash or pulverize them), then add the long beans and pound lightly to bruise them (they should not break into pieces or dramatically flatten).

Halve the cucumber lengthwise and cut it into angled, irregular 3/4- to 1-inch chunks. Add the cucumber, both fish sauces, and lime juice. The next step is easy but subtle. You want to use the pestle to barely bruise the cucumber (lightly pounding at a slight angle, not directly up-and-down) for about 10 seconds, while simultaneously using a large spoon to scoop up from the bottom of the mortar, essentially tossing the cucumber, palm sugar mixture, and the other ingredients as you pound. Do not smash the cucumber.

Add the tomatoes and pound lightly, just to release the juices. Add the peanuts and mix briefly but well with the spoon.

If you're using the noodles, put them on a plate with raised edges or in a shallow bowl. Spoon the contents of the mortar, liquid and all, over them. Stir well before you eat.

YAM
Thai "salads"

Yam is often translated in English as "salad," because we lack a better word to describe this category in the Thai repertoire. The word *yam* has a more expansive meaning—it suggests aromatics, as in the ubiquitous soup *tom yam*, or if you will "boiled salad," and it can mean, essentially, "to mix." In this context, however, it refers to ingredients (typically warm or room-temperature proteins or vegetables mixed with herbs and shallots) dressed with a mixture that almost always includes fish sauce, lime juice, palm sugar, fresh Thai chiles, and garlic. Cooks vary these elements, perhaps omitting one, adding another, or tweaking the balance among them all, to accommodate the main ingredients. (*Som tam*, aka papaya salad and its ilk, are not thought of as *yam*; the pounding method they employ sets them apart.) Anyone expecting from *yam* something akin to a Caesar or bowl of baby spinach will be thoroughly disappointed, but the "salad" translation really isn't so far off.

Yam Khai Dao

In the past, Ban Pae was probably a fishing village. Today it's a tiny town whose sole purpose seems to be as the place to catch a boat to Ko Samet, which has the nicest beaches within a few hours of Bangkok. Years ago I took the three-hour bus ride from the capital to Ban Pae, arriving with a couple of hours to spare before the afternoon boat left. Enough time for lunch.

The bus stop area where I was let off, like so many in Thailand, contained a few tiny restaurants selling snacks and simple lunches. The food at these can be surprisingly good, though typically you order in the hope that, at best, whatever you order won't suck. I chose a spot, more or less at random, sat myself down on a comically tiny chair, and took in the menu, a document smattered with English including the strange but inviting "fried egg salad." I'd try that.

What arrived were rice and an unassuming plate of herbs, lettuce, and carrot tossed with fried egg. The white was crispy at the edges. (The *khai dao* in the name means "star-shaped egg," a poetic way to refer to the way the whites spread out while frying in a hot wok.) The yolk was just set, not runny but not chalky either, and the vivid-orange color I've come to expect in Thailand, the result apparently of feeding chickens shrimp shells. Each bite was bright and fiery, thanks to a dressing made of little more than lime juice, palm sugar, and fresh chile—a familiar combination to even novice Thai food lovers and perfectly calibrated here.

The dish so exceeded my expectations that, for a second, I thought that maybe I'd happened upon the inventor of the dish or at least a restaurant that specialized in it. But as with many of my revelations, once a new dish appeared on my radar, I started to see it everywhere. What I discovered was just a common offering, a simple, delicious thing that any careful cook can execute well.

That's what I found when I returned to Portland and set out to recreate this salad. As long as you make sure to fry the eggs in plenty of hot, hot oil—to achieve those crispy edges—you'd be hard pressed to screw this one up. It's so simple and yet so distinctive that it became a dish that I'd make at Pok Pok, sure, but also one I make all the time at home.

Flavor Profile NEARLY EQUAL PARTS SWEET, SOUR, SPICY, SALTY

Try It With Kaeng Khiaw Waan Luuk Chin Plaa (Green curry with fish balls and eggplant), page 161, or Sii Khrong Muu Yaang (Thai-style pork ribs), page 128, and Khao Hom Mali (Jasmine rice), page 31.

{continued}

**SERVES 2 TO 6
AS PART OF A MEAL;
THE RECIPE IS
EASILY DOUBLED**

EGGS

2 large eggs, at room temperature

1/4 to 1/3 cup vegetable oil

DRESSING

1 1/2 tablespoons lime juice (preferably from Key limes or spiked with a small squeeze of Meyer lemon juice)

1 1/2 tablespoons Naam Cheuam Naam Taan Piip (Palm sugar simple syrup), page 275

1 tablespoon Thai fish sauce

3 grams peeled garlic, halved lengthwise and very thinly sliced (about 1 1/2 teaspoons)

2 grams fresh Thai chiles (about 2 small), preferably green, thinly sliced

SALAD

14 grams green leaf lettuce, cut into 2-inch-thick pieces (about 1 cup, lightly packed)

1 ounce peeled yellow onion, thinly sliced with the grain (about 1/4 cup, lightly packed)

14 grams peeled carrot, cut into long (about 3-inch), thin (about 1/8-inch) strips (about 1/4 cup, lightly packed)

1/4 cup very coarsely chopped Chinese celery (thin stems and leaves), lightly packed

1/4 cup very coarsely chopped cilantro (thin stems and leaves), lightly packed

FRY THE EGGS

Heat a wok or nonstick frying pan over high heat, then add just enough oil to reach a depth of a generous 1/4 inch. Once the oil begins to smoke, carefully crack in the eggs (holding them close to the oil to avoid splatter) and decrease the heat to medium. The eggs should spit, bubble, and crackle wildly. The whites should puff and develop large transparent bubbles.

Once the whites get crispy and deep golden brown at the edges, 45 seconds to 1 minute, use a spatula to flip the eggs (try not to break the yolks, but if you do, it's fine) and keep cooking until the bottom is golden brown and the yolks are set but still molten, 30 to 45 seconds more. Transfer the eggs to paper towels to drain. Discard the oil, then rinse and wipe out the wok and let it cool. You can fry the eggs up to 15 minutes or so before you make the salad.

MAKE THE DRESSING AND ASSEMBLE THE SALAD

Add the lime juice, simple syrup, fish sauce, garlic, and chiles to the wok, set it over medium heat, and heat the mixture just until it's warm to the touch, 15 seconds or so. Turn off the heat.

Quarter the eggs through the yolks and add them to the wok along with the remaining ingredients. Stir gently but well, then transfer the salad, liquid and all, to a plate in a low heap, so that most of the herbs end up near the top, and serve.

Yam Tuna

Not long ago I was at a Thai friend's house for dinner. He employed a fantastic Isaan cook, who brought out dish after awesome dish, including one that would become a favorite of mine. It looked like a typical *yam*, what we translate into English as "salad," except that the main ingredient looked a lot like canned tuna.

Can't be, I thought. In Thailand, your mind often plays tricks on you. What looks like beef could very well be water buffalo. What you assume is green papaya turns out to be white turmeric. I took a bite. No question, it was canned tuna. And it was fucking delicious.

Once I'd eaten it, I started seeing how common canned fish is in Thai food. This is one of those weird and wonderful dishes that are testaments to the fact that Thai cooks can take just about any ingredient you give them and seamlessly incorporate it into their culinary lexicon. It proves yet again that modern Thai food is fusion food, in the best sense of the term.

While tuna isn't a particularly popular fish in Thailand, the country happens to be a major exporter of the canned stuff. I still don't know whether the dish has its roots as a *yam* made with fresh fish or with a creative and convenience-oriented young cook who was trying to make dinner on the cheap and thought, *Hey, why not?*

Back in Portland, I put it on Pok Pok's menu as a special, thinking customers would get a kick out of an offbeat combination. Now, it's a staple there. Typically, I look to local canneries that process tasty local albacore caught off the coast. But when I come across great fresh albacore, I grill it and use that instead. You should do the same.

Flavor Profile TART, SPICY, SLIGHTLY FISHY, SALTY

Try It With Phat Phak Ruam Mit (Stir-fried mixed vegetables), page 98, or Naam Phrik Plaa Thuu (Grilled-fish dip), page 177, and Khao Hom Mali (Jasmine rice), page 31, or Khao Niaw (Sticky rice), page 33.

SERVES 2 TO 6 AS PART OF A MEAL; THE RECIPE IS EASILY DOUBLED

DRESSING

2 tablespoons Thai fish sauce

2 tablespoons lime juice (preferably from Key limes or spiked with a small squeeze of Meyer lemon juice)

1 tablespoon Naam Cheuam Naam Taan Piip (Palm sugar simple syrup), page 275

1 (14-gram) piece peeled ginger, cut into long (about 1¹/₂-inch), thin (about ¹/₈-inch), matchsticks (about 2 tablespoons, lightly packed)

7 grams peeled garlic cloves, halved lengthwise and thinly sliced (about 1 tablespoon)

6 grams fresh Thai chiles (about 4), preferably green, thinly sliced

SALAD

1 (5-ounce) can solid light tuna packed in water, drained and broken into large pieces

2 ounces cherry tomatoes (about 4), halved, or quartered if large

7 grams thinly sliced lemongrass (tender parts only), from about 1 large stalk (about 1 tablespoon)

14 grams peeled yellow onion, thinly sliced with the grain (about 2 tablespoons)

1 tablespoon coarsely chopped cilantro (thin stems and leaves), lightly packed

1 tablespoon coarsely chopped Chinese celery (thin stems and leaves), lightly packed

1 tablespoon thinly sliced green onions, lightly packed

MAKE THE DRESSING

Combine the fish sauce, lime juice, simple syrup, ginger, garlic, and chiles in a medium pot, set it over medium heat, and heat the mixture just until it's warm to the touch, 15 seconds or so. Turn off the heat.

ASSEMBLE THE SALAD

Add the remaining ingredients to the pot with the dressing and toss gently but well. Transfer the salad, liquid and all, to a plate in a heap, and serve.

Yam Wun Sen "Chao Wang"

SUNNY'S FANCY GLASS NOODLE SALAD

SPECIAL EQUIPMENT

- **A Thai granite mortar and pestle**
- **A long-handled noodle basket**

My friend Sunny, who has taught me so much about Thai food, is very opinionated—to say the least. When we cook together, he is quick to scold me when I try to take a shortcut. I once asked whether instead of painstakingly crushing melon by hand for Khanom Bataeng Laai (page 254), I could use a blender. "No, can not!" he said, horrified. What about using a whisk to mix the ingredients for Sankhaya Turian (page 260)? *"Mai aroy!"* he cried ("Not delicious!"). Sometimes, he'll skip the verbal reprimand and just hit me with a cucumber.

I usually listen, because Sunny has great taste in food. His preferences tend toward the *chao wang* (fancy), probably because he learned to cook from his mother and aunts, who were employed as cooks by Thai royalty. That's why he insists on mincing pork so finely for *laap*. And that's one reason his version of glass noodle salad is particularly awesome. While you don't have to add as many goodies as he does, the fresh shrimp, ground pork, pork roll, pickled garlic, and fried garlic and shallots do make a memorable combination.

Flavor Profile SPICY, SOUR, AROMATIC, UMAMI-RICH

Try It With Sii Khrong Muu Yaang (Thai-style pork ribs), page 128, or other grilled meat, and Jaw Phak Kat (Northern Thai mustard green soup with tamarind and pork ribs), page 151, or Phat Fak Thawng (Northern Thai-style stir-fried squash), page 94.

{continued}

SERVES 2 TO 6 AS PART OF A MEAL; THE RECIPE IS EASILY DOUBLED

PORK AND DRIED SHRIMP

1/2 teaspoon vegetable oil

Scant 2 ounces ground pork

A few dashes Thai fish sauce

1 tablespoon medium-size dried shrimp, rinsed and patted dry

DRESSING

3 grams fresh Thai chiles (about 2), preferably green, thinly sliced

7 grams peeled garlic (about 2 medium cloves), halved lengthwise

1 tablespoon lime juice (preferably from Key limes or spiked with a small squeeze of Meyer lemon juice)

1 tablespoon Thai fish sauce

1 1/2 teaspoons liquid from Thai pickled garlic (straight from the jar)

1/2 teaspoon granulated sugar

1 1/2 teaspoons water

SALAD

1 1/4 ounces dried glass noodles (also called bean thread or cellophane noodles), soaked in lukewarm water until very pliable, about 8 minutes, drained well, and snipped into irregular 4- to 6-inch lengths

2 ounces medium shrimp (about 4), shelled, halved lengthwise, and deveined

1 (2-ounce) piece Vietnamese pork roll (called giò lụa or chả lụa in Vietnamese and muu yaw in Thai), quartered lengthwise and cut into 1/4-inch-thick slices

1 tablespoon Naam Man Krathiem (Fried-garlic oil), page 272, or Naam Man Hom Daeng (Fried-shallot oil), page 273

14 grams peeled carrots, cut into long (about 3-inch), thin (about 1/8-inch) strips (about 1/4 cup, lightly packed)

14 grams peeled small shallots, preferably Asian, or very small red onions, halved lengthwise and thinly sliced with the grain (about 2 tablespoons)

2 tablespoons coarsely chopped cilantro (thin stems and leaves), lightly packed, plus an extra pinch

2 tablespoons coarsely chopped Chinese celery (thin stems and leaves), lightly packed

8 grams unpeeled jarred pickled garlic head, very thinly sliced crosswise (about 1 tablespoon, lightly packed)

Pinch ground white pepper

1 tablespoon Hom Daeng Jiaw (Fried shallots), page 273

1 tablespoon Krathiem Jiaw (Fried garlic), page 272

COOK THE PORK AND DRY-FRY THE SHRIMP

Heat the vegetable oil in a small pan over medium-high heat until it shimmers, add the pork, and cook (stirring, breaking up the meat, and about halfway through, adding a couple dashes of fish sauce) just until it's cooked through, about 1 minute.

Heat a small dry pan or wok over medium heat, add the dried shrimp, and cook, stirring frequently, until they're dry all the way through and slightly crispy, about 5 minutes. Set them aside in a small bowl to cool. They'll keep covered at room temperature for up to 1 week.

MAKE THE DRESSING

Pound the chiles and garlic in a granite mortar to a very coarse paste, about 15 seconds. Add 2 teaspoons of this mixture to a wok or medium pan along with the lime juice, fish sauce, pickled garlic liquid, sugar, the 1 1/2 teaspoons water, and 1/4 cup of the cooked pork. Set it aside for the moment.

MAKE THE SALAD

Bring a medium pot of water to a gentle simmer. Put the noodles, raw shrimp, and pork roll in a long-handled noodle basket and put the basket in the water. Cook, gently shaking the basket frequently to move the ingredients around, just until the shrimp is cooked through, the pork is warm, and the noodles are tender, about 30 seconds. Firmly shake the basket to drain well.

Set the wok or pan containing the chile mixture over medium heat, and heat the mixture just until it's warm to the touch, 15 seconds or so. Turn off the heat. Add the noodles, shrimp, and pork roll to the wok with the chile mixture. Add the garlic or shallot oil and toss well, then add the carrots, shallots, cilantro, Chinese celery, dried shrimp, pickled garlic, and white pepper and toss well once more.

Transfer to a shallow bowl and sprinkle with the fried shallots, fried garlic, and an extra pinch cilantro. Stir again before eating.

Yam Makheua Yao

GRILLED EGGPLANT SALAD

SPECIAL EQUIPMENT

- A charcoal grill (highly recommended)

I'm halfway through one of the most memorable dinners I'd ever have when I hear yelling. I'm in Isaan, having traveled along the border Thailand shares with Cambodia and stopped for a day in Si Sa Ket, a small countryside town. I had been prowling the streets around dusk with dinner on my mind, and one restaurant's massive grill pit beckoned with green eggplants, each more than a foot long, charring on the rack. I ordered a sort of salad made with them that I'd first encountered a year or two earlier. That version was good, but this one was on another level. The eggplants had picked up an incredibly smoky flavor and, instead of turning to mush, stayed juicy and fleshy. If this were Italy, a cook might just drizzle nice olive oil on something this spectacular. But this is Thailand, so there was a dressing bright with lime and fragrant from chiles. There was the richness of crumbled hard-boiled egg and the salty, umami punch of dried shrimp. I sat outside looking onto the town's main drag, tearing through that eggplant along with sticky rice and a small plate of grilled meat, consumed by the all-is-well-with-the-world feeling food this great breeds.

I turn toward the ruckus, just fifty feet away. A cop is screaming at a thirty-something woman. She's screaming back. Suddenly, people who had been strolling the street are now hunched over and running. Others have taken cover behind chairs, under tables. I'm peeking out from behind a car. The cop has pulled out his service revolver and pointed it at the woman's face. Incredibly, she takes this in, sticks her fingers in her ears, makes a 180-degree turn, and walks slowly toward her truck. After a harrowing half minute—cop still screaming, following her, and aiming the gun point-blank at the back of her head—she gets in and drives away. The cop sits down and continues his drinking, like nothing happened.

It's funny how food memory becomes inextricably linked with other memories—how a smell can evoke your grandmother at the stove, how I can't eat *yam makheua yao* without thinking about that woman and that gun. Nor can I cook *yam makheua yao* without thinking about the rendition I had that day. It's the one I aspire to, superior even to the more fanciful versions I've had with ground pork and fresh shrimp.

Long green eggplants can be hard to locate back home, though they do show up at Asian markets and even some farmers' markets. Somehow, they resist turning into mush. They're useful in this recipe, because the eggplant must be cooked over very high heat to char its skin but without losing the meaty texture of the flesh. That said, the more common long purple eggplants require a little more vigilance, but they do the trick.

Flavor Profile SMOKY, SPICY, SOUR, SLIGHTLY SWEET

Try It With Muu Kham Waan (Grilled pork neck with spicy dipping sauce and iced greens), page 125, Sii Khrong Muu Yaang (Thai-style pork ribs), page 128, or Kai Yaang (Whole roasted young chicken), page 135. Needs Khao Niaw (Sticky rice), page 33.

{continued}

{Grilled eggplant salad, continued}

1 tablespoon medium-size dried shrimp, rinsed and patted dry

12 ounces long Asian eggplants (2 or 3), preferably green

1 large egg, at room temperature

1½ tablespoons lime juice (preferably from Key limes or spiked with a small squeeze of Meyer lemon juice)

1½ tablespoons Naam Cheuam Naam Taan Piip (Palm sugar simple syrup), page 275

1 tablespoon Thai fish sauce

2 grams fresh Thai chiles (about 2 small), preferably green, thinly sliced

14 grams peeled small shallots, preferably Asian, or very small red onions, halved lengthwise and thinly sliced with the grain (about 2 tablespoons

1 tablespoon Krathiem Jiaw (Fried garlic), page 272

2 tablespoons coarsely chopped cilantro (thin stems and leaves), lightly packed

SERVES 2 TO 6 AS PART OF A MEAL; THE RECIPE IS EASILY DOUBLED

DRY-FRY THE SHRIMP

Heat a small dry pan or wok over medium heat, add the dried shrimp, and cook, stirring frequently, until they're dry all the way through and slightly crispy, about 5 minutes. Set them aside in a small bowl to cool. They'll keep covered at room temperature for up to 1 week.

COOK, PEEL, AND CUT THE EGGPLANTS

Cook the eggplants either on the grill (highly recommended) or in the oven.

ON THE GRILL: Prepare a charcoal grill and ignite the coals (see page 124). (Hardwood charcoal burns hot and is ideal for this recipe.) Once the coals have begun to turn gray but are still flaming, grill the eggplants directly on the coals, turning frequently, until the skin has almost completely blackened and the flesh is very soft (it should meet with almost no resistance when you poke it with a sharp knife), about 4 minutes. The goal is to fully char the skin before the flesh gets mushy.

IN THE OVEN: Preheat the broiler to high and position a rack as close as you can to the heat source. Put the eggplants on a baking tray lined with aluminum foil (or, even better, on a wire rack on the baking tray) and broil, turning them over once, until the skin has blistered and mostly blackened and the flesh is very soft (it should meet with almost no resistance when you poke it with a sharp knife) but not mushy, about 6 to 12 minutes total, depending on the size of the eggplants and the distance from the heat source.

Let the eggplants cool for 10 minutes or so. This will make them easier to peel and allow the flesh to firm up slightly. Use your fingers to peel off the skin (don't go crazy removing every last bit), trying your best to keep the flesh intact. Do not run the eggplants under water. Cut the eggplants crosswise (on the diagonal, if you're feeling fancy) into 2-inch slices and arrange them on a serving plate.

COOK THE EGG

Prepare a bowl of ice water. Bring a small pot of water to a full boil, gently add the whole egg, and cook for 10 minutes. Your goal is a fully cooked egg whose yolk hasn't become dry and powdery. Transfer the egg to the ice water and once the egg is cool to the touch, peel and coarsely chop the white and yolk into small pieces.

ASSEMBLE THE SALAD

Combine the lime juice, simple syrup, fish sauce, and chiles in a small saucepan or wok, set it over medium heat, and heat the mixture just until it's warm to the touch, 15 seconds or so. Pour the warm mixture over the eggplant. Sprinkle on the egg, shallots, dried shrimp, fried garlic, and finally cilantro.

SUNNY

Sunny, my friend for more than fifteen years, is also my go-to guy in Chiang Mai, the curator of some of my most formative food experiences in Northern Thailand. Besides his extensive knowledge of food, he possesses charm that can penetrate even the surliest street vendor. He's a fantastic, intuitive cook. I've never seen him pull out a recipe. He and I cook together often when I visit, and like a good older brother, which is essentially what he has become for me, he affectionately chides me for everything from my heavy hand with seasoning to my "bad organization." I love every minute of it.

Sunny grew up in a small village near Chiang Mai, which was transplanted a few decades back after major flooding, to another spot a half an hour's drive southwest of the city, earning its name Ban Mai, or "new village." Before cities expanded their sprawl and lured rural Thais with opportunity, much of Thai life took place in long-lived, self-sustaining communities like this one. The fraternity of families who live here today has been intact for generations.

Sunny's father was a rice farmer. His mother worked at the country house of Chiang Mai's royal family as a kitchen assistant, helping to prepare their meals. She worked from the early morning to night for, Sunny tells me, less than a dollar a day. To supplement her income, she went to the local market before work to sell vegetables she grew. To fund Sunny's eldest brother's education in Bangkok, a big deal at the time, the family kept a few pigs to slaughter and sell every month. A luxurious life theirs was not.

Still, they ate well, if modestly. For dinner, the family typically gathered around a large basket of sticky rice and one simple boiled curry. They ate with their hands, as Northern Thais do, with just one spoon between them for any necessary scooping. They had plenty of fish from the nearby Ping River. Sunny tells me, as if it were the most normal thing in the world, that his dad would jump in and catch fish by hand. Frogs, too, were a staple—grilled or hacked up in curries and soups. They'd eat *yam hok*, a soup made with herbs and water buffalo fetus. To some people, that sounds gross. Others might smell a "delicacy." Yet it's clear how the dish developed. A buffalo miscarried. Meat is scarce. You eat what you can. Once in a while, his father would come home with a treat: pig's ear stewed with five spice, an essentially Chinese dish that wasn't easy to find in those days.

In the house there was almost always *naam phrik taa daeng*, a dense, dark paste made with dried chiles. It kept for a week, despite the heat. He'd eat it in the mornings, with sticky rice and boiled eggs, then after school, he'd come home, grab a handful of sticky rice and mold it around the same *naam phrik*, making a sort of sandwich the way an American kid might make himself a peanut butter and jelly.

Between his mother's experience with royal cuisine and a rich aunt, his family occasionally indulged in luxuries like massaman curry, which was relatively meat heavy. They occasionally ate noodles, which were expensive enough for them at the time that the family couldn't fill up on them alone. So they served sticky rice, too, dipping it into the noodle soup as if it were a curry.

Sunny did his best to help the family, though not without, as he readily admits, the typical grumblings of a kid. He wasn't allowed out of the house to play or watch television at a comparatively wealthy neighbor's house. He split his time between school, a forty-minute bike ride away, studying, and chores. Sunny would come home after school to haul in water from the nearby well. He woke up early to cook sticky rice. He grudgingly helped his mother and aunts prepare family meals, rummaging in the garden and through bushes to find whatever herbs and leaves they sent him to fetch and pounding whatever they asked him to pound. Occasionally, he had to kill one of the scrawny chickens that ran wild in his village, a horrible task for an animal lover like Sunny. (Today he has about twelve dogs, cooks all of their food himself, trains electric fans on their cages during the especially hot months, and turns on music for them when he leaves.) Learning to cook, he explained, wasn't the romantic endeavor we in the West sometimes imagine it to be. They didn't teach him; they told him. *Pound this. Gather that.* For poor families, having kids who could cook was invaluable. His parents worked late. How else would dinner be ready? Sunny transcended the typical gender roles, which had girls working in the kitchen and boys starting the cooking fires and doing other manual labor. By the time he was ten or so, he was tasked with making *laap* for special guests.

Today he's grateful for having been forced into culinary servitude. From junior high school through college, he and his sister earned money cooking and delivering lunches and dinners. In college, he began to make and sell *khanom*, Thai sweets. I can attest to the intense deliciousness of his *khanom*, so I wasn't surprised that

he took in about three hundred baht a day in profit. Now, Sunny essentially works as a private cook. Young people today, he says, don't know the same deprivation and they aren't forced to cook. He sums us their existence pithily: "They have MAMA"—instant noodles.

* * *

To come to the village where Sunny grew up is to see a typical Northern Thai community. To walk the streets with him is to glimpse real life in Thailand, and to begin to understand why Northerners eat the way they do. I know it helped me. You wonder why this herb and this root end up together in so many dishes, then you see them growing wild next to one another. It provided contemporary context to supplement the fascinating but abstract facts and dates that I'd read about.

In the old days, just about everyone in Ban Mai had rice fields. Each family tended its own crops, but the harvest was communal and the profits shared, a type of collectivity with a long tradition in Thailand. Today there are still rice fields, but rice is by no means the only source of commerce. Modernity has intervened. The cost of living has risen. Trucks and TVs need fixing. Kids are going to college rather than staying to tend the family business.

So people have diversified their industries. And almost everyone has a sideline, a hustle. Some moonlight as masseuses or midwives. One woman in Ban Mai makes curry paste and sells it to local markets. A man does the same with rice whiskey, supplying the village from his makeshift distillery just a stroll away.

Sunny has since moved away, but one brother and two sisters still live in Ban Mai. The ground floor of his eldest sister's home serves as a sort of all-purpose shop, the Thai version of a small-town general store or big-city bodega. Her retired husband tends the operation, watching TV on the couch and feeding his caged songbirds as neighbors drop by to buy soap or charcoal, cigarettes or palm sugar. Men come to knock back drams of the local rice whiskey, almost always taken along with a pinch of shrimp paste or a few *mayom* (a tiny, sour applelike fruit). They might linger for a minute before they slap seven baht on the counter and head back to work. Virtually everyone here speaks to each other in Northern Thai, which I can barely understand. For older residents, it is their first language. Central Thai is their second, something only their children excel at.

Peer into Sunny's sister's yard and you might see a slab of corrugated steel roofing on the stone patio strewn with small red chiles, picked just feet away and now drying in the sun. Other chiles, *phrik chii faa*, still green, grow toward the sky on shoulder-high bushes. Scattered on a plate next to the roofing is *makhwen*, also grabbed from a nearby tree. These tiny berries clustered on branches are also sun-dried and taste a bit like Sichuan peppercorn, bitter with a heat that numbs rather than scalds.

The paved roads are narrow with lush vegetation overtaking each side. There are few recognizably tended gardens or orchards. Instead, it all just grows. There are trees everywhere, heavy with longan, a lycheelike fruit sold in American Chinatowns, as well as fruits that never make it out of the Northern Thailand. We pass two women who have set down their sun umbrellas to pluck ripe star fruit from a neighbor's tree. Another tree looks like it's sprouting plastic bags. Actually, someone has wrapped a bag around every mango, a pricey variety, to protect them from greedy bugs. Notably, you don't see many coconut trees. No wonder coconut milk and cream aren't common features in the food of the North.

Locals use multiple parts of the plants here for cooking. There are kaffir lime trees, used for their bumpy fruits and glossy leaves. There are banana trees, which yield fruit, leaves, shoots, and blossoms. Amid the greenscape are galangal plants, known best for their knobby rhizome, but also popular here for their pink shoots and peppery flowers. To me, it's incredible that these plants grow here. In the US, I have to form a search party to unearth them at markets. Here, they grow wild, and Sunny will nod to lemongrass and betel leaf the way a Mainer might point out yet another blueberry bush.

And perhaps most striking are all the plants that aren't so obviously edible. As you stroll, Sunny will occasionally reach into the brush or squat down beneath a tree and pluck up some unremarkable-looking leaf. "Sweet," he might say with a puckish smirk as he hands it to you. You'll eagerly chomp on it, only to find that it's incredibly bitter or that it has a tannic quality that dries out your mouth, as if you'd bitten into a banana peel. Surprisingly to me at first, people here like this sensation. There are sweet leaves, too, and those that are peppery or spicy. There's even one, *khao tong* in Thai, that the Vietnamese call *diếp cá* or "fish herb," which tastes, bizarrely, like grilled fish. These leaves often have no names, or at least not for Sunny. Ask him to name one and he'll reply, "*Kin kap laap*," a general title that means, more or less, "stuff to eat with *laap*." Indeed, the night before, we'd gone to a restaurant specializing in Laap Meuang (page 106), the Northern dish of minced meat. The dish invariably comes with sticky rice and a plate of herbs and leaves, including many that grow wild in roadside patches—like those here in Sunny's village.

After a tour from Sunny, you can almost see how subsistence living worked here long ago. People were poor, but they had access to a bounty of fruits, vegetables, and wild herbs. Perhaps they had a chicken or two running around. Maybe a neighbor had a pig. Frogs and fish were free. His mother would slather fish with a simple curry paste, put it in hollowed-out bamboo, and lean it over fire to cook.

That he can so readily recognize all of these plants and leaves in the dense greenery is notable because Sunny is not a naturalist. He hasn't studied botany, nor have his neighbors. People of his generation were brought up knowing this stuff. The new generation, however, seems to have chosen a different life. Kids are decamping to cities and no longer eating the food their families eat, let alone learning how to cook it. The chain by which recipes are passed between generations is breaking. The food culture I saw just twenty years ago is disappearing. This is not by any means a uniquely Thai phenomenon. When was the last time a teenager in the US identified dandelions as anything but a weed?

We've become desensitized to what's growing around us. I'm as guilty of this as anyone. My mom was a state park naturalist with a particular interest in edibles. When I was a kid, she'd walk me through the woods in Vermont, pointing out fiddlehead ferns and plucking up wild onions. I could've marveled at her skill and set about learning it myself, but at the time all I wanted to do was ride my bike and throw rocks at shit. Lately, we've come to think of foraging for food as the stuff of culinary romance. In the West we fetishize wild foods like ramps and chanterelles. We deify those chefs, like René Redzepi, who make elaborate dishes from neglected edibles like tree bark, grasses, and forgotten fruits, because it's a sort of elegant throwback to an earlier age of eating. In parts of Thailand, though, this has always been the way. Foraging never stopped, so it never had a chance to return, triumphantly, to vogue.

Yam Samun Phrai

NORTHERN THAI-STYLE HERBAL SALAD

THE PLAN

- Up to 2 weeks in advance: Make the palm sugar simple syrup

- Up to 2 days in advance: Make the fried shallots, cook the pork, and make the dried-shrimp powder

- Up to a few hours in advance: Peel and prep the vegetables

Even after twenty-odd years of traveling to Thailand, I still come across unfamiliar dishes just about every time I go. Some are compelling precisely because they take your assumptions about Thai food—any food really—and smash them to pieces. Spicy, salty, sweet? Try bitter, pungent, and bracingly tart. Whether you immediately like the food is not the point. You eat it and your realm of possibilities expands.

Some dishes, though, hit that sweet spot between exotic and familiar. They take you somewhere you've never been before but make the trip easy. For me, this salad was like a first-class seat. I first tasted it at a highway restaurant in Chiang Mai specializing in *aahaan meuang*, the food of the North.

As soon as I sat, waiters brought a basket full of edible leaves and a pitcher of water infused with the ricelike flavor of pandan leaf. Among the bowls and plates that soon cluttered the table, this salad, one of the restaurant's specialties, stood out. Heaped on a small plate were thin slivers of what looked like carrot and green papaya. There were shreds of herbs and a sprinkling of fried shallots. A few cashews had tumbled off the pile.

I took a bite: boisterously sweet and slightly tart, crunchy and crispy, rich and bright. I had no idea what I was eating, but I don't think I've ever encountered anything that tasted this unique but also this immediately approachable. I ate the dish again and again and with the help of friends, parsed its composition, identifying each ingredient. That unfamiliar herb? Betel leaf. Those slivers of what I assumed was green papaya? Fresh white turmeric. With all these healthy ingredients—vegetables, herbs, nuts, seeds— it's easy to understand why the Thais call it, roughly, "herbal" or "medicinal salad." When I opened Pok Pok, probably a decade after first tasting this salad, I knew it had to be on the menu, even if I had to ape the sharp, slightly sweet flavor of white turmeric (not exactly common in Portland) with a combination of raw parsnips and young ginger.

The only challenge in recreating the dish at home is rounding up the laundry list of ingredients, only a few of which might require searching beyond a good Asian grocery store. Once you shop, you basically just toss everything together.

Flavor Profile HERBACEOUS, SLIGHTLY SWEET, NUTTY, BRIGHT, VERY MILDLY SPICY

Try It With Northern Thai dishes like Kaeng Hung Leh (Burmese-style pork belly curry), page 170, and/or Jaw Phak Kat (Northern Thai mustard green soup with tamarind and pork ribs), page 151. Needs Khao Niaw (Sticky rice), page 33.

{continued}

{Northern Thai-style herbal salad, continued}

PORK AND DRIED SHRIMP

1/2 teaspoon vegetable oil

1 ounce ground pork

A few dashes Thai fish sauce

2 tablespoons medium-size dried shrimp, rinsed and patted dry

DRESSING

1 tablespoon Thai fish sauce

1 1/2 tablespoons Naam Cheuam Naam Taan Piip (Palm sugar simple syrup), page 275

1 1/2 tablespoons lime juice (preferably from Key limes or spiked with a small squeeze of Meyer lemon juice)

1 tablespoon coconut milk (preferably boxed)

2 grams fresh Thai chiles (about 2 small), preferably green, thinly sliced

SERVES 2 TO 6 AS PART OF A MEAL; THE RECIPE IS EASILY DOUBLED

SALAD

2 ounces peeled carrot, cut into long (about 3-inch), thin (about 1/8-inch) strips (about 1 cup, lightly packed)

1 ounce peeled yellow onion, thinly sliced with the grain (about 1/4 cup, lightly packed)

1 1/2 ounces peeled white turmeric, cut into long (about 3-inch), thin (about 1/8-inch) strips (about 3/4 cup, lightly packed), see **NOTE**

7 grams thinly sliced lemongrass (tender parts only), from about 1 large stalk (about 1 tablespoon)

1 generous tablespoon coarsely chopped unsalted roasted peanuts

1 generous tablespoon unsalted roasted whole cashews

1/2 teaspoon very thinly sliced fresh or frozen kaffir lime leaves (stems removed if thick), lightly packed

1 teaspoon thinly sliced fresh betel leaf, lightly packed

1 teaspoon thinly sliced sawtooth herb, lightly packed

2 teaspoons thinly sliced Thai basil, lightly packed

1 heaping tablespoon Hom Daeng Jiaw (Fried shallots), page 273

1/2 teaspoon toasted sesame seeds

NOTE: You're most likely to find fresh white turmeric (also called mango ginger and amba haldi in Hindi) at Indian markets or online at indianblend.com. If you can't, substitute 1 ounce peeled parsnip and 14 grams peeled young ginger, cut into the same long, thin strips. Young or "new" ginger has thinner, smoother skin (you might also spot some pink skin and shoots) and a dramatically milder flavor than mature ginger.

COOK THE PORK AND DRY-FRY THE SHRIMP

Heat the oil in a small pan over medium-high heat until it shimmers, add the pork, and cook (stirring, breaking up the meat, and about halfway through, adding a couple dashes of the fish sauce) just until it's cooked through, about 1 minute.

Heat a small dry pan or wok over medium heat, add the dried shrimp, and cook, stirring frequently, until they're dry all the way through and slightly crispy, about 5 minutes. Set them aside in a small bowl to cool. Once the shrimp have cooled, pound them in a granite mortar (or grind them in a spice grinder) to a fairly fine, fluffy powder. It keeps for weeks in an airtight container stored at room temperature.

MAKE THE DRESSING

When you're ready to make the salad, combine the fish sauce, simple syrup, lime juice, coconut milk, chiles, and 2 tablespoons of the cooked pork in a wok or medium pan, set it over medium heat, and heat the mixture just until it's warm to the touch, 15 seconds or so. Turn off the heat.

ASSEMBLE THE SALAD

Add the carrots, onion, white turmeric, lemongrass, peanuts, and 1 teaspoon of the pounded dried shrimp (reserve the rest for another use) to the wok and toss gently but well.

Transfer the salad, liquid and all, to a plate in a heap, then sprinkle with, in this order, the cashews, herbs, fried shallots, and toasted sesame seeds. Toss well before eating.

Neua Naam Tok

ISAAN STEAK SALAD

The translation of *naam tok* is "waterfall," which sounds poetic until you learn that the waterfall it refers to is the blood that spills from meat as it grills. The term has come to refer to a particular flavor profile achieved by a collection of ingredients, including lemongrass, lime, dried chiles, fresh herbs, and sometimes toasted rice powder. In typical Northeastern Thai fashion, the resulting dish, what we in the West call a "salad" and what Central Thais might categorize as a *yam*, is one of sticky rice's best friends: vibrantly spicy, tart, and salty with just a spot of sugar for balance.

Flavor Profile SPICY, TART, AROMATIC, SALTY, UMAMI-RICH

Try It With Any Som Tam (Papaya salad and family), page 35, and/or Phak Buung Fai Daeng (Stir-fried water spinach), page 97. Needs Khao Niaw (Sticky rice), page 33.

SERVES 2 TO 6 AS PART OF A MEAL; THE RECIPE IS EASILY DOUBLED

STEAK

2¹⁄₂ grams lemongrass (tender parts only), thinly sliced (about 1 generous teaspoon)

2 black peppercorns

Scant 4 ounces flank steak, butterflied if necessary to ¹⁄₂-inch thickness

1¹⁄₂ teaspoons Thai thin soy sauce

DRESSING

1¹⁄₂ tablespoons lime juice (preferably from Key limes or spiked with a small squeeze of Meyer lemon juice)

1¹⁄₂ tablespoons Thai fish sauce

1 tablespoon beef stock (purchased or homemade; see NOTE) or water

1 teaspoon granulated sugar

1 teaspoon Phrik Phon Khua (Toasted-chile powder), page 270

14 grams thinly sliced lemongrass (tender parts only), from about 2 large stalks (about 2 tablespoons)

SALAD

1 ounce peeled small shallots, preferably Asian, or very small red onions, halved lengthwise and thinly sliced with the grain (about ¹⁄₄ cup, lightly packed)

¹⁄₄ cup small mint leaves, lightly packed

¹⁄₄ cup coarsely chopped cilantro (thin stems and leaves), lightly packed

1 heaping teaspoon Khao Khua (Toasted–sticky rice powder, page 271), plus a few pinches for finishing

NOTE: To boost the flavor, grill any steak trimmings until they're lightly charred and cooked through, then put them in a pot with enough water to cover and simmer for 15 minutes or so. Spoon out 1 tablespoon of the liquid for the dressing.

MARINATE THE STEAK

Combine the 2¹⁄₂ grams of lemongrass and the peppercorns in a granite mortar and pound to a coarse paste, about 15 seconds. Scrape it into a bowl with the steak, add the soy sauce, and use your hands to massage the steak until it's well coated with the marinade. Cover and refrigerate for at least 30 minutes or up to 1 hour.

COOK THE STEAK

Prepare a grill, preferably charcoal, to cook with medium heat (see page 124). Or preheat a lightly oiled grill pan or heavy skillet over medium heat.

Grill the steak, flipping once, until well browned and lightly charred on both sides and just barely pink inside, 6 to 8 minutes total. Transfer the steak to a cutting board, let it rest for about 5 minutes, then cut it against the grain into slices that are somewhere between $1/8$ and $1/4$ inch thick.

MAKE THE DRESSING

Combine the lime juice, fish sauce, beef stock, sugar, chile powder, and the 14 grams of lemongrass in a medium pan, set it over medium heat, and heat the mixture just until it's warm to the touch, 15 seconds or so. Turn off the heat.

ASSEMBLE THE SALAD

Add the steak slices to the pan along with the shallots, mint, cilantro, and rice powder, toss well, and transfer the salad to a plate in a low heap, pulling most of the herbs toward the top. Sprinkle on another pinch or two of rice powder, and serve.

Het Paa Naam Tok

ISAAN-STYLE FOREST MUSHROOM SALAD

SPECIAL
EQUIPMENT

**SPECIAL
EQUIPMENT**

- A charcoal grill (highly recommended), grates oiled

The recipe for steak salad is a classic, but *naam tok* made with mushrooms is less common. Yet mushrooms are everywhere in Thailand and echo the texture and even the umami-rich flavor of animal flesh. Thailand has a long history of vegetarian food, for strict Buddhists and those celebrating Buddhist holidays. And while I rarely spend time considering the needs of vegetarians, I figured that if I swapped out the fish sauce in the original for thin soy sauce, then they'd have something to eat at Pok Pok.

Flavor Profile SPICY, TART, AROMATIC, SALTY, UMAMI-RICH

Try It With Any Som Tam (Papaya salad and family), page 35, and/or Phat Khanaeng (Stir-fried Brussels sprouts), page 91. Needs Khao Niaw (Sticky rice), page 33.

SERVES 2 TO 6 AS PART OF A MEAL; THE RECIPE IS EASILY DOUBLED

MUSHROOMS

10 ounces meaty mixed mushrooms (such as oyster, king oyster, cremini, and/or wild mushrooms), tough stems trimmed and any large mushrooms halved through the stem (trimmings reserved; see NOTE)

A generous drizzle of vegetable oil

Kosher salt and freshly ground black pepper

NOTE: If you'd like, briefly grill the mushroom trimmings, put them in a pot with enough water to cover, and simmer for 15 minutes or so. Spoon out 1 tablespoon of the liquid for the dressing.

DRESSING

1½ tablespoons lime juice (preferably from Key limes or spiked with a small squeeze of Meyer lemon juice)

1½ tablespoons Thai thin soy sauce

1 tablespoon mushroom stock (purchased or homemade; see NOTE) or water

1 teaspoon granulated sugar

1 teaspoon Phrik Phon Khua (Toasted-chile powder), page 270

14 grams thinly sliced lemongrass (tender parts only), from about 2 large stalks (about 2 tablespoons)

SALAD

1 ounce peeled small shallots, preferably Asian, or very small red onions, halved lengthwise and thinly sliced with the grain (about ¼ cup, lightly packed)

¼ cup coarsely chopped mint leaves (the smaller the better), lightly packed

¼ cup coarsely chopped cilantro (thin stems and leaves), lightly packed

1 heaping teaspoon Khao Khua (Toasted–sticky rice powder, page 271), plus a few pinches for finishing

COOK THE MUSHROOMS

Prepare a grill, preferably charcoal, to cook with medium heat (see page 124). Or preheat a grill pan or heavy skillet over medium heat.

Toss the mushrooms in a bowl along with just enough oil to lightly coat them. Season generously with salt and pepper and toss again. Grill the mushrooms, turning them over occasionally, until they're cooked through and deep golden brown in spots, 5 to 10 minutes, depending on the size of the mushrooms, transferring them as they're cooked to a cutting board. Cut any large mushrooms into bite-size slices, about ½ inch thick. Leave any small mushrooms whole. You should have about 1 cup of chopped, cooked mushrooms. Let them cool slightly as you make the dressing.

MAKE THE DRESSING

Combine the lime juice, soy sauce, mushroom stock, sugar, chile powder, and lemongrass in a wok or medium pan, set it over medium heat, and heat the mixture just until it's warm to the touch, 15 seconds or so. Turn off the heat.

ASSEMBLE THE SALAD

Add the mushrooms to the pan along with the shallots, mint, cilantro, and rice powder, toss well, and transfer to a plate in a low heap so that most of the herbs end up near the top. Sprinkle on another pinch or two of rice powder, and serve.

PLAA

Fish

This chapter includes just a small sampling of recipes that celebrate Thai cooks' dexterity with fish. At my restaurants, selling some of these dishes has at times proved challenging. Despite my evangelizing, fried fish outsells steamed four to one at Pok Pok, and we will never move whole fish like we could fillets. The former is probably due to the general American preference for crispy over soft and fear of skin (unless it's hidden under fry), and the latter to our squeamishness about digging into faces, tails, and bones. We eat fish. But we don't always like to be reminded that we do. Which is too bad, because to me, the best way to cook fish is whole.

Plaa Neung

STEAMED FISH, TWO WAYS

Before I had my conversion, I thought steamed fish sounded like a small step above steamed broccoli. Why steam fish, a method that seemed fit only for someone on a diet, when you can batter chunks and immerse them in hot oil? When you can grill it over charcoal? When you can, as I did time and time again as a line cook at French-inspired restaurants, griddle fillets to crisp-skinned glory with the help of fist-size hunks of butter? Steaming, I assumed, was a cop-out, the refuge of the picky, the dieting, and the dull. Then I saw the light.

All over Thailand—from beachside towns to rural villages in Northern Thailand to the center of Bangkok—I found myself face to fish face, gazing at whole steamed tilapia and snapper and bass. Whether the fish were scattered with chopped garlic, cilantro, and fresh chiles or oyster mushrooms, ginger, and green onions, the toppings were just supporting players working to highlight the star of the show—that pristine fish. Don't get me wrong, I still love fish that's been fried, grilled, or butter basted. Yet the experience is entirely different than what you get when you steam. Instead of tasting the batter, the smoke of the coals, or the richness of the dairy, you get the unobstructed flavor of the fish. Now it strikes me as incredible that steamed fish is so rare outside of Asian restaurants. And that we Americans so rarely cook it at home.

Steaming is easy once you have the right vessel. Ideally, you'll get a large, round aluminum Chinese steamer, which is cheap and widely available. (Save the bamboo steamers for dumplings.) It should be 11 to 16 inches in diameter, which will accommodate a 2-pound whole fish with a little room to spare. The holes in the steamer tray should be about 1/2 inch in diameter (tiny holes don't let as much steam through). Of course, just about any wide pot can be jerry-rigged for steaming with a rack and a lid. Don't skimp on the amount of steaming water. Too little won't provide enough heat, plus it could evaporate before the fish has fully cooked.

After you've got this stuff sorted, then in goes the fish and a handful of ingredients—I've provide two variations, one bright and spicy and the other salty and aromatic—and out comes the fish, sauced and ready to eat.

Plaa Neung Manao

STEAMED WHOLE FISH WITH LIME AND CHILES

SPECIAL EQUIPMENT

- A Thai granite mortar and pestle
- A wide aluminum Chinese steamer

SERVES 2 TO 6 AS PART OF A MEAL

Flavor Profile TART, SPICY, UMAMI-RICH

Try It With Phat Phak Ruam Mit (Stir-fried mixed vegetables), page 98, and/or Kaeng Jeut Wun Sen ("Bland" soup with glass noodles), page 149. Needs Khao Hom Mali (Jasmine rice), page 31.

12 grams fresh green Thai chiles (about 8), thinly sliced

1 ounce peeled garlic (about 8 medium cloves), halved lengthwise

3 grams cilantro roots, thinly sliced (about 1 generous teaspoon)

3 tablespoons Thai fish sauce

3 tablespoons lime juice (preferably from Key limes or spiked with a small squeeze of Meyer lemon juice)

2 tablespoons Sup Kraduuk Muu (Pork stock), page 268, or water

1½ teaspoons granulated sugar

¼ teaspoon ground white pepper

1 (1½- to 2-pound) whole striped bass, golden or black tilapia, grouper, barramundi, or trout, scaled, gutted, and cleaned

Large pinch torn cilantro leaves

2 lime wedges (preferably from Key limes)

Pour about 3 inches of water into a wide aluminum Chinese steamer (it should be wide enough to accommodate the fish with a few inches to spare), insert the steamer layer, cover, and bring the water to a boil over high heat.

Combine the chiles, garlic, and cilantro roots in a granite mortar and pound just until the garlic is in small pieces and you have a slightly wet-looking mixture (not a paste), about 45 seconds. Add the fish sauce, lime juice, stock, sugar, and white pepper, and stir well.

Using a sharp knife to make vertical cuts (going from back to belly), score both sides of the fish every inch or so starting from the gills and going all the way to the tail, cutting deep enough so that you hit bone. Put the fish on a heatproof plate with raised edges (it's okay if the head and tail hang over the edge a little) and spoon all the chile mixture (solids and liquid) evenly over the fish. The liquid will pool on the plate.

Decrease the heat slightly so the water is still boiling but not wildly. Carefully place the plate in the steamer basket, cover the steamer, and cook just until the fish is cooked through, 12 to 18 minutes, depending on the size and weight of the fish. To be sure, use tongs to gently peek at the flesh at the thickest part of the fish (behind the head at the fish's back). The flesh should be opaque.

Carefully remove the plate from the steamer (it'll be hot) and if you'd like, transfer the fish, liquid and all, to a serving plate. Sprinkle on the cilantro and serve with lime wedges.

Plaa Neung Si Ew

STEAMED WHOLE FISH WITH SOY SAUCE, GINGER, AND VEGETABLES

SPECIAL EQUIPMENT

- **A Thai granite mortar and pestle**
- **A wide aluminum Chinese steamer**

SERVES 2 TO 6 AS PART OF A MEAL

Flavor Profile SLIGHTLY SALTY AND SWEET, UMAMI-RICH, AROMATIC

Try It With Phak Buung Fai Daeng (Stir-fried water spinach), page 97, and/or Khanom Jiin Naam Yaa (Thai rice noodles with fish-and-krachai curry), page 232. Needs Khao Hom Mali (Jasmine rice), page 31.

1 (1¹/₂- to 2-pound) whole striped bass, golden or black tilapia, grouper, barramundi, or trout, gutted, scaled, and cleaned

2 tablespoons Thai thin soy sauce

2 tablespoons Sup Kraduuk Muu (Pork stock), page 268, or water

1 teaspoon granulated sugar

¹/₄ teaspoon ground white pepper

11 grams peeled garlic cloves, halved lengthwise and lightly crushed into small pieces in a mortar (about 1 tablespoon)

1 (1-ounce) piece peeled ginger, cut into long (about 1¹/₂-inch), thin (¹/₈-inch) matchsticks (about ¹/₄ cup, lightly packed)

7 grams Chinese celery (thin stems and leaves), coarsely chopped (about ¹/₂ cup, lightly packed), plus 1 tablespoon torn leaves for finishing

1 ounce green onions, cut into 2-inch lengths (about ¹/₂ cup, lightly packed), plus 1 tablespoon chopped green parts for finishing

3 ounces trimmed oyster mushrooms, cut into 1¹/₂-inch pieces if necessary (about 1¹/₂ cups, lightly packed)

Pour about 3 inches of water into a wide aluminum Chinese steamer (it should be wide enough to accommodate the fish with a few inches to spare), insert the steamer layer, cover, and bring the water to a boil over high heat.

Using a sharp knife to make vertical cuts (going from back to belly), score both sides of the fish every inch or so starting from the gills and going all the way to the tail, cutting deep enough so that you hit bone. Put the fish on a heatproof plate with raised edges (it's okay if the head and tail hang over the edge a little).

Evenly spoon the soy sauce and stock over the fish (most of it will pool on the plate), then sprinkle on the sugar and white pepper. Finally, sprinkle the garlic, ginger, Chinese celery, green onions, and mushrooms onto the fish. It's okay if some of these tumble onto the plate.

Decrease the heat slightly so the water is still boiling but not wildly. Carefully place the plate in the steamer basket, cover the steamer, and cook just until the fish is cooked through, 12 to 18 minutes, depending on the size and weight of the fish. To be sure, use tongs to gently peek at the flesh at the thickest part of the fish (behind the head at the fish's back). The flesh should be opaque.

Carefully remove the plate from the steamer (it'll be hot) and if you'd like, transfer the fish, liquid and all, to a serving plate. Sprinkle on the remaining celery leaves and green onions, and serve.

Plaa Phao Kleua

GRILLED SALT-CRUSTED FISH WITH CHILE DIPPING SAUCE

Many cultures have come up with their version of salt-crusted fish, an excellent way of cooking whole fish (the crust keeps the flesh moist) and probably, in decades past, of preserving the flesh. The Thai version, sold at seafood restaurants and at to-go stands in markets and on the side of the road, is not so different from the European ones. There's only the thinner salt crust (still, don't eat it; it's salty), the lemongrass stalk that impales the fish, and the fiery, tart dipping sauce that's served alongside.

Flavor Profile UMAMI-RICH AND SLIGHTLY SALTY (THE FISH): SPICY, SOUR, SWEET (THE SAUCE)

Try It With A DIY spread, including lettuce leaves, bite-size pieces of cucumber, herbs like mint and cilantro, and Khanom Jiin (Thai rice noodles), page 231. Have guests make lettuce-leaf bundles.

SERVES 2 TO 6 AS PART OF A MEAL

1 (1½- to 2-pound) whole tilapia, porgy, or red snapper, scaled, gutted, and cleaned	1 large stalk lemongrass, outer layer, bottom ½ inch and top 4 inches removed	1 egg white, beaten
	2 cups kosher salt	½ cup Naam Jim Seafood (Spicy, tart dipping sauce for seafood), page 280

Dry the fish well with a towel. Using a pestle or heavy pan, whack the thick end of the lemongrass several times to bruise it, which releases some of its oils. Insert the stalk through the fish's belly so that the thin end comes out of the fish's mouth. (You may have to use a knife to clear a path from belly to mouth.) Pull the thin end of the lemongrass firmly but gently so as much of the stalk sticks out of the mouth as possible, and tuck the thick end into the belly until it's no longer visible.

Spread the salt on a large plate. Using a brush or your hands, coat the fish on one side with the beaten egg white in a thin layer from the head to the tip of the tail. Lay the fish, egg white–brushed side down, onto the bed of salt, gently pushing down on the fish so the salt adheres. Brush the other side with the egg white (there's no need to use it all), flip the fish over, and use your hands to pat the salt on the fish to form a more or less even layer (thick enough to partially obscure the color of the skin, but not as thick as a European salt crust), enlisting some salt from the plate if necessary. Flip the fish once more and do the same on the other side. There will be a lot of salt left over. That's fine.

At this point, you can keep the fish in the fridge for 30 minutes to help the crust firm up or cook it right away.

NOTE: Because the crust makes it difficult to inspect the flesh, the best way to check doneness is to use a thin, instant-read thermometer. The fish is done when the thermometer inserted into the flesh at the thickest part of the fish (behind the head at the fish's back) registers 125°F.

ON THE GRILL (HIGHLY RECOMMENDED): Prepare a grill, preferably charcoal, to cook over high—but not blazing hot—heat (see page 124). Put the fish directly on the grill grates and cook, without messing with it, for at least 6 minutes (otherwise, the crust could break). Then begin checking the underside, and when it's light golden brown with a few darker brown patches, use the spatula and a pair of tongs to carefully turn it over and cook until both sides are golden brown and the fish is just cooked through to the bone, about 16 to 20 minutes total (see **NOTE**, above).

IN THE OVEN: Preheat the oven broiler to high and position the oven rack as far as possible from the heat source. Line a baking sheet with aluminum foil and add a wire rack. Put the fish on the wire rack and broil, using a spatula and a pair of tongs to carefully turn it over once, but only after the crust has firmed up, until both sides are golden brown and the fish is just cooked through to the bone, 16 to 20 minutes (see **NOTE**, above).

Right before you serve it (perhaps at the table for dramatic effect), remove the crust (it's too salty to eat and it's very easy to do): Using the tip of a sharp knife, make an L-shaped cut just through the salt-crust, starting at the tail, cutting along the back toward the gills, then down toward the bottom of the fish. Peel back the skin in one piece, do the same on the other side of the fish, and discard both pieces or leave them on the plate as garnish.

Serve with a bowl of the dipping sauce.

Plaa Thawt Lat Phrik

DEEP-FRIED WHOLE FISH WITH CHILE SAUCE

SPECIAL EQUIPMENT

- **A deep-fry thermometer**
- **A large spider skimmer (recommended)**

Nothing turns fillet-loving friends into whole fish fiends like this dish, a head-on, tail-on two-pounder, crispy and golden brown. When it comes to swaying reluctant eaters, a little battering and frying works even better than whiskey. That and the addictive sweet-spicy sauce spooned on top. This fried fish is a thrilling way to round out a Thai meal of rice, stir-fried vegetables, and some sort of bright, spicy salad.

Deep-frying has a reputation for being onerous, but really, it's hard to mess up. Grab a wide deep pot and a deep-fry thermometer, and you're golden. Once you get the hang of it, you won't even need the thermometer. You won't see any of the old hands who fry up fish at markets peeking at temperature gauges. They just toss in a bit of batter or some other edible detritus and let the bubbles announce when the oil has reached the right temperature. One vendor takes deep-frying expertise to its extreme: Kann Trichan, Chiang Mai's very own Internet celebrity, grabs crispy chicken from a wok of bubbling fat with his bare hands.

The key to successful deep-frying is consistent temperature. Don't start frying until the temperature levels out, and occasionally stir the oil while it heats up, because the oil might have cooler or hotter pockets that the prong of the thermometer won't pick up.

Flavor Profile SWEET, TART, SPICY, SALTY, RICH

Try It With Phat Khanaeng (Stir-fried Brussels sprouts), page 91, and/or Yam Khai Dao (Fried egg salad), page 51. Needs Khao Hom Mali (Jasmine rice), page 31.

SERVES 2 TO 6 AS PART OF A MEAL

SAUCE

1½ teaspoons vegetable oil

2 tablespoons minced shallots, preferably Asian

1 tablespoon finely chopped fresh (or drained pickled) red Thai chiles

1 tablespoon minced cilantro roots

1 tablespoon minced garlic cloves

¼ cup Naam Makham (Tamarind water), page 275

2 tablespoons Thai fish sauce

2 tablespoons granulated sugar

FISH

Vegetable oil, preferably rice bran or palm oil, for deep-frying (about 8 cups)

1 (1½- to 2-pound) whole tilapia, porgy, or red snapper, scaled, gutted, and cleaned

½ cup white rice flour (*not* glutinous rice flour)

2 tablespoons tempura batter mix (preferably Gogi brand)

1 generous tablespoon very coarsely chopped cilantro leaves

MAKE THE SAUCE

Heat the oil in a small saucepan over high heat until it shimmers. Add the shallots, chiles, cilantro roots, and garlic, decrease the heat to medium-low, and cook, stirring occasionally, just until the shallots are translucent, about 2 minutes.

Add the tamarind water, fish sauce, and sugar. Increase the heat and bring the mixture to a boil,

stirring occasionally; then decrease the heat again to maintain a steady simmer until the mixture has thickened slightly, about 2 minutes. You'll have about ½ cup of sauce.

Use it right away or let it sit for up to an hour and gently reheat before serving.

{continued}

{Deep-fried whole fish with chile sauce, continued}

FRY THE FISH

Pour enough of the oil into a wok, Dutch oven, or wide pot to reach a depth that will completely submerge the fish, about 2 inches.

Set the pot over medium-high heat. Bring the oil to 350°F (use a deep-fry thermometer), carefully stirring the oil occasionally to ensure a consistent temperature, and adjust the heat to maintain the temperature.

While the oil is heating, pat the fish dry with paper towels. Using a sharp knife held at a 45-degree angle, vertically score both sides of the fish every inch or so starting from the gills and going all the way to the tail, cutting deep enough to hit bone.

In a wide bowl, mix the rice flour and tempura mix together well, then add the fish and turn it in the flour mixture to coat, using your fingers to make sure the flour gets inside the vertical slits. Lightly pat the fish so any excess flour falls back into the bowl.

When the temperature of the oil is steady at 350°F, carefully add the fish to the oil. (The oil temperature will drop slightly, but will rise again after a minute or so.) Fry the fish, carefully turning it over with tongs or a spider skimmer after 4 minutes and adjusting the heat if necessary to maintain the temperature, until the fish is evenly golden brown and cooked to the bone at the thickest part, about 8 minutes total. You can remove the fish to check its doneness, then add it back to the oil, if need be. Carefully peek at the flesh at the thickest part of the fish (behind the head at the fish's back). The flesh should be opaque.

Transfer the fish (this is easiest with a spider skimmer) to paper towels to drain. The fish will stay crisp and hot for about 15 minutes. I don't like to eat it right out of the oil, when it's screaming hot.

ASSEMBLE THE DISH

When you're ready to serve the fish, transfer it to a serving plate, spoon on the sauce, and sprinkle on the cilantro.

Aep Plaa

CURRIED FISH GRILLED IN BANANA LEAVES

SPECIAL EQUIPMENT

- A Thai granite mortar and pestle
- 3 wood skewers, broken into approximately 5-inch pieces
- A charcoal grill (highly recommended), grates oiled

When you're new to Thailand, every plate that appears on your table can seem like a mystery: a brackish soup crowded with bones or a white dish with a dollop of dark paste made from lord knows what. For an outsider, the cuisine can be difficult to penetrate, guarded by several language barriers (even if you speak Thai, you might not recognize the dialect-heavy names of regional dishes), the Thai alphabet (no Roman characters to spot on menus and signs), and the food's unfamiliar appearance. Having friends to guide you, as I have, helps a lot. Yet sometimes you just have to set out to explore a new world with your spoon.

In that spirit, I've found myself opening many charred banana-leaf packages—and being thrilled by what's inside. In the north of the country, the technique of wrapping and slow grilling, typically over charcoal, is known as *aep*. Inside is typically a curry paste–slathered protein, which could be anything from pig brain or prawns to fish or frog, or even dozens of tadpoles.

This is rustic food, a window into an old way of eating. I like to imagine a worker, in the days before there were noodle shops serving lunch, heading out to the fields for his day's labor. When he leaves in the morning, he packs a basket of sticky rice and his *aep*, the cooking vessel now the packaging. Or maybe he brings not the premade *aep* but just the aromatic paste. When he gets hungry, he snags a frog or fish from the rice paddies and cuts a banana leaf from a nearby tree. He builds a fire, assembles and cooks the package, and eats it with rice and herbs plucked from bushes and trees.

The version here calls for fish cut into small steaks, which can be bony. Thais are not as afraid of bones as we are. In Thailand, you'll often find whole fish prepared this way as well. Cooking bone-in fish gives you a moister, more flavorful product, but if some of you want to use fillets, don't let me stop you.

Flavor Profile SALTY, SLIGHTLY SPICY, UMAMI-RICH, AROMATIC

Try It With Jaw Phak Kat (Northern Thai mustard green soup with tamarind and pork ribs), page 151, and/or Phat Fak Thawng (Northern Thai-style stir-fried squash), page 94, and Khao Niaw (Sticky rice), page 33.

{continued}

{Curried fish grilled in banana leaves, continued}

MAKES 4 PACKAGES
AND SERVES 3 TO 6
AS PART OF A MEAL;
THE RECIPE IS
EASILY DOUBLED

PASTE

7 grams stemmed dried Mexican puya chiles (about 4)

1 teaspoon kosher salt

1¹/₄ ounces thinly sliced lemongrass (tender parts only), from about 5 large stalks

1 (1¹/₄-ounce) piece peeled fresh or frozen (not defrosted) galangal, cut against the grain into thin slices

1 (1-ounce) piece peeled fresh or frozen (not defrosted) yellow turmeric root, cut against the grain into thin slices

1¹/₂ ounces peeled garlic cloves, halved lengthwise

1¹/₂ ounces peeled Asian shallots, thinly sliced against the grain

1¹/₂ teaspoons Kapi Kung (Homemade shrimp paste), page 274

FISH

1 (2-pound) whole small Asian catfish, or 1 (1¹/₄- to 1¹/₂-pound) whole trout, bass or another meaty freshwater fish (scaled, gutted, cleaned, head removed, and body cut crosswise into ³/₄-inch-thick steaks by the fishmonger)

Kosher salt

8 (12- by 9-inch) pieces fresh or defrosted frozen banana leaves

30 or so large Thai basil leaves

TO SERVE ALONGSIDE

Phrik Naam Plaa (Fish sauce–soaked chiles), page 286, optional

MAKE THE PASTE

Combine the dried chiles in a granite mortar with the salt and pound firmly for about 5 minutes, scraping and stirring with a spoon after about 3 minutes, until you have a fairly fine powder (some larger flecks are fine). Add the lemongrass and pound, occasionally stopping to scrape down the sides of the mortar, until you have a fairly smooth, slightly fibrous paste, about 2 minutes. Do the same with the galangal, then the turmeric, then the garlic, and then the shallots, fully pounding each ingredient before moving on to the next. Finally, pound in the shrimp paste until it's fully incorporated, about 1 minute.

You'll have about ³/₄ cup of paste and will need ¹/₄ cup for this recipe. Store the remaining paste in an airtight container in the fridge for up to 1 week, or in the freezer for up to 6 months.

COOK THE FISH

Combine 1 pound of the fish steaks and ¹/₄ cup of the paste in a medium mixing bowl, season lightly with salt, and use your hands to mix gently and well, coating the fish.

Trim any stems from the banana leaves. Unless the leaves are exceptionally fresh and supple, pass both sides very briefly over a gas flame to make them more pliable and less likely to break when you fold them.

Put one piece of banana leaf shiny side down so that the ridges are running toward you. Put another piece shiny side up on top of the first piece so the ridges are perpendicular to those beneath. This will make your packages stronger. Put a quarter of the fish mixture in a tidy pile on the center and top with 8 or so basil leaves. Now you're going to make a neat, compact package. Starting with the edge closest to you, fold both layers of banana leaf over the fish to enclose it, then fold over the edge farthest from you. Carefully flip over the rectangular package, then fold the short edges over one another to create a tidy package. Use a piece of skewer to stitch together the two pieces you just folded so the package stays closed (do not puncture the part of the package that contains the fish). Repeat with the remaining banana leaves, fish, basil, and skewers.

Prepare a grill, preferably charcoal, or grill pan to cook over low to medium-low heat (see page 124). Add the packages seam side up and cook, carefully turning them over every 5 minutes, until the banana leaf packages are charred and mostly black on both sides and the fish is cooked through, 20 to 25 minutes.

If the packages start to char after only 5 minutes, the heat is too high. Resist the temptation to open the packages to check on the fish. Keep in mind that you're cooking relatively forgiving fish and not shooting for precise doneness. If you're eager to check, insert a thermometer. The fish should register about 145°F when it's done. Serve right away.

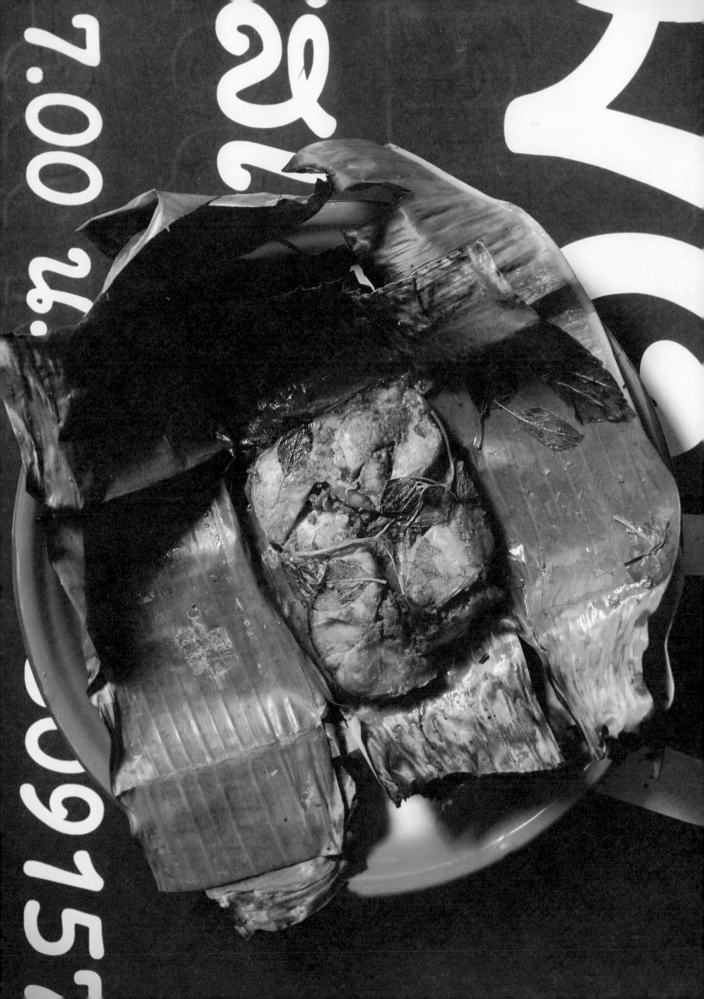

PHAT

Stir-fries

The technique of cooking in a scalding-hot wok is a Chinese import to the Thai repertoire. High heat isn't just part of the cooking method—it's an ingredient, adding a sought-after and elusive quality known in Chinese as *wok hay*.

Anyone who has seen this technique in action understands that the roaring flame enveloping the wok isn't attainable with most home-kitchen setups. Home stoves max out at about 12,000 BTUs, the units used to measure a burner's heat output. At Pok Pok, we cook with as much as 150,000 BTUs. So for the vast majority of home cooks, that *wok hay* stuff is just not going to happen. (For the slim minority intent on recreating stir-fries worthy of a great street vendor, flip to page 90 to learn how to use a *tao* as a mighty burner.)

Here's the good news: In Thailand, cooks tend to stir-fry at lower temperatures than the classic Chinese technique requires. So at home, you'll get a damn good result with a gas stovetop burner turned up as high as it can go. The stir-fry recipes in this book were developed using a gas stove and a carbon steel wok.

THE TECHNIQUE

We call it "stir-fry" for a reason. The technique involves cooking in a little oil and stirring—using a wok spatula to push, scoop, and flip the ingredients—more or less the whole time. As you stir, keep in mind the purpose of the technique: to use a very hot wok to cook ingredients briefly, stirring to ensure all the ingredients make plenty of contact with the hot surface and don't have a chance to burn or stick. Occasionally, scrape the bottom of the pan as you stir. There's no need for any fancy wrist-flicking and tossing.

Because you're cooking with very high heat, the process goes quickly. Some steps take no more than thirty seconds each. So it's especially important to fully read the recipe and to prep and organize the ingredients before you even turn on the heat. For the first few times you stir-fry, have all the liquid ingredients measured out, too. Once you've gotten more comfortable with the process, you'll be able to measure them as you're ready to add them, pouring them directly onto a wok spatula resting in the pan, without risking disaster.

NOTE: Stir-Frying on Electric Burners

A gas burner is ideal for stir-frying, but you can get a good result on stoves with electric burners. As you stir-fry, keep in mind that the electric burners take longer to heat up and take longer to respond when you adjust the heat and that as soon as you lift the wok from the stove, it will cool down considerably. Electric burners also won't maintain the necessary high heat: when you add a bunch of ingredients to the wok, not only will the wok itself cool down, but the electric heating element will, too. To combat this, consider using a cast-iron wok, which holds heat better than a thin steel or aluminum wok (though takes longer to respond to changes in heat). If you do, you'll have to adjust the cooking times provided in the recipes.

BUY A WOK AND A WOK SPATULA

There are endless options for those looking for a wok. Instead of attempting a comprehensive review, here's my take on your options if you want to cook the stir-fry dishes in this book.

In the US, few stoves have racks meant to cradle the classic round-bottomed wok. If you're dead-set on using one of these woks, you must buy an inexpensive wok ring or a *tao* (Thai-style charcoal stove). However, I recommend buying a flat-bottomed wok pan, which is widely available and works best on a Western stovetop.

By now, most people are familiar with the wok's shape, but not necessarily with its purpose. For this style of cooking, you want a wok that conducts heat, not one that holds heat. So cast-iron woks, though they have their advantages, are not essential or ideal for the stir-fry recipes in this book—unless you're stuck with an electric stove.

Look for an 11- to 14-inch flat-bottomed wok pan made from aluminum, stainless steel, or carbon steel. At the moment, my preferred brand for home use is Vollrath. Avoid those with plastic on the handle. Scrub and wash the wok well before you cook with it. Nonstick woks are convenient and, in the case of just a handful of recipes, highly recommended. If you'd rather not buy nonstick, you'll have to season your wok to create an almost-nonstick surface: Heat it over high heat, add a few tablespoons of vegetable oil, swirl to coat the pan, let the oil begin to smoke, then pour off the oil. Wipe the wok dry with a towel. Repeat once more with fresh oil.

Wok spatulas resemble small, long-handled shovels. If you have a nonstick wok, use a wooden wok spatula. Otherwise, use a metal one. Whatever it's made of, the spatula should be sturdy and rigid, because you'll be using it not just to stir but also to lift and flip ingredients as well as, occasionally, to break them up.

USING A TAO

The Thai clay cooking vessel called a *tao* can act like a grill—just set a rack on top—but a grill can't act like a *tao*. It has a relatively narrow body, a mouth meant to cradle a wok, and an opening on its side, which gives you the opportunity to stoke the flame. If you add a good pile of red-hot hardwood coals and train an electric fan on this opening (old-school vendors use small powerful industrial blowers that resemble hairdryers), the *tao* becomes a powerful burner, the flames screaming like those of a rocket booster. It probably goes without saying, but this method is not for beginners or inferno-phobes. But if you want to stir-fry like a street vendor at home, it's your best bet.

A *tao* costs about thirty dollars at Thai markets or from www.templeofthai.com.

Phat Khanaeng

STIR-FRIED BRUSSELS SPROUTS

SPECIAL EQUIPMENT

- **A Thai granite mortar and pestle**
- **A wok and wok spatula**

A visit to a Thai market will always remind you how much you don't know. At Chiang Mai's vast wholesale emporium Talaat Meuang Mai, for instance, you'll pass vendor after vendor exhibiting piles of green things—feathery flora and serpentine stalks, wide blades of what looks like grass, and pudgy-stemmed Chinese-broccoli doppelgangers. There are sundry leaves—some spindly and bitter, some succulent and tart, some strangely sweet—and other plants, plucked from overgrown patches by the side of the road, foraged from forests, or harvested from farm fields.

Some day I'm going to stop inquiring about them. For years, I've asked friends, restaurant owners, and vendors at local markets to identify every novelty I've come across. And instead of a simple name, I get one of three answers. "That?" I'll hear in Thai. "You eat it raw along with *laap*," the minced meat, blood-spiked Northern staple (page 106). Or you eat it steamed along with *naam phrik*, the diverse category of chile-based relishes. Or you eat it stir-fried with oyster sauce. So I still don't know the names of most of these alien vegetables. I'm not sure they even have names.

Once in a while, though, you'll be surprised by what you do recognize. During a trip to Phrae, an hour's drive from Chiang Mai, I went to a restaurant and asked what vegetables they offered for a simple stir-fry. "Very local vegetable," said my waiter. "Then that's what I want," I said. Minutes later, out came a plate of fiddlehead ferns. Turns out that the furled young ferns that overflow crates in springtime markets in Portland, Oregon, and elsewhere throughout the US, also pop up in Northern Thailand.

Another favorite vegetable common in stir-fries is *khanaeng*, which looks like a cross between a Brussels sprout and bok choy. You can't find it in the US, so at Pok Pok I sub regular old Brussels sprouts, which turn out great, and I call for them here. Of course, as my fruitless inquiries suggest, you can apply this method of cooking and saucing (a Chinese-Thai merging of oyster sauce and fish sauce) to almost any vegetable to delicious effect. Briefly blanched (I subscribe to the theory of deep-water blanching, so use a pasta pot full of water for a pound of vegetables), broccoli, green beans, cauliflower, or a mix of several types all work well.

Flavor Profile SWEET AND SALTY, SLIGHTLY SPICY, SMOKY

Try It With Puu Phat Phong Karii (Crab stir-fried with curry powder), page 101, or Yam Khai Dao (Fried egg salad), page 51. Needs Khao Hom Mali (Jasmine rice), page 31, or Khao Niaw (Sticky rice), page 33.

{continued}

| SERVES 2 TO 6 AS PART OF A MEAL | 10 ounces Brussels sprouts, bottoms trimmed, outer leaves removed, halved lengthwise (about 2 cups)

Kosher salt

2 tablespoons Thai oyster sauce

1 teaspoon Thai fish sauce | 1 teaspoon Thai thin soy sauce

Small pinch ground white pepper

2 tablespoons vegetable oil

11 grams peeled garlic cloves, halved lengthwise and lightly crushed into small pieces in a mortar (about 1 tablespoon) | 6 grams fresh Thai chiles (about 4), preferably red, thinly sliced

1/4 cup Sup Kraduuk Muu (Pork stock), page 268, or water

1 teaspoon granulated sugar |

BRIEFLY COOK THE BRUSSELS SPROUTS

Bring a large pot of water to a boil, and add enough salt to make it taste slightly salty. Add the Brussels sprouts and cook just until they're no longer raw but still crunchy, 30 seconds to 1 minute, depending on their size. Drain them well. If you're not stir-frying them right away, shock them in ice water.

STIR-FRY AND SERVE THE DISH

Combine the oyster sauce, fish sauce, soy sauce, and white pepper in a small bowl and stir well.

Heat a wok over very high heat, add the oil, and swirl it in the wok to coat the sides. When it begins to smoke lightly, add the garlic, take the wok off the heat, and let the garlic sizzle, stirring often, until it's fragrant but not colored, about 15 seconds.

Put the wok back on the heat, and add the Brussels sprouts and chiles. Stir-fry (constantly stirring, scooping, and flipping the ingredients) for 30 seconds to infuse the sprouts with the garlic flavor. Add the oyster sauce mixture (plus a splash of water, if necessary, to make sure nothing's left behind in the bowl), and stir-fry until the Brussels sprouts are tender but still crunchy and the liquid in the pan has almost completely evaporated, about 45 seconds.

Add the stock, then add the sugar and stir-fry until the Brussels sprouts are tender with a slight crunch and the sauce has thickened slightly but is still very liquidy, about 30 seconds. Transfer the vegetables and sauce to a plate in a low mound, and serve.

Phat Fak Thawng

NORTHERN THAI-STYLE STIR-FRIED SQUASH

SPECIAL EQUIPMENT

- **A Thai granite mortar and pestle**
- **A wok and wok spatula**

I love visiting my friend Sunny in the village of Ban Pa Du, near Chiang Mai, because I know I'll eat well. While I thrill at the prospect of chipping in to make his elaborate *laap*, even the simplest dishes in his repertoire are a pleasure to cook and devour. Take this one: pumpkin stir-fried with an aromatic paste, then dusted with fried shallots. I had always assumed that squash required long cooking. Standing at the gas-powered range in his modern kitchen, Sunny convinced me that soft, creamy flesh wasn't the be-all and end-all of good squash—instead, he turned out slices with texture, that still retained a slight snap to them. Back home, I opt for kabocha or, even better, delicata squash, which shows up in fall farmers' markets and which you don't even have to peel.

Flavor Profile SWEET, SPICY, SALTY AND SLIGHTLY FUNKY

Try It With Laap Meuang (Northen Thai minced pork salad), page 106, and/or Kaeng Hung Leh (Burmese-style pork belly curry), page 170. Needs Khao Niaw (Sticky rice), page 33.

SERVES 2 TO 6 AS PART OF A MEAL

PASTE	STIR-FRY	
7 grams thinly sliced green Thai chiles	**10 ounces seeded unpeeled delicata or peeled kabocha squash, cut into approximately 2- by 1- by 1/4-inch slices (about 2 cups)**	**2 tablespoons Sup Kraduuk Muu (Pork stock), page 268, or water**
6 grams peeled garlic cloves, halved lengthwise		**1 teaspoon granulated sugar**
5 grams peeled Asian shallots, thinly sliced against the grain	**2 tablespoons Naam Man Krathiem (Fried-garlic oil), page 272, or Naam Man Hom Daeng (Fried-shallot oil), page 273**	**1/4 teaspoon kosher salt**
1 teaspoon Kapi Kung (Homemade shrimp paste), page 274		**A small bowl of water**
		1 tablespoon Hom Daeng Jiaw (Fried shallots), page 273

MAKE THE PASTE

Pound the chiles to a coarse paste in a granite mortar, about 20 seconds. Add the garlic and pound until it breaks down and you can see only small bits of garlic, about 30 seconds, then do the same with the shallots. Add the shrimp paste and pound until it's just incorporated, about 10 seconds. The paste should still be fairly coarse, not smooth or homogenous in appearance. You'll have 1 tablespoon of paste.

BRIEFLY COOK THE SQUASH

Bring a large pot of water to a boil, add the squash, wait 15 seconds, then drain it well.

STIR-FRY AND SERVE THE DISH

Heat a wok over medium heat, add the oil, and swirl it in the wok to coat the sides. When the oil is hot, add all of the paste, take the wok off the heat, and cook, stirring constantly and quickly until the paste is fragrant but not colored, about 30 seconds to 1 minute. Do yourself a favor and avoid taking too dramatic or close a sniff—pounded chiles plus heat equals coughing fit.

Put the wok back on the heat, turn the heat to high, add the squash, and stir-fry (constantly stirring, scooping, and flipping) the ingredients for a minute or so to coat the squash and let the flavor of the paste infuse it. Add the stock, sugar, and salt, and continue to stir-fry just until the squash is tender but not mushy or falling apart, 3 to 5 minutes. Every 30 seconds or so, consider adding a splash of water to keep the ingredients moist, though once the squash is ready, there should be no liquid in the wok.

Transfer it all to a plate, sprinkle on the fried shallots, and serve.

Phak Buung Fai Daeng

STIR-FRIED WATER SPINACH

SPECIAL EQUIPMENT

- **A Thai granite mortar and pestle**
- **A wok and wok spatula**

You have to get to know water spinach, if you haven't already. Sold in generous bunches in just about any Asian market, the vegetable is one of the best things ever to hit a hot wok. The mild leaves soak up the flavor of sauce, in this case an umami-rich mixture of oyster sauce, fish sauce, and yellow bean sauce, and the hollow stems have an awesome snap to them. Vendors of this dish often engage in a little showmanship, flinging the stir-fried vegetable into the air for a waiter to catch on a plate. The *fai daeng* in the title means "red fire," which refers not to the stir-fry's spiciness but to the trademark flames that terrifyingly explode from the wok as it's cooked. I don't recommend trying that at home.

Flavor Profile SALTY, SPICY, UMAMI-RICH, SMOKY

Try It With Plaa Thawt Lat Phrik (Deep-fried whole fish with chile sauce), page 83, plus Khao Hom Mali (Jasmine rice), page 31, or Khao Niaw (Sticky rice), page 33.

SERVES 2 TO 6 AS PART OF A MEAL

2 tablespoons Thai oyster sauce	11 grams peeled garlic cloves, halved lengthwise and lightly crushed into small pieces in a mortar (about 1 tablespoon)	3 or 4 dried Thai chiles, broken in half
Scant tablespoon Thai fish sauce		1/4 cup Sup Kraduuk Muu (Pork stock), page 268, or water
1 teaspoon Thai yellow bean sauce	6 ounces water spinach, thin stems (no more than 1/4-inch thick) and leaves only, cut into 2-inch lengths (about 6 cups, lightly packed)	
1 teaspoon granulated sugar		
2 tablespoons vegetable oil		

Combine the oyster sauce, fish sauce, bean sauce, and sugar in a small bowl and stir well.

Heat a wok over very high heat, add the oil, and swirl it in the wok to coat the sides. When it begins to smoke lightly, add the garlic, take the wok off the heat, and let the garlic sizzle, stirring often, until it turns light golden brown, about 30 seconds.

Put the wok back on the heat, add the water spinach, and stir until the leaves begin to wilt, about 15 seconds. Add the oyster sauce mixture (plus a splash of water, if necessary, to make sure nothing's left behind in the bowl) and the chiles. Stir-fry (constantly stirring, scooping, and flipping the ingredients) until the leaves have fully wilted, about 45 seconds.

Add 2 tablespoons of the stock and stir-fry until the stems are just tender with a slight crunch, about 45 seconds more. You should end up with about 1/4 cup of liquid in the wok with the water spinach. If the liquid looks like it will reduce to less than that, gradually add more stock as you stir-fry.

Transfer the water spinach and sauce to a plate in a low mound and serve.

Phat Phak Ruam Mit

STIR-FRIED MIXED VEGETABLES

SPECIAL
EQUIPMENT

• A Thai granite mortar
  and pestle

• A wok and wok spatula

This dish is cursed by its weak English translation. Before I understood its potential, I would see it on menus in the US and in Thailand and assume it was the refuge of the dull diner. When you can order Chinese broccoli with hunks of crispy pork belly, why settle for cabbage and baby corn? Turns out that in the hands of a good cook, this stir-fry transcends its name and earns its place at the table. Addictively salty-sweet and packed with umami from oyster and fish sauce, the vegetables conspire to create a flavorful foil to any meal heavy on rich proteins, though at home I'd easily burn through a plate of it by myself for dinner, along with jasmine rice and perhaps amped up with Phrik Naam Plaa (page 286).

For a vegetarian version, use vegetarian oyster sauce (often made from mushrooms), leave out the fish sauce, and use purchased fried tofu instead of shrimp. The vegetables in this recipe are just a jumping-off point (most mixtures of about 2^1/$_2$ cups will do), though they do provide a particularly fine array of textures and flavors. And yes, I like baby corn, fresh or defrosted. You didn't think it grew in cans, did you?

Flavor Profile SLIGHTLY SALTY AND SWEET, UMAMI-RICH, SLIGHTLY SMOKY

Try It With Yam Tuna (Thai tuna salad), page 54, or Kung Op Wun Sen (Shrimp and glass noodles baked in a clay pot), page 210. Plus Khao Hom Mali (Jasmine rice), page 31.

{continued}

{Stir-fried mixed vegetables, continued}

SERVES 2 TO 6 AS PART OF A MEAL

VEGETABLES

Kosher salt

1¼ ounces Chinese broccoli (gai lan), stems cut diagonally into long, ¼-inch-thick slices and leaves cut into 3-inch pieces (about ½ cup)

1¼ ounces fresh or defrosted frozen baby corn (about 3), quartered lengthwise

1¼ ounces white or green cabbage (not savoy), cut into 1-inch pieces (about ½ cup)

1¼ ounces peeled yellow onion, cut into ½-inch wedges (about ½ cup)

21 grams peeled carrot, cut diagonally into ¼-inch-thick half-moon slices (about ¼ cup)

21 grams trimmed snow peas (about 7)

21 grams oyster, king oyster, or cremini mushrooms, trimmed and cut diagonally into ¼-inch-thick slices (about ⅓ cup)

14 grams Chinese celery (thin stems and leaves), very coarsely chopped (about ¼ cup)

STIR-FRY

2 tablespoons Thai oyster sauce

1 teaspoon Thai fish sauce

1 teaspoon Thai thin soy sauce

1 teaspoon granulated sugar

Pinch white pepper

2 tablespoons vegetable oil

22 grams peeled garlic cloves, halved lengthwise and lightly crushed into small pieces (about 2 tablespoons)

2 ounces medium shrimp (about 4), shelled, halved lengthwise, and deveined

¼ cup shrimp stock (see NOTE) or reserved blanching water

NOTE: Using shrimp stock multiplies the umami. Next time you buy a bunch of shrimp, keep the shells (in the freezer, if need be), heat them in a dry pan for a few minutes until they turn pink and fragrant, add just enough water to cover them, and simmer for 10 minutes or so. Strain and use or freeze in small portions.

BRIEFLY COOK THE VEGETABLES

Bring a large pot of water to a boil, and add enough salt to make it taste slightly salty. Add all the vegetables, and cook just until they lose a little of their rawness but are still crunchy, 15 to 30 seconds. Drain them well, reserving ¼ cup of the blanching water if you're not using shrimp stock. If you're not stir-frying them right away, shock them in ice water.

STIR-FRY AND SERVE THE DISH

Combine the oyster sauce, fish sauce, soy sauce, sugar, and pepper in a small bowl and stir well.

Heat a wok over very high heat, add the oil, and swirl it in the wok to coat the sides. When it begins to smoke lightly, add the garlic, take the wok off the heat, and let the garlic sizzle, stirring often, until it's fragrant but not colored, about 15 seconds.

Put the wok back on the heat, then add the vegetables and stir-fry (constantly stirring, scooping, and flipping the ingredients) for about 30 seconds. Add the oyster sauce mixture (plus a splash of water, if necessary, to make sure nothing's left behind in the bowl) and stir well.

Add the shrimp and stir-fry so the shrimp make plenty of contact with the hot wok until they begin to turn pink on both sides, about 45 seconds.

Add the shrimp stock and stir-fry until the vegetables are cooked but still slightly crunchy, the shrimp is just cooked through, and the sauce has thickened just slighty but is still liquidy, about 1 minute. Put it on a plate, liquid and all, and serve.

Puu Phat Phong Karii

CRAB STIR-FRIED WITH CURRY POWDER

SPECIAL EQUIPMENT

- A cleaver or heavy knife

- A Thai granite mortar and pestle

- A wok and wok spatula

I used to go to a Bangkok restaurant called Teng Hong Seng. My friend Chris would take me to this sprawling place, about a mile from his house and not far from Soi Cowboy, a neon-lit street full of bars and other establishments focused on male-geared entertainment. Among the families and friends who packed the restaurant's tables, you'd occasionally spot a few past-their-prime tourists dining with scantily clad bar girls.

The restaurant specialized in *aahaan tham sang*, food made to order. Laid out on ice, meat, seafood, and vegetables waited to be pointed at by customers. The place was family run. Dad presided over the dining room. The son manned the counter, prepping those ingredients and running them to the kitchen to be cooked. Grandpa hung out in the corner. There was also a waiter of indeterminate age—every time I went he was my waiter; he might have been the only waiter—who'd hand out wet wipes, squeezing each plastic packet with one hand so it puffed and then striking it with his elbow to open it with a loud pop.

We needed those wipes, because Chris would always order a version of this messy dish, a yellowish, oily jumble of shell-on crustacean, egg, and green onion. The color that ultimately stains your fingers comes from a good dose of curry powder.

You could order the dish to your specifications—no chiles! extra curry powder!—and Chris usually opted for giant prawns. When I returned without him, I got hooked on crab, which the counterman would wisely crack slightly with a cleaver before it hit the wok. Back in Portland, I take advantage of the glut of Dungeness crab, though you could use any meaty whole crab, snow crab legs, or king crab claws, and even lobster or those four-to-a-pound giant shrimp.

Flavor Profile RICH, HIGHLY SPICED (BUT NOT VERY SPICY), SLIGHTLY SWEET

Try It With Phak Buung Fai Daeng (Stir-fried water spinach), page 97, or Plaa Neung Si Ew (Steamed whole fish with soy sauce, ginger, and vegetables), page 79, and Khao Hom Mali (Jasmine rice), page 31.

{continued}

{Crab stir-fried with curry powder, continued}

SERVES 2 TO 6 AS PART OF A MEAL

TO COOK THE CRAB

1 gallon water

1/4 cup kosher salt

1 (2-pound) live Dungeness crab or another large meaty crab, claws bound

STIR-FRY

1/2 cup evaporated milk

4 large eggs, at room temperature

2 tablespoons Thai fish sauce

2 tablespoons Thai oyster sauce

2 teaspoons granulated sugar

5 tablespoons Naam Man Krathiem (Fried-garlic oil), page 272

11 grams peeled garlic cloves, halved lengthwise and lightly crushed into small pieces in a mortar (about 1 tablespoon)

1 tablespoon plus 1 teaspoon mild Indian curry powder

1 1/2 ounces peeled yellow onion, thinly sliced with grain (about a heaping 1/4 cup)

14 grams Chinese celery (thin stems and leaves), cut into 2-inch lengths (about 1 cup, lightly packed), plus a large pinch coarsely chopped leaves for finishing

14 grams green onions, cut into 2-inch lengths (about 1/4 cup, lightly packed)

7 grams fresh red Thai chiles (about 5), lightly whacked with a pestle, pan, or flat part of a knife blade

KILL THE CRAB

Here's a quick, humane way to kill the crab: Turn it on its back on a cutting board so that its eyes are facing you. With one firm whack, strike the crab between the eyes, using the sharp edge of a knife blade. (You're not trying to cut the crab in half, though, so only use about 1 1/2 inches of the blade.)

COOK THE CRAB

Combine the water and salt in a large pot and bring the water to a boil over high heat. Prepare a large bowl of ice water. Add the crab to the boiling water, cover the pot, cook for 8 minutes for a 2 to 2 1/2-pound crab, and transfer the crab to the ice water. Adjust the boiling time for smaller or larger crustaceans, keeping in mind it's better to slightly undercook the crab than overcook it, since you'll be cooking it again.

When it's cool enough to handle, hold the crab topside down and use a spoon or knife to pry off the triangular piece (often called the "apron"). Next, use your hands to pry off the top shell (the "carapace"), then use a spoon to scrape out the gills. If there's yellow gunk (politely known as "crab butter") in the top shell, scoop out it out, reserve it, and stir it into the evaporated milk and egg mixture later. Discard the top shell.

Transfer the crab to a cutting board and use a heavy knife to halve the crab lengthwise then cut the halves widthwise into three pieces. Use the back of a heavy knife's blade or a pestle to strike the thick legs and claws to crack them slightly, so you'll have an easier time getting at the meat later.

STIR-FRY AND SERVE THE DISH

Beat the evaporated milk with the eggs in a bowl. Combine the fish sauce, oyster sauce, and sugar in a separate bowl and stir well.

Heat a wok over very high heat, add 4 tablespoons of the oil, and swirl it in the wok to coat the sides. When it begins to smoke lightly, add the crab, garlic, and curry powder and stir-fry (constantly stirring, scooping, and flipping the ingredients) for 1 minute.

Decrease the heat to medium, add the onion, celery, green onions, and chiles, and stir-fry for 10 seconds, then add the fish sauce mixture (plus a splash of water, if necessary, to make sure nothing's left behind in the bowl). Increase the heat to high again and stir-fry for 45 seconds.

Push the crab to one side of the wok, add the remaining 1 tablespoon of oil, then pour in the egg mixture. Stir-fry everything until the egg is just barely set (you'll see very small curds) and the eggy sauce is still slightly creamy but not runny, about 30 seconds more.

Transfer the stir-fry—crab, vegetables, yellow curds, and all—to a large plate. Sprinkle on the remaining large pinch Chinese celery leaves, and serve.

LAAP
Thai minced-meat salads

Laap, like *yam*, is another distinct category of Thai food on which we in the West typically foist the translation "salad." I'll admit "minced-meat salad" was the best description of *laap* I could manage using just a few words. Now to employ a few more: The Thai word "laap" basically means "to chop up" and has come to refer to dishes made from meat that's been, well, chopped up. Typically the chopping is done with a massive knife that looks like something out of the Iron Age and is used exclusively for making *laap*. Of course, *laap* takes many forms and has many variations. The protein of choice (be it duck or fish, pork or beef) and the peculiarities of the cook aside, *laap* can be divided into two basic groups: the version from Isaan, the northeast of Thailand, which tends to be lime-spiked, fiery, and mixed with an aromatic powder made from toasted sticky rice; and the version from the North, which is typically seasoned with fresh herbs, a paste that's heavy on dried spices, and fried shallots and garlic. The ingredient lists and flavor profiles are so different that, aside from the chopped meat, the two versions seem like they could come from two separate countries.

The few *laap* constants are 1) the sticky rice that comes alongside to be used as an edible eating implement, and 2) *aahaan kin kap laap* (essentially, "things to eat with *laap*"). The latter is to be eaten between bites. These things to eat with *laap* might be whole cloves of mellow raw garlic, mouth-scalding *phrik khii nuu* (which translates, evocatively, to "rat-shit chiles"), raw vegetables, and virtually any green herblike thing imaginable. These plants and leaves, often plucked from bushes and trees on the roadside nearby, can taste intense—some saccharine, some licorice-like, others bracingly bitter or sour. I began to understand how inclusive this category of accompaniments really is after a few strolls with my friend Sunny through his village. Nearly every one of

my "What's that?" questions was followed by a familiar refrain: Oh, that jungle herb in the market? *Aroy kin kap laap* ("delicious with laap"). That bush by the side of the road? *Kin kap laap* ("eat with laap"). The leaves on that tree? You guessed it. I swear I could've closed my eyes, pointed, and gotten the same answer. I go through great pains to find American-grown versions of these wild herbs and plants in the US, shipping them in from a farm in Florida or a woman's garden in Pennsylvania. (Still, most customers push them aside as if they were sprigs of curly parsley at a restaurant from the 1980s.) You don't have to go to such lengths—use cilantro, Thai basil, long beans, raw Thai eggplants, white cabbage, anything that adds contrast in flavor or texture.

Laap Meuang

NORTHERN THAI MINCED PORK SALAD

For what seemed like a very long time, I'd been hacking at a kilo of pork shoulder with a sort of scimitar-shaped cleaver, trying to reduce it to a level of mince that would satisfy Da Chom, my friend Lakhana's father. At first, I went at it in the choppity-chop Western style until he frowned, snatched the knife, and showed me the Thai way. I finally graduated to a point where he felt comfortable leaving the room, popping back in occasionally to peer at my wad of meat and gesture in a way that said, *Keep going, you're not there yet.* Not that I'm complaining. This was labor of my own making. At dinner the night before, I had tasted his *laap*, and knew immediately that I had to learn how he made it.

After I'd incorporated some beet-red pig's blood and hacked it all up some more, Da Chom deemed my pork sufficiently minced. Now the next task began. I sat on the concrete floor in front of a large mortar. He squatted next to me, looking on as I pounded away, slowly reducing garlic and shallots, galangal and lemongrass, spices, dried chiles, and shrimp paste to smooth *naam phrik laap*, the paste used to season the meat. I stirred in the minced meat and some boiled innards, massaging it with the paste. Da Chom swiped a bit of the mixture with his fingers and tasted it, tuning the flavor with fish sauce. He nodded to suggest that I do the same. I didn't want to. I was unsettled by all that rawness. Soon I learned that old-timers often ate the dish at this stage, mixed with fried garlic and shallots, snipped herbs, and tiny dried chiles. They call it *laap dip* (or "raw *laap*"). Instead of eating it then and there, we added the burgundy mixture to a wok set over a charcoal fire. As it sizzled, we added spoonfuls of the liquid we'd used to boil pork innards, letting it all simmer until the *laap* gradually turned deep brown, the color of cooked blood.

If I had any remaining preconceived notions about what Thai food was, Da Chom's *laap* totally demolished them. When I first heard about Northern Thai laap, I imagined a slight variation on the pleasant, lime-spiked plate of chopped meat we've all eaten in the States, which I would come to understand is based on an Isaan dish. But here was this pile of nearly black meat that tasted nothing like sweet-tart salads and rainbow curries, or the noodle soups and stir-fries I'd had on the streets of Bangkok. It was fragrant, pungent, bitter—and wonderful. There was no obvious sweetness, except from the crunchy bits of fried garlic and shallots scattered on top. There was definitely no lime or coconut milk. If I hadn't been eating it at the home of my friend Chris and his wife, Lakhana, in Chiang Mai, I would never even have identified it as Thai.

Today, if I had to choose my last meal before I were shot into space, it would be this jumble of minced meat. It's a dish worthy of its own establishment; just as we in the West have temples to burgers, pizza, and barbecue, there are restaurants all over the North that specialize in this concoction. Whether you encounter it in a restaurant or in someone's home, you'll always find sticky rice and a heap of foraged herbs and vegetables alongside. Unlike its Isaan counterpart, you rarely see it outside of Northern Thailand. And if you want a crash course on the flavors of Northern Thai food, you'll make it. Now.

* * *

Da Chom makes *laap meuang*, the sophisticated *laap* found in Northern Thailand. While the renditions in the northeastern region of Isaan reflect an unfussy, fiery peasant cuisine, here the *laap* betrays the influence of the old royal court once established in the North. Instead of the lime and fish sauce dressing you encounter in the Isaan (and at most restaurants in the US), Da Chom mixes the meat with a curry paste that makes use of spices like cardamom, star anise, and cumin.

But after spending a ton of time in Thailand, I've learned enough to give up on the idea of ever fully understanding anything. The *laap* variants are endless, changing from region to region, town to town, cook to cook. I've noticed that the number of ingredients in the *naam phrik laap* shrinks the further you go from Chiang Mai. And as you traverse the north, its composition changes, too. For instance, in the same kitchen where I made my first *laap* with Da Chom, his son-in-law showed me how to make a version from the city of Nan, right near the border with Laos, with a *naam phrik laap* unmistakably heavy on *makhwen*, the seeds from a type of prickly ash native to Northern Thailand, and a must for Chiang Mai– and Nan-style laap. Unusually, this version of *laap* also contained kaffir lime leaves, lemongrass, and boiled innards that had all been deep fried. A friend recently brought me a *naam phrik laap* from a market in Lampang that lacked any *makhwen* whatsoever. You could smell its absence.

At the homes of friends and at the restaurants that specialize in it, I've eaten Northern Thai *laap* made with catfish *(laap plaa duuk)*, chicken *(laap kai)*, or bitter *laap (laap khom)*, which gets its characteristic flavor from beef bile. Northern Thai laap can be raw *(laap dip)*, simmered and liquidy *(laap suk)*, or cooked in a dry skillet *(laap khua)*. Just last year, I met an older man who told me his family once made sour *laap (laap som)* that relies on banana flower to produce the mouth-drying sensation known as *faht*—familiar to anyone who has ever accidentally bitten into banana peel. He's promised to teach me to make it, and I plan on showing up at his doorstep with a bottle of Scotch to grease the skids.

* * *

Unless you're in the countryside, you're not likely to see teenagers gathered around tables heaving with dishes that include *laap meuang*. Like kids just about everywhere nowadays, they'd rather go to KFC, McDonald's, or the national noodle franchise than hang out at the local *laap* restaurant, where you'd sooner find families and groups of middle-aged drinking buddies.

That's because *laap* is fast becoming a folk dish. It's labor intensive, probably the toughest recipe in this book. A relatively *chao wang* (sophisticated and elaborate) version of *laap suk*, this dish is an all-day endeavor.

The real challenge is hacking up the pork to a fine mince. Your arm will get tired. You might find out whether you're ambidextrous. I still occasionally try to stop early, then my friend Sunny, who has taken over for Da Chom as my *laap* tutor, hits me with a daikon radish. You might be wondering, Why can't I start with ground pork and chop it for much less time? When meat is ground, it's effectively smashed by the grinder, which gives you a different texture than hand chopping with a sharp, heavy cleaver. If you want to make this dish, you've got to get chopping.

Rounding up the ingredients, too, can prove difficult, though I'm constantly surprised by how a blend of mostly familiar spices adds up to such an exotic flavor. The good news is that you can make the spice paste a few days (or really, up to a few weeks) before chopping and cooking the meat.

{continued on page 110}

laap

Ingredients for Naam Phrik Laap

pork skin

pork intestines

raw pork blood

pork loin

pork liver

Laap prepared for cooking (after the "*yam*" stage)

Finished *laap* with its requisite partners:
sticky rice and a plate of raw vegetables and herbs

{Northern Thai minced pork salad, continued}

Because of the effort involved, I suggest using a pound of meat (at restaurants, portions are closer to 6 ounces) and treat this dish as the centerpiece to a dinner with many friends. Whereas the table at a *laap* restaurant in Thailand might be crowded with several other dishes, you can make a meal of *laap* by serving just Khao Niaw (Sticky rice) page 33, fresh herbs on the stem, such as Thai basil, sawtooth, cilantro, and Vietnamese mint (*rau ram*); and raw vegetables, such as wedges of cabbage, quartered Thai apple eggplant, cucumber spears, and 3-inch lengths of long bean. And beer. Lots of beer.

FINDING INNARDS AND BLOOD: Your best bets for finding pork innards and fresh or frozen raw pork blood are higher-end butcher shops, Asian and Russian markets, and anywhere else where blood sausage is made. The blood may be liquid or have a gelatinous texture. There is no substitute. If you must, you could leave it out, though you'll end up with a less rich and swarthy (but still very tasty) version.

Flavor Profile INTENSELY SPICED, UMAMI-RICH, MODERATELY SPICY, SLIGHTLY BITTER

Try It With Yam Makheua Thet (Fish sauce-soaked tomatoes), page 282, and raw vegetables and herbs like cucumber, Thai eggplant, white cabbage, Vietnamese mint, and Thai basil, as well as Yam Jin Kai (Northern Thai chicken soup), page 158. Needs Khao Niaw (Sticky rice), page 33.

THE PLAN

- **Up to a week in advance:** Make the laap seasoning paste

- **Up to 2 days in advance:** Make the fried garlic, fried shallots, and fried-shallot oil

- **Up to a few hours in advance:** Cook the offal and chop the pork

SPECIAL EQUIPMENT

- **A Thai granite mortar and pestle**

- **A solid wood chopping block (not made of bamboo), recommended**

- **A meat cleaver or another large heavy knife**

SERVES 6 TO 12 AS PART OF A MEAL

NAAM PHRIK LAAP (LAAP SEASONING PASTE)

1 ounce stemmed dried Mexican puya chiles (about 12)

1 tablespoon makhwen (see NOTE), black Sichuan peppercorns, or whole black peppercorns

1 tablespoon coriander seeds

1 teaspoon fennel seeds

1/2 teaspoon ground dried galangal

1/2 teaspoon ground dried lemongrass

1/2 teaspoon black peppercorns

1/4 teaspoon cumin seeds

1/8 teaspoon freshly grated nutmeg

4 cloves

2 dried Indonesian long peppers (called pippali in Indian and Malay markets, dippli in Thai markets, and tiêu lốp in Vietnamese markets)

1 star anise

1 whole mace

1 cardamom pod, preferably the white, rounder Thai variety

1 teaspoon kosher salt

1 ounce peeled garlic, halved lengthwise

2 ounces peeled Asian shallots, thinly sliced against the grain

1 tablespoon Kapi Kung (Homemade shrimp paste), page 274

OFFAL

2 ounces pork small intestine, cut into a few pieces

2 ounces pork skin, cut into a few pieces

1 (2-ounce) piece pork liver

1 teaspoon Kapi Kung (Homemade shrimp paste), page 274

1 (14-gram) piece unpeeled fresh or frozen (not defrosted) galangal, coarsely sliced

1 large stalk lemongrass, outer layer removed, halved crosswise, and lightly smashed with a pestle, pan, or flat part of a knife blade

3 1/2 cups water

PORK

1 large stalk lemongrass, outer layer removed, halved crosswise, and lightly smashed with a pestle, pan, or flat part of a knife blade

2 cups fresh or defrosted frozen raw pork blood

1 pound boneless pork loin, trimmed of any large fat deposits if necessary and cut against the grain into approximately 1/2-inch-thick slices

NOTE: Makhwen, the seeds of the Northern Thai prickly ash tree, are hard but not impossible to find in the West. (Ask around at Thai markets and you might get lucky.) The flavor shares some qualities with Sichuan peppercorn, but there is no real substitute.

TO PREPARE THE
LAAP FOR COOKING

1/2 cup reserved offal
cooking liquid

1/2 teaspoon kosher salt

2 tablespoons thinly sliced
green onion, lightly packed

2 tablespoons thinly sliced
sawtooth herb, lightly
packed

2 tablespoons coarsely
chopped cilantro (thin stems
and leaves), lightly packed

2 tablespoons coarsely
chopped Vietnamese mint
leaves, lightly packed

2 tablespoons Hom Daeng
Jiaw (Fried shallots),
page 273

1 tablespoon Krathiem Jiaw
(Fried garlic), page 272

TO SERVE THE LAAP

2 tablespoons Naam Man
Hom Daeng (Fried-shallot
oil), page 273, or Naam Man
Krathiem (Fried-garlic oil),
page 272

1 1/2 cups reserved offal
cooking liquid

3 tablespoons thinly sliced
green onions, lightly packed

3 tablespoons thinly sliced
sawtooth herb, lightly packed

3 tablespoons coarsely
chopped cilantro (thin stems
and leaves), lightly packed

3 tablespoons coarsely
chopped Vietnamese mint
leaves, lightly packed

3 tablespoons Hom Daeng
Jiaw (Fried shallots),
page 273

3 tablespoons Krathiem Jiaw
(Fried garlic), page 272

3 tablespoons very coarsely
chopped (about 1/4-inch
pieces) unseasoned pork
cracklings, preferably with
some meat attached

MAKE THE NAAM PHRIK LAAP (LAAP SEASONING PASTE)

Put the chiles in a small dry pan or wok, increase the heat to high to get the pan hot, then decrease the heat to low. Cook, stirring and flipping them frequently to make sure both sides of the chiles make contact with the hot pan, until the chiles are brittle and very dark brown (nearly black) all over, 15 to 20 minutes. Remove the chiles from the pan as they're finished. (Discard any seeds that escape the chiles, because they'll be burnt and bitter.) Set the chiles aside.

Combine the makhwen, coriander seeds, fennel seeds, ground galangal, ground lemongrass, black peppercorns, cumin seeds, nutmeg, cloves, long peppers, star anise, mace, and cardamom in a small pan, set the pan over low heat, and cook, stirring and tossing often, until they're very fragrant, about 5 minutes. Turn off the heat and stir for another minute. Grind them in a spice grinder (or pound them in a granite mortar) to a fairly fine powder.

Combine the dried chiles and salt in a granite mortar and pound firmly, scraping the mortar and stirring the mixture once or twice, until you have a fairly fine powder, about 5 minutes. Add the garlic and pound, occasionally stopping to scrape down the sides of the mortar, until you have a fairly smooth paste, about 2 minutes. Do the same with the shallots. Next, add the ground spice mixture and pound until it's well incorporated into the paste, about 2 minutes. Finally, pound in the shrimp paste until it's fully incorporated, about 30 seconds.

You'll have about 1/2 cup of paste. You can use it right away, or store the paste in the fridge for up to 1 week or in the freezer for up to 6 months. It helps to freeze the paste in small portions. You'll need about 6 tablespoons of paste for enough laap to serve 6 to 12 people.

COOK THE OFFAL

Combine the intestines, skin, liver, shrimp paste, galangal, lemongrass, and water in a small pot. Set the pot over high heat and bring the water to a strong simmer. Check the pork liver. Once it's cooked through (firm and just barely pink in the center), transfer it to a cutting board. Decrease the heat to maintain a gentle but steady simmer, skimming off any surface scum.

Keep cooking until the skin is translucent and soft enough to easily slice, about 20 minutes. Transfer the intestines and skin to the cutting board with the liver and reserve 2 cups of the liquid. When they're all cool enough to handle, slice the intestines and liver into small bite-size pieces. Slice the skin into thin 2-inch-long strips.

CHOP ("LAAP") THE PORK

Clear your appointments for the next 45 minutes.

Combine the lemongrass and blood in a mixing bowl and use your hand to squeeze and squish the lemongrass stalk for about a minute. You're helping to release the essence of the lemongrass, which tones down the flavor of the blood and keeps the blood liquid. Leave the lemongrass in the blood for now, but avoid it when you spoon out the blood later.

{continued}

{Northern Thai minced pork salad, continued}

Put the pork slices on a solid wood chopping block or cutting board. Use a heavy knife or cleaver to chop the pork, lifting the knife off the block with each chop and working methodically from one side of the expanse of meat to the other, then working your way back. (How hard should you chop? Pretend you want to hack a medium-size carrot into two pieces with each chop. Rely on your wrist for motion and the weight of the knife for most of your power.) Every 15 seconds or so, use the knife to scoop up some of the meat and fold it back onto the rest. Make sure you're not neglecting any spots.

Once the meat is coarsely chopped, after about 5 minutes, drizzle on 2 tablespoons of the blood (leaving behind the lemongrass), and keep chopping and folding as before to incorporate the blood and to continue chopping the meat more and more finely. Keep at it, adding another 2 tablespoons of blood every 5 minutes but stopping once you've used a total of 1/2 cup, until the blood is completely incorporated (the meat will be a deep purple reminiscent of beets), and the meat is very finely minced (you're shooting for a level several times finer than that of store-bought ground meat). After 15 minutes, you'll have reached hamburger texture. Keep going. It requires about 30 to 40 minutes of chopping, depending on your facility for it.

Discard the rest of the blood. (Don't worry, blood isn't expensive.) Transfer the minced meat mixture to a bowl. You've just spent more time and expended more energy than most people do preparing and eating an entire meal, so it should go without saying that you don't want to leave any of your hard-won mince on either the chopping block or your knife. Do, however, discard any waxy fat that might have collected on your knife blade.

PREPARE THE LAAP FOR COOKING ("YAM" THE LAAP)

In a medium mixing bowl, stir together the 1/2 cup of reserved offal cooking liquid with the 1/2 teaspoon of salt and 5 to 7 tablespoons of the laap seasoning paste, depending on how intensely flavored you want the final dish to be, until they're well mixed. Add all of the raw meat mixture and cooked offal, then stir gently but well. Add the salt, green onions, and herbs, stir well, then add the fried shallots and garlic and stir well.

At this point, the average Northern Thai cook would taste the mixture and adjust the seasoning, adding salt (or less typically in the North, fish sauce) if it isn't salty

enough and more naam phrik laap if it is not spicy or intense enough. If you're brave, go ahead. (If not, you can season it later, as it cooks.) Raw laap is delicious and rich. Northern Thai men of a certain generation would say it is superior to the cooked version. And I agree.

COOK AND SERVE THE LAAP

Heat a wok or large pan over high heat, add the oil, and swirl it in the wok to coat the sides. When the oil begins to smoke lightly, add the meat mixture, stir well, then add 1 1/2 cups of the reserved offal cooking liquid.

Cook, stirring constantly and breaking up the meat to ensure that it doesn't clump, until the meat is cooked, the liquid begins to simmer vigorously, and the mixture looks slightly soupy as the meat gives up its water, about 5 minutes. Taste and season with more salt or laap seasoning paste.

Keep cooking at a vigorous simmer, stirring often, so the flavors have a chance to meld, about 3 minutes more.

Spoon the laap onto a large plate or platter in a low mound. There should be some liquid pooling at the edges. Let it cool to just above room temperature, then sprinkle on the green onions, herbs, fried shallots and garlic, and pork cracklings, and serve.

Da Chom making *laap*

DA CHOM

When Da Chom invited me into his kitchen, I was lucky for the opportunity to watch him make *laap* before he hung up his knife for good. More generally, I was fortunate to catch a glimpse of a generation of Thais that has lived life on both sides of modernity.

Da Chom (*Da* means grandfather, a term of respect) was born in 1925 in the village of Muu Ban Saluang Nai, where he has lived, more or less, his entire life. Life in his early years was uncomplicated but difficult. There was no electricity (the village only got it thirty years ago). At the time, he told me, a child's education typically ended after fourth grade. Many families couldn't afford to lose the extra hands at home. He and his four siblings chipped in to do chores. "In the past, countryside kids didn't have toys," he told me in Thai. "Instead we helped our parents raise cows." His parents sent their children to gather herbs and leaves that grew nearby. Those green things would appear on the table along with classic Northern Thai food like sticky rice, *laap*, and Yam Jin Kai (page 158), and nearly extinct dishes like *yam salai*, a sort of salad made from a local river weed. No longer can you find this weed at markets, he told me. To get it, you'd have to trudge into a stream and pull it out yourself. When he was a teenager, he graduated from picking herbs and leaves to helping his parents make *laap*. At the time, the meat they minced was typically pork or water buffalo, though they occasionally used barking deer or boar.

When he was fourteen, his parents surprised him by giving him permission to study in Chiang Mai, agreeing to fund the 18 baht (about 50 cents) yearly tuition. To get there, he walked five miles to a place where he could hitch a ride by truck into the city.

As soon as he'd finished school, he returned to the village, where he eventually found a job as headmaster of the local elementary school, got married, and soon after found a plot beside a rice field where he built a home (where, incidentally, the recipes in this book were given a final cook-through). He and his wife had three children and couldn't get by on his teacher's salary alone. He took a second job at the local rice mill and operated a sundry store out of his home, selling everything from darning needles to shrimp paste. His wife took odd sewing jobs.

They raised their children in a different world than the one in which they grew up. His son, Tri, became a professional *muay thai* boxer and now trains young fighters. His daughter, Lakhana, went to college, became a teacher, and married my friend Chris. When she brought Chris home for the first time, Da Chom welcomed him into the family, in part because he could speak the local dialect but perhaps more important, because "he would eat just about anything."

This anything included Da Chom's *laap*, which he became justly famous for among his family. Notably, he didn't teach his children to make *laap*. He didn't have the chance. They studied at school during the days and worked at night. He's proud of what they've become.

He was in his late sixties when I watched him make *laap*. Until recently, when the family gathered for special occasions, his *laap* was at the center of the table. Now that he's in his eighties, he can only rarely summon the energy to make it. He still eats *laap* and prefers the uncooked version, though his kids urge him to avoid it after news, rumor or not, hit the village that people were going deaf from eating it. For those who balk at the idea of eating raw meat and blood, of trying food done the old way with all of the risks and rewards it brings, he has some advice: "It helps to drink a lot of booze first."

Laap Isaan

TWO ISAAN MINCED MEAT SALADS

It was New Year's Eve 1999, and I had been drifting around Southeast Asia for months. A cab from Vientiane, Laos, took me over the Friendship Bridge, still relatively new then, the first to connect Laos and Thailand over the Mekong River. Waylaid by a busted throttle cable, the cab finally dropped me in the city of Nong Khai, in Isaan. From there, I continued south by sluggish train and slow bus along the northeastern edge of Thailand, following the border formed by the Mekong and avoiding the backpacker ghettos as best I could.

My dog-eared *Lonely Planet* showed me how to get from city to city, and helped me decide where to go—and where not to. I was attracted to sleepy towns mentioned in the guidebook as having no ruins, no attractions to speak of—perfect for someone looking to elude tourists. But I couldn't resist the lure of Ubon Ratchathani, in part because it's one of the largest cities in Isaan but mainly because, as the guidebook noted, it was home to a restaurant that served the be-all, end-all duck *laap*.

I'd heard of *laap* before. Like most adventurous eaters in the US, I recognized it as a sort of minced meat "salad," the Thai menu staple often transliterated as "larb." (The spelling seems like a mistake, since speaking the Thai word requires no r-sound at all. My hunch is that this spelling was a Brit's doing: Say "larb" in an English accent and you're pretty close to the proper pronunciation.) But I'd never heard of a version made with duck. I had to try it.

That the restaurant's rendition made little impression, the details of my meal now lost to time, speaks to an unromantic reality of eating abroad. There are many reasons a talked-up restaurant can disappoint. Perhaps this one had lost its skilled cook or the guidebook nod had caused a tourist stampede and an inevitable dumbing down. Or maybe I ate an impeccable version and didn't know it. Like a kid wincing after a sip of his dad's coffee, maybe my assessment of this new-to-me food was so colored by my preconceived notions or expectations that I couldn't tell bad from good from great. And just as the watched pot never boils, sometimes when you seek out a revelation, you can't find it.

It wasn't until many years later, when Thailand had become more second home than vacation fodder, that I found myself speeding along a two-lane highway toward Loei province, in Isaan, and the best version of duck *laap* I've ever eaten. My friend Sunny and I had just crossed the border to Thailand on the way back from Laos, both of us eager for lunch. The road wended through small roadside towns, bursts of commerce punctuated by rice fields. Suddenly Sunny shouted from the passenger's seat, "There! *Laap pet!*" Duck *laap*. Whenever Sunny shouted and pointed, it meant, "Pull over," because there was something worth eating.

We parked in the dirt lot, and took seats in the more or less empty restaurant, a concrete floor covered by a patchwork canopy of metal sheets and shingles. We were presented with little baskets of sticky rice and a plate containing a low heap of chopped meat littered with fresh herbs and, ominously, lots of whole dried chiles.

As we dug in, pinching off little orbs of rice and using them to grab bites, I got to know the components with each mouthful: The jumble of duck pieces the size of the very tip of my pinky (a common way, I've learned, for Thai people to describe anything of small size); the chewy, squidgy bits of skin and rich entrails; the fiery, tart dressing; and the fragrant dusting of toasted rice crushed into powder. Beside the rice and duck was a plate of raw vegetables and herbs piled high, to be eaten between bites. By the time we'd finished, Sunny was sated and becoming fast friends with the middle-aged couple who ran the place, just steps from their modest house, inviting them to visit us in Chiang Mai. He's good like that. Whether I'd been primed by Sunny's approval, shocked by how much this lunch had surpassed my expectations (we were hungry; we just wanted lunch), or blessed to be in the presence of undeniably great *laap pet*, with my mouth still burning, I knew I had found my paragon.

* * *

I've included two renditions—one made with duck, one with catfish—of *laap isaan*, which comes from the northeastern region of Thailand and is different in nearly all aspects from the *laap* of Northern Thailand (page 106). Because Isaan people have become the country's primary source for manual labor, they've traveled in droves to Bangkok and beyond, bringing their food with them to virtually every corner of the kingdom. Today classic Isaan dishes like papaya salad and *laap* are almost as well known in Thailand and the US as the ubiquitous Central Thai dishes like *tom yam* and *phat thai*. The people of Isaan, primarily ethnic Lao and Khmer with different languages and cultures than their Central, Southern, and Northern Thai brethren, have a particular affinity for fiery, funky flavors, and their *laap*—also made from pork, water buffalo, and chicken—is indeed fiercely hot and imbued with the profound pungency of the unrefined fermented fish sludge called *plaa raa*. It is inseparable from mounds of sticky rice and cold beer.

{continued}

laap

Laap Pet Isaan

ISAAN MINCED DUCK SALAD

Flavor Profile TART, FIERY, AROMATIC, SALTY

Try It With Som Tam Lao (Lao/Isaan-style papaya salad), page 40, or Phak Buung Fai Daeng (Stir-fried water spinach), page 97. Needs Khao Niaw (Sticky rice), page 33.

NOTE: Despite its eager export, laap doesn't always arrive in the US intact. The off-cuts—the bits of skin, intestines, and liver—that you'd find in Thailand in the minced meat provide a richness and textural variety that I miss in most American versions. If you're up for it, I recommend using just 4 ounces of duck meat and supplementing it with a generous 1/4 cup of prepared offal and skin. The ingredients and method are listed below, and while they are "optional," I encourage you to try this version out.

THE PLAN

- Up to 2 weeks in advance: Make the toasted-chile powder and toasted–sticky rice powder
- Up to 1 week in advance: Make the galangal paste and fry the dried chiles
- Up to 1 day in advance: Chop the duck

SPECIAL EQUIPMENT

- A grill, preferably charcoal (optional), grates oiled
- 2 wood skewers (but only if you're grilling), soaked in tepid water for 30 minutes
- A Thai granite mortar and pestle
- A solid wood chopping block (not made of bamboo), recommended
- A meat cleaver or another large heavy knife

SERVES 2 TO 6 AS PART OF A MEAL; THE RECIPE IS EASILY DOUBLED

GALANGAL PASTE

1 ounce unpeeled garlic cloves

1 ounce unpeeled Asian shallots

1 (14-gram) piece peeled fresh or frozen (not defrosted) galangal, cut against the grain into 1/4-inch-thick slices

DUCK

If you're not using the offal:

1 (5 1/2-ounce) piece skinned duck breast (or meat cut from duck legs)

If you're using the offal:

1 (4-ounce) piece skinned duck breast (or meat cut from duck legs), skin reserved

SKIN AND OFFAL (OPTIONAL)

2 ounces duck skin reserved from the breast or leg

1 ounce mixed duck liver and heart

A few dashes Thai fish sauce

LAAP

1 tablespoon vegetable oil

6 dried Thai chiles, fried (page 12)

2 tablespoons lime juice (preferably from Key limes or spiked with a small squeeze of Meyer lemon juice)

2 tablespoons Thai fish sauce

1/2 teaspoon granulated sugar

14 grams peeled small shallots, preferably Asian, or very small red onions, halved lengthwise and thinly sliced with the grain (about 2 tablespoons)

7 grams thinly sliced lemongrass (tender parts only), from about 1 large stalk (about 1 tablespoon)

1 tablespoon Khao Khua (Toasted–sticky rice powder), page 271, plus a large pinch for finishing

1 tablespoon Phrik Phon Khua (Toasted-chile powder), page 270

1 tablespoon fresh or frozen kaffir lime leaves (stems removed if thick), very lightly packed

2 tablespoons very thinly sliced green onions, lightly packed

2 tablespoons thinly sliced sawtooth herb, very lightly packed

2 tablespoons very coarsely chopped cilantro (thin stems and leaves), lightly packed

2 tablespoons mint leaves (the smaller the better), very lightly packed, torn at last minute if large

MAKE THE GALANGAL PASTE

Prepare a grill, preferably charcoal, or grill pan to cook over medium heat (see page 124). Skewer the garlic and shallots separately (if you're grilling), then grill the shallots, garlic, and (unskewered) galangal, turning them over once or twice, until the galangal is cooked through and looks dry on both sides (don't let it char or brown), about 5 minutes, and until the garlic and shallots' skin is charred in spots, and they are fully soft but still hold their shape, 15 to 20 minutes. Let them cool to room temperature.

Pound the galangal in a granite mortar to a fairly smooth, fibrous paste, about 2 minutes. Then slip the

{continued}

{Isaan minced duck salad, continued}

skins off the garlic and pound the garlic until it's fully incorporated, 1 to 2 minutes. Do the same with the shallots and pound to a fairly smooth, slightly fibrous paste, 2 to 3 minutes. You'll have about 2 tablespoons of paste. You can use it right away, or store the paste in the fridge for up to 1 week or in the freezer for up to 6 months. It helps to freeze the paste in small portions in airtight containers. You'll need 1 tablespoon for this recipe.

CHOP ("LAAP") THE DUCK

Put the duck meat on a solid wood chopping block or cutting board.

Cut the meat against the grain into 1-inch-thick slices. Use a heavy knife or cleaver to chop the duck, relying on your wrist for motion and the weight of the knife for most of your power. (How hard should you chop? Pretend you want to hack a medium-size carrot into two pieces with each chop.) Work methodically from one side of the expanse of meat to the other, lifting the knife off the board with each chop, then work your way back. Every 10 seconds or so, use the knife to scoop up some of the meat and fold it back onto the rest. Keep at it until the meat looks like a coarse tartar, 5 to 8 minutes.

If you'd like, you can store the duck meat in an airtight container in the fridge for up to 1 day.

PREPARE THE SKIN AND OFFAL (OPTIONAL)

Combine the skin, liver, heart, and fish sauce in a small pot with enough water to cover them by about an inch (it's fine if the skin floats). Set the pot over high heat, bring the water to a strong simmer, then decrease the heat to maintain a gentle, steady simmer. Skim off any surface scum and check the duck liver. When it's cooked through (firm and just barely pink in the center), transfer it to a cutting board.

Keep cooking, turning the skin over occasionally, until the skin is slightly translucent and soft enough to easily slice, about 15 minutes. Transfer the heart and skin to the cutting board with the liver. When they're all cool enough to handle, thinly slice the heart and cut the liver into small bite-size pieces. Slice the skin into thin 2-inch-long strips.

COOK AND SERVE THE LAAP

Heat a wok or pan over high heat, pour in the oil, and swirl to coat the wok. When the oil begins to smoke lightly, add the chopped duck meat and 1 tablespoon of the galangal paste. Stir-fry (constantly stirring, scooping, and flipping the ingredients) and break up the meat to avoid clumps, until the duck is just barely cooked through, about 45 seconds. You are not trying to brown the duck.

Remove the wok from the heat, add the fried chiles, lime juice, fish sauce, and sugar, then return the wok to the high heat. Cook at a vigorous simmer, stirring constantly at first and then occasionally, until the liquid is almost completely gone but the meat still looks moist, 2 to 3 minutes. Turn off the heat and let the mixture cool to just above room temperature in the wok.

Add the duck skin and offal (if using), shallots, lemongrass, rice powder, chile powder, kaffir lime leaf, and 1 tablespoon of each of the remaining herbs to the wok. Stir well, then transfer the laap to a plate and sprinkle on the remaining herbs and rice powder, and serve.

Laap Plaa Duuk Isaan

ISAAN MINCED CATFISH SALAD

Flavor Profile TART, FIERY, AROMATIC, SALTY, SLIGHTLY SMOKY

Try It With Som Tam Lao (Lao/Isaan-style papaya salad), page 40, or Naam Phrik Plaa Thuu (Grilled-fish dip), page 177. Needs Khao Niaw (Sticky rice), page 33.

THE PLAN

- Up to 2 weeks in advance: Make the toasted-chile powder and toasted–sticky rice powder
- Up to 1 week in advance: Fry the dried chiles
- Up to a few hours in advance: Cook the fish

SPECIAL EQUIPMENT

- A charcoal grill (highly recommended), grates oiled
- A solid wood chopping block (not made of bamboo), recommended
- A meat cleaver or another large heavy knife

SERVES 4 TO 8 AS PART OF A MEAL

FISH

1 (3¹/₂- to 4-pound) whole Asian catfish (see **NOTE**), gutted and cleaned

1 (14-gram) piece peeled fresh or frozen (not defrosted) galangal, cut against the grain into thin slices

LAAP

About 1 tablespoon vegetable oil

¹/₄ cup lime juice (preferably from Key limes or spiked with a small squeeze of Meyer lemon juice)

3 tablespoons Thai fish sauce

1 teaspoon granulated sugar

1 ounce peeled small shallots, preferably Asian, or very small red onions, halved lengthwise and thinly sliced with the grain (about ¹/₄ cup)

14 grams thinly sliced lemongrass (tender parts only), from about 2 large stalks (about 2 tablespoons)

2 tablespoons very thinly sliced green onions, very lightly packed

2 tablespoons mint leaves (the smaller the better), very lightly packed and coarsely chopped at the last minute if large

2 tablespoons thinly sliced sawtooth herb, very lightly packed

2 tablespoons very coarsely chopped cilantro (thin stems and leaves), lightly packed

2 tablespoons Khao Khua (Toasted–sticky rice powder), page 271, plus a few pinches for finishing

2 teaspoons to 2 tablespoons Phrik Phon Khua (Toasted-chile powder), page 270

2 teaspoons very thinly sliced fresh or frozen kaffir lime leaves (stems removed if thick), very lightly packed

6 dried Thai chiles, fried (page 12)

NOTE: For this dish, there is no substitute for what I call "Asian catfish," for lack of a better term. It goes by many names, including cá bông lau in Vietnamese, but there most likely won't be any particularly helpful signage at the Asian fish markets where it's sold. Once you're there, buy the whole catfish you see on ice or alive in tanks.

COOK AND CHOP ("LAAP") THE FISH

Prepare a grill, preferably charcoal, or a lightly oiled grill pan to cook with high heat (see page 124). Grill the fish, turning it over once or twice but only after 10 minutes or so, until the skin is golden brown and slightly crispy and the flesh is cooked to the bone but not dried out, about 30 minutes. It's not important to keep the fish perfectly intact.

When the fish is cool enough to handle, remove and discard the head, pull off the skin (you can deep-fry it as a garnish; otherwise, discard it), and use a fork to pull the meat from the bones in large chunks. You'll have about 1 pound of flesh. Measure 12 ounces of flesh (about

2 cups, lightly packed), reserving the rest to snack on. Take a look at the mixture and pick out any stray bones.

Use a heavy knife or cleaver to roughly chop the galangal on a solid wood chopping block or cutting board. Add the 12 ounces of fish to the board and chop, lifting the knife off the board with each chop, working methodically from one side of the pile to the other and occasionally using the knife to scoop up some of the mixture and fold it back onto the rest, until it's coarsely chopped (a mixture of small chunks and medium ones no larger than an inch), and the galangal is finely chopped and well incorporated, about 45 seconds.

{continued}

{Isaan minced catfish salad, continued}

COOK AND SERVE THE LAAP

Heat a wok or pan over high heat, pour in about a tablespoon of oil, swirl to coat the wok, then pour out the oil. Add the chopped fish mixture and cook, stirring constantly and scraping the bottom of the wok, for about 30 seconds. (You're not trying to brown the fish.) Add the lime juice, fish sauce, and sugar and cook, constantly stirring, scooping, and flipping the ingredients and breaking up the fish as you do, until the fish has absorbed all of the liquid, the pan looks dry, but the fish still looks moist, about 2 to 4 minutes more.

Transfer the fish to a mixing bowl and let it cool slightly. Add the remaining ingredients, stir really well, and transfer to a plate along with an extra sprinkle of toasted rice powder and then serve.

KHONG YAANG
Grilled foods

A lot of the cooking at Pok Pok happens outdoors. Every day we get a big charcoal fire going. Once the flames go out, we scorch long eggplants over the red-hot coals for Yam Makheua Yao (page 59). Soon, the coals ash over and we grill mushrooms for Het Paa Naam Tok (page 70) and char chiles, garlic, and shallots for Naam Phrik Num (page 174). When the heat of the coals dies down, on goes meat like pork neck for Muu Kham Waan (page 125), not to sear but to absorb a little charcoal smoke as it slowly cooks.

The fragrance and flavor that charcoal grills impart are important elements of so many Thai dishes, so let me get this out of the way: Every dish in this book can be cooked without a grill. I provide the option, for instance, to char fresh chiles in a stovetop pan and to cook ribs in the oven. But I can't stress this enough: the dozen or so recipes that call for a grill will turn out much better if you use a charcoal grill. Gas power gives you easy temperature control. Charcoal asks more of you, but gives more back. Besides a grill, you'll need a sturdy pair of grill tongs and a heatproof implement that you can use to push, prod, and maybe scoop coals.

Building a fire and employing its heat take practice. There are approximately a billion grilling and barbecue books on the market. This is not a book on either. To learn about the subtleties of cooking with charcoal, I suggest you buy at least one—because here you'll find only what you need to know to cook the food in this book.

BUYING A GRILL

Some recipes in this book ask you to cook directly over the coals, typically with relatively high heat; some ask you to cook covered and "indirectly" (so whatever you're cooking is not directly above the coals), a method closer to oven cooking than grilling but one with the added benefit of charcoal flavor.

To perform both tasks with one piece of equipment, buy a simple, inexpensive charcoal grill. A Weber kettle grill, no bells or whistles required, does the trick. A step up in expense is a cooker that has both a small firebox and a larger drum grill chamber, because it'll make indirect cooking even easier. At Pok Pok, we use a simple Brinkmann cooker that I bought at Home Depot.

For direct cooking only, a cast-iron hibachi is great. It allows you to raise and lower the grill grates, giving you the ability to easily control the temperature at which you grill.

CHOOSING AND LIGHTING CHARCOAL

I like hardwood charcoal best. Lump and mesquite are perhaps the most readily available; *binchotan* rocks, if you can find it and feel like splurging, because it burns hotter and longer than just about anything else. Briquettes work fine, too.

My preferred way to light a fire is with a so-called chimney starter, available wherever grills are sold. You put crumpled newspaper in the chamber, heap on charcoal, and use a match to ignite the paper from the bottom. Wait until the coals catch, let the flames die down slightly, then carefully dump the glowing red, graying coals into the grill in a pile.

Alternatively, pile unlit coals in the grill and hit them with a blowtorch until they ignite. I'm even okay with using lighter fluid as long as you let the fluid burn off before you start cooking. But the other methods are so easy, why bother?

PREPARING THE GRILL

It might sounds obvious but it's worth the reminder. Before you grill, clean the grates, then oil them. The easiest way to oil the grates is to rub them with a clean rag or paper towel soaked with vegetable oil.

CONTROLLING HEAT

This is the task that requires the most practice to do well. The concepts, however, are relatively straightforward.

The first and most obvious way to adjust the heat of the grill is by relying on the heat produced by the coals. Right after they've ignited, the coals will be glowing red and have some contained flames. These are very hot coals. Soon the flame will completely die and the coals will turn gray (or "ash over")—they'll still be really, really hot. But wait a little while and the heat will begin to decrease, then decrease more and more. To raise the heat, add more coals or stoke the coals, introducing oxygen by fanning them. To quickly reduce the heat, sprinkle on some damp ash. I always keep a small bucket of ash near the grill.

The second way is by adjusting the distance between those coals and whatever you're cooking. Make a tall pile of coals, which decreases the distance between them and whatever you're cooking, and you'll be cooking at a higher heat. Flatten out the pile, which increases the distance, and you'll be cooking at a lower heat. Same goes for adjusting the height of the grill rack or cooking on a part of the grill that has no coals beneath it: the farther away from the fire, the lower the cooking heat.

COVERED GRILLING

In some cases, you'll be cooking on the grill using ambient temperature rather than the direct heat of the coals. Assessing this heat is easy, since most grills have a built-in thermometer. If yours doesn't, buy an oven thermometer and stick it inside.

This kind of grilling isn't typically used for quick cooking, so your task is to maintain the proper heat for an hour or two. To do this, you'll have to add more charcoal (unlit is fine) to the fire every now and then. Knowing exactly how much to add and how often takes practice, since a host of factors—the type of charcoal you use, how densely the charcoal is packed, the weather, the cooker, and so on—determine how long your fire will last. But you'll probably want to light a second batch of charcoal right after the first, so you can easily replenish the coals as necessary.

Once you're cooking, you can also regulate the temperature by playing with the grill's vents. Open them (a crack, halfway, all the way) and the rush of oxygen will increase the heat accordingly and also make the coals burn more quickly. It will also create a sort of convection cooking, pulling heat and smoke toward or away from what you're cooking.

Muu Kham Waan

GRILLED PORK NECK WITH SPICY DIPPING SAUCE AND ICED GREENS

There's nothing better to snack on while you drain tall bottles of Leo beer at a late-night (or late-afternoon) drinking joint. This is boozing food, without a doubt, a thirst-inducing combination of heat and meat—and awesomely chewy meat at that, not a cut that's going to fall apart when you so much as look at it.

Along with those slices of neck (a common sight in Thailand) comes a dead-simple dipping sauce whose requisite flavors are sour, salty, and viciously spicy. At Pok Pok, we pour the sauce over the pork, even though you rarely, if ever, see it served that way in Thailand. That's because no one in Southeast Asia's going to tentatively dip a corner of the pork, as whiteys tend to. The dish must be spicy. That's its purpose. So I force the issue. I also include a plate of raw *yu choy* heaped with ice, an element borrowed from the swank athletic club in Chiang Mai where I first tried the dish and just about every iteration I've had thereafter. Each bite of these greens is a crisp, cold antidote to the chile-bombed sauce's fire.

At Pok Pok, we go the extra mile and use boar meat (*muu paa*) rather than straight-up pork, because boar is common in Northern Thailand. I suggest you attempt the same. Yet whether you want to use boar or not, I don't think I need to point out that neck does not exactly pack butcher cases at Safeway and Trader Joe's. To find the cut, which has tons of flavor and long, lovely striations of fat, you need to have a chat with a real butcher, preferably one who deals with whole animals. If you can't find it, pork shoulder makes a fine stand-in.

Flavor Profile MEATY, FIERY, SOUR, SLIGHTLY HERBACEOUS AND PEPPERY

Try It With Khao Phot Ping (Grilled corn with salty coconut cream), page 144, or Phat Khanom Jiin (Stir-fried Thai rice noodles), page 238. Needs lots of beer and Khao Niaw (Sticky rice), page 33.

{continued}

khong yaang

{Grilled pork neck with spicy dipping sauce and iced greens, continued}

PORK	DIPPING SAUCE	TO SERVE ALONGSIDE
4 grams peeled garlic, halved lengthwise	3 tablespoons Thai fish sauce	About 12 leafy stalks yu choy or baby Chinese broccoli
2 grams cilantro roots, thinly sliced	3 tablespoons lime juice (preferably from Key limes or spiked with a small squeeze of Meyer lemon juice)	About 3 cups crushed ice
12 black peppercorns	2 tablespoons minced garlic	
1 pound boneless pork neck or shoulder, sliced with the grain into 1/2-inch-thick slabs	12 grams fresh Thai chiles (about 8), preferably red, thinly sliced	
1 tablespoon plus 1 teaspoon Thai seasoning sauce	1 tablespoon plus 1 teaspoon granulated sugar	
2 teaspoons granulated sugar	1/4 cup finely chopped cilantro (thin stems and leaves), lightly packed	

SERVES 4 TO 8 AS PART OF A MEAL; THE RECIPE IS EASILY DOUBLED

MARINATE AND COOK THE PORK

Combine the garlic, cilantro roots, and peppercorns in a granite mortar and pound to a coarse paste, about 45 seconds. Combine the pork in a mixing bowl with the paste, seasoning sauce, and sugar and massage with your hands to coat the pork well with the seasonings. Cover and refrigerate for up to 1 hour.

Prepare a grill, preferably charcoal, or a lightly oiled grill pan to cook over medium heat (see page 124). Cook the pork, flipping once, until it's well browned on both sides, slightly charred, and just cooked through, about 8 minutes total. Transfer the pork to a cutting board to rest for a few minutes, then cut it against the grain into slices that are about 3 inches long and 1/8 to 1/4 inch thick.

MAKE THE DIPPING SAUCE

Combine the fish sauce, lime juice, garlic, chiles, and sugar in a bowl and stir well. Right before you're ready to serve, stir in the cilantro.

SERVE THE DISH

Arrange the pork slices on a plate. Serve with the dipping sauce in a small bowl and a plate of yu choy covered with a heap of crushed ice.

Sii Khrong Muu Yaang

{Pictured on page 130}

THAI-STYLE PORK RIBS

SPECIAL EQUIPMENT

• A charcoal grill (highly recommended), grates oiled

There are many battles I've chosen not to fight at Pok Pok. I don't serve the herbaceous Northern Thai curries floating with hacked-up frog (I just use the legs). I don't offer up incendiary Southern stir-fries or *luu*, a soup of raw blood. But I will not change the way I cook these ribs. They represent one front in my offensive against the status quo.

When most Americans hear "pork ribs," they imagine either the sauce-slathered, falling-off-the-bone version that's the centerpiece of so many back-yard barbecues or those you'd demolish at some great dive in Memphis, the meat coming away with a gentle tug from teeth. These ribs, the kind you'd find at booze-heavy, grill-focused Thai establishments, are decidedly different. Cut across the bone into pieces just a few inches long and marinated in a Chinese-influenced mixture of whiskey, honey, and ginger, they're grilled over charcoal until they're just tender—not spoon-tender, not falling-off-the-bone tender. Or to put it less generously, as some do, they're too chewy. These ribs, to be clear, are not chewy. They just don't disintegrate when your teeth hit them.

This is one of those moments when the preferences of Thais conflict with ours. Westerners tend to prefer predictably tender meat to all else. Thais eagerly gnaw on bones, suck at gristle, and crunch through cartilage. They chew comically tough but incredibly flavorful strips of beef—called "crying tiger" in Thai, because (or so I've heard) not even a tiger could chew them. The fact that these ribs have some chew to them makes them vulnerable to criticism, but also makes them that much more welcome with beer.

Still, customers occasionally put up a fight. Sometimes I'm tempted to just give in, to make them more tender. But sometimes I have to stand my ground and say this is what the food is. If you don't like it, tell you what, order the chicken wings. You'll like those.

Flavor Profile MEATY, UMAMI-RICH, SWEET AND SALTY, SMOKY

Try It With Tam Taeng Kwaa (Thai cucumber salad), page 45, or Yam Makheua Yao (Grilled eggplant salad), page 59; Khao Phot Ping (Grilled corn with salty coconut cream), page 144; and Khao Niaw (Sticky rice), page 33.

RIBS	⅛ teaspoon ground Ceylon or Mexican cinnamon	TO SERVE ALONGSIDE
6 tablespoons honey		½ cup Jaew (Spicy, tart dipping sauce for meat), page 278, optional
2 tablespoons Thai thin soy sauce	Pinch grated nutmeg	
2 tablespoons Shaoxing wine	2 pounds pork spareribs, cut lengthwise across the bone into 2-inch-wide racks by your butcher (most Asian butchers sell them already cut)	
1 tablespoon finely grated ginger		
½ teaspoon Asian sesame oil (look for brands that are 100 percent sesame oil)	2 tablespoons hot water	
¼ teaspoon ground white pepper		

MAKES ABOUT 20 RIBLETS (ENOUGH FOR 4 TO 8 AS PART OF A MEAL); THE RECIPE IS EASILY DOUBLED

MARINATE THE RIBS

Whisk 2 tablespoons of the honey with the soy sauce, Shaoxing wine, ginger, sesame oil, pepper, cinnamon, and nutmeg in a bowl until the honey has dissolved. Put the ribs in a large resealable bag, pour in the marinade, force out the air, and seal the bag. Put the bag in the fridge to marinate, turning the bag over occasionally, for at least 2 hours or as long as overnight.

COOK THE RIBS

In a small bowl, stir together the remaining 4 tablespoons of honey with the hot water until the honey has dissolved. You'll brush the ribs with this mixture when they're almost finished cooking.

ON THE GRILL (HIGHLY RECOMMENDED): Prepare a charcoal grill to cook at 200°F to 250°F (see page 124). If your grill doesn't have a firebox, which allows for easy indirect cooking, push the coals to one side of the grill and form them into a mound. Add the ribs, meat side up, to the area of the grill rack opposite the charcoal. Rotate the grill top if possible so the vents are directly over the ribs, open the vents, and cover the grill. Positioning the open vents above the ribs will pull the charcoal smoke toward them, giving the ribs an especially smoky flavor.

Cook the ribs, flipping the racks over occasionally and rotating them 180 degrees when you do, until they're a mahogany color with crisp, slightly charred edges, 2 to 2¼ hours, adding more charcoal as necessary to maintain the temperature. (Pinch a piece off the corner. The meat should be tender with a slight pleasant chewiness, not falling off the bone.) Thirty minutes or so before they're done, begin brushing the ribs with the honey mixture every 10 minutes or so.

IN THE OVEN: Preheat the oven to 250°F. Put the ribs on a foil-lined baking sheet, leaving at least an inch between the two racks. Bake for 2 hours, turning the rib racks over and rotating the baking sheet once or twice. Increase the heat to 300°F. Brush the ribs with some of the honey mixture and continue baking, brushing them every 10 minutes or so, until the ribs have a lacquered, mahogany surface and the meat is tender with a pleasant chewiness, not falling off the bone, 30 minutes to 1 hour more.

Transfer the ribs to a cutting board, let them rest for a few minutes, then slice them into individual ribs. Serve them alongside a bowl of the dipping sauce.

Sai Ua Samun Phrai

{Pictured on page 131}

NORTHERN THAI-STYLE HERBAL SAUSAGE

I have never eaten any sausage quite like *sai ua samun phrai*, and to this day I have eaten none tastier than the version made by a grumpy man in a market on the outskirts of Chiang Mai. He grills the coils of meat over a low fire and sells them by the kilo until they're gone, typically by 3 p.m. You'd be grumpy too if you stood over hot charcoal all day.

Before you even take a bite, you know this isn't your average sausage. A cross section looks like a mosaic—green specks of herbs, red flecks of chile, and yellow-tinged pork separated by patches of white fat. The Thai name means, basically, "stuffed intestines, lots of herbs," and a bite reveals why: the loose, crumbly sausage explodes with bright flavor, an alchemy brought about by lemongrass, galangal, kaffir lime leaf, and other aromatics. There's another layer too, a richness and depth from spices like turmeric and curry powder.

As far as I can tell, the sausage is particular to Northern Thailand, though you'll occasionally spot different sausages sold by the same name in Isaan. If you find a decent version at a restaurant in the US, text me immediately. Until then, you're stuck making your own, which—let's be clear—is a royal pain to do. Well worth it, too.

NOTE: I strongly recommend a meat grinder for this recipe, because it'll make your life infinitely easier. Yet, since this is a chunky, not emulsified, sausage, you can get away with chopping the meat on a sturdy wood cutting board as you would the duck for Laap Pet (page 117) until it's about four times coarser than store-bought ground meat, 5 to 8 minutes.

Flavor Profile HERBACEOUS, MEATY, RICH, AROMATIC, SALTY

Try It With Naam Phrik Num (Green Chile Dip), page 174, and steamed vegetables like long beans, cabbage, and winter squash. Needs Khao Niaw (Sticky rice), page 33.

THE PLAN

- Up to 1 week in advance: Make the paste
- The night before: Grind the meat and stuff the sausage
- Up to a few hours in advance: Steam the sausage

SPECIAL EQUIPMENT

- A charcoal grill (highly recommended), grates oiled
- 2 or 3 wood skewers (but only if you're grilling), soaked in tepid water for 30 minutes
- A Thai granite mortar and pestle
- A meat grinder or meat grinder attachment
- A sausage maker or small funnel
- A wide aluminum Chinese steamer

MAKES ABOUT
2 POUNDS OF SAUSAGE;
SERVES 8 TO 12 PEOPLE
AS PART OF A MEAL

PASTE

2 ounces unpeeled garlic cloves

1 1/2 ounces unpeeled Asian shallots

1 (1-ounce) piece peeled fresh or frozen (not defrosted) galangal, cut against the grain into 1/4-inch-thick slices

1 (14-gram) piece peeled fresh or frozen (not defrosted) yellow turmeric root, cut against the grain into 1/4-inch-thick slices

14 grams stemmed dried Mexican puya chiles (about 8), slit open and seeded

1 1/3 ounces thinly sliced lemongrass (tender parts only), from about 6 large stalks

18 grams cilantro roots, thinly sliced

2 grams finely grated zest from fresh or defrosted frozen kaffir lime

SAUSAGE

1 pound boneless pork shoulder, cut into approximately 1 1/2-inch chunks

1 pound skinless pork belly, cut into approximately 1 1/2-inch chunks

1/2 cup very coarsely chopped cilantro (thin stems and leaves), lightly packed

1/4 cup Thai fish sauce

1 generous tablespoon very thinly sliced fresh or frozen kaffir lime leaves (stems removed if thick)

1 1/2 teaspoons mild Indian curry powder

1 teaspoon ground black pepper

About 6 feet natural sausage casings, about 1 inch in diameter (available at good butcher shops), defrosted in water if frozen or soaked for 5 minutes if salted

MAKE THE PASTE

Prepare a grill, preferably charcoal, or grill pan to cook over medium heat (see page 124). Skewer the garlic and shallots separately (if you're grilling). Cook the garlic, shallots, galangal, and turmeric, turning them over once or twice, until the galangal and turmeric are cooked through and look dry on both sides (don't let them char or brown), about 5 minutes, and until the garlic and shallots' skin is charred in spots, and they are fully soft but still hold their shape, 15 to 20 minutes. Transfer the grilled items to a plate as they're finished and let them cool to room temperature. Roughly chop the galangal and turmeric and peel the garlic and shallots.

Firmly pound the dried chiles in the mortar, scraping the mortar and stirring the mixture once or twice, until you have a fairly fine powder, about 5 minutes. One by one, pound in the lemongrass, then the cilantro roots, then the galangal and turmeric, then the garlic, and then the shallots to a fairly smooth, slightly fibrous paste, fully pounding each ingredient before moving on to the next, 2 to 3 minutes per ingredient. Finally, pound in the kaffir lime zest until it's well incorporated, about 30 seconds.

You'll have a generous 1/2 cup of paste. You can use it right away, or store the paste in an airtight container in the fridge for up to 1 week or in the freezer for up to 6 months.

MAKE THE SAUSAGE MIXTURE

Put the pork shoulder, belly, and the meat grinder (or meat grinder attachment) in the freezer just until the edges of the meat are frozen. Grind the meat once through a grinder plate with 1/2-inch holes and add it to a large mixing bowl.

Add all of the seasoning paste, cilantro, fish sauce, kaffir lime leaf, curry powder, and black pepper to the bowl and mix gently but well with your hands for no more than a minute or so. Overworking the mixture will give the sausage too dense a texture. (At this point, you'll want to fry up a generous teaspoon of the mixture and taste it to check the seasoning. Once the mixture is in the casing, you won't be able to adjust the seasoning. If you'd like, mix in some toasted-chile powder, page 270, or fish sauce to adjust the seasoning.)

MAKE THE SAUSAGE

Rinse the casings well under running water, then rinse the insides by putting one end around the mouth of a faucet and letting the water run through for a few minutes. This will also show you whether the casing is broken. Find an unbroken length of about 4 1/2 feet for your sausage. Discard the broken parts. That's why you bought so many feet of casings.

If you have a sausage maker, good for you. If not, you can stuff the casings with the help of a "sausage-stuffer" funnel or regular funnel. First, tie a tight knot at one end of the casing and gather as much of the casing as you can onto the funnel. Insert the narrow end of the funnel into the open end of the casing. Push the meat a few tablespoons at a time through the funnel and into the casing. Whenever you have a good 6 inches or so of meat in the casing, stop for a moment, hold the open end of the casing with one hand and use the other hand to gently but firmly force the meat toward the knotted end. Your first time will take a while, though the process will get easier as you go.

When you've used all of the meat mixture, use a toothpick or bamboo skewer to prick the casings near any air bubbles you spot. Then slowly run one hand along the sausage from opening end to knotted end, to ensure the meat is as evenly distributed as possible and to eliminate any remaining pockets of air. Lay the sausage on a large plate in one big coil and use the knife tip to prick the casing every inch or so on the top of the coil so the sausage won't burst when you grill it.

Let the sausage sit in the fridge for at least a few hours or as long as overnight. At this point, you can freeze some or all of the sausage for up to 3 months. Fully defrost it in the fridge before proceeding.

STEAM, THEN GRILL THE SAUSAGE

Pour about 3 inches of water into a wide aluminum Chinese steamer (it should be wide enough to fit the plate with a few inches to spare), insert the steamer layer, cover, and bring the water to a boil over high heat. Add the sausage directly to the steamer basket, cover the steamer, and cook just until the sausage is firm and springy to the touch, though still not fully cooked in the center, 6 to 10 minutes.

Prepare a grill, preferably charcoal, to cook over medium heat (see page 124). Or preheat a very large grill pan or griddle over medium heat. Cook, carefully turning the coil over once, until both sides are light brown with dark brown patches and the sausage is cooked through, 15 to 20 minutes. The sausage won't be bursting with juice like a European sausage.

Let the sausage cool until it's just warm (call it "Thai room temperature"), then cut it into approximately 1/2-inch-thick slices and serve.

khong yaang

Kai Yaang

WHOLE ROASTED YOUNG CHICKEN

It all started with these roasted birds.

Even when I finally decided to open a restaurant, back in 2005, I didn't know what kind. I was considering a Mexican joint until I saw the big house on SE Division Street, in Portland, with a funky little hovel out front. That was when my blurry vision for a restaurant came into focus: *Forget tacos*, I thought. *That's a chicken shack if it's anything.*

Almost two decades ago, I'd befriended a colorful character named Chavalit Van—Mr. Lit, for short. He ran SP Chicken, a restaurant on the moat road in Chiang Mai. I had been staying nearby and had read about the restaurant in a guidebook, of all things. I wasn't expecting much. Yet when I got there, I was entranced by a row of pint-sized chickens rotating on a vertical spit beside a wall of glowing charcoal.

I'd eaten dozens of versions of this chicken, an Isaan classic, but none came close to this one. The others were typically spatch-cocked and grilled or roasted intact but on the increasingly popular gas-fired rotisserie. Every time I was in Chiang Mai, I found myself at a table at SP Chicken in front of one of those birds, hacked-up, mahogany skin capping the juicy flesh, and a little heap of the garlicky, lemongrass-packed stuffing—fibrous but incredibly flavorful. Alongside were a little dish of sweet-tart chile sauce, sticky rice, and perhaps papaya salad.

After a dozen visits, I resolved to figure out what made these birds this good. During each visit, I noticed the same man tending the chickens, mopping them with some mysterious liquid as they browned. Once my Thai had improved from nonexistent to merely woeful, I decided to approach him. I did my halting best, butchering word after word until I'd spit out a sentence or two. He responded in impeccable English.

Soon after, we struck up a friendship. Besides showing me his collection of charged political "Letters to the Editor" published in the *Bangkok Post* and the *Nation*, he told me about the chicken. He was circumspect about the precise details—of course, I never expected him to share the recipe—but when I decided to open Pok Pok, he told me where to find the right rotisserie, deep in the bowels of Bangkok Chinatown, and more important, how to modify it. Straight out of the box, these rotisseries were wonky: Everything seemed in order until you started cooking. Then all hell broke loose. Thanks to him, I replaced the skewers meant to hold the birds, installed a variable-speed motor, made new drain pans so the grease wasn't leaking everywhere—a litany of alterations all made in the name of fine chicken cookery. I've since shipped half a dozen of these rotisseries to the US. My homage to his rotisserie birds was one of a handful of menu items on the original menu at Pok Pok.

Yet I was inspired as much by his ethos as I was by his method. It took two years of culinary experimentation, he told me, before he was happy enough with his product to offer it for sale. And he hasn't changed a thing about it since he opened in 1977. I love that. No ego, no weekly changing menu, no look-at-me dishes. Just the same thing, done well, for decades. SP Chicken became not only my model for chicken, but also for what a restaurant's food

{continued}

should be: simple, delicious, consistent. This endless repetition—Mr. Lit estimates that he has cooked and sold more than six hundred thousand chickens—is why he can tell when a bird is done just by lifting it, by sensing the infinitesimal difference in weight. It's remarkable, not least because it's no longer how businesses typically operate. A couple of years ago, Mr. Lit retired, leaving the day-to-day operation to his wife and daughter. But when I go, I almost always spot him out back, hanging with his grandson.

My plan was never to duplicate his chicken. My rendition is a composite, a picking and choosing of my favorite qualities. But the spirit of the dish is intact. And of course, I don't expect you to buy and build out a rotisserie. I've come up with a way to achieve—well, almost—the same juicy, flavor-packed birds in an oven.

NOTE: If you don't have a brush for marinating and basting, you can fashion one from a lemongrass stalk. Trim off the bottom 1/2 inch, remove the outer layer, and use a small knife to make inch-or-so-deep perpendicular cuts in the thicker bottom until it resembles the bristles of a brush.

Flavor Profile AROMATIC, UMAMI-RICH, SALTY, SLIGHTLY SWEET

Try It With Any Som Tam (Papaya Salad and Family), page 35, and Khao Niaw (Sticky rice), page 33.

THE PLAN

- **Up to 1 week in advance:** Make the fried-shallot or fried-garlic oil and the dipping sauces
- **The night before:** Brine the birds
- **The morning of:** Stuff the birds and let them dry out in the fridge
- **2 hours before:** Marinate the birds

SPECIAL EQUIPMENT

- **A Thai granite mortar and pestle**
- **A charcoal grill (highly recommended), grates oiled**
- **A food-safe brush (or lemongrass brush; see NOTE)**

SERVES 4 TO 8 PEOPLE AS PART OF A MEAL; THE RECIPE IS EASILY DOUBLED

2 Cornish game hens or poussins (1 1/4 to 1 1/2 pounds each), rinsed inside and out

BRINE

1/2 cup kosher salt

1/4 cup superfine sugar

10 cups tepid water

5 or 6 unpeeled garlic cloves

1 teaspoon white peppercorns

A thumb-size hunk of unpeeled ginger, coarsely sliced against the grain

1 large unpeeled stalk lemongrass, cut into 2-inch lengths

A small handful cilantro stems, preferably with roots attached, torn in half

2 or 3 whole green onions, torn in half

STUFFING

3 large stalks lemongrass, outer layer, bottom 1/2 inch, and top 4 inches removed

3 3/4 ounces unpeeled garlic cloves, halved lengthwise (about 3/4 cup)

1 tablespoon kosher salt

1 teaspoon ground white pepper

2 ounces thinly sliced cilantro stems (about 1/2 cup)

MARINADE

2 tablespoons Thai fish sauce

2 tablespoons Thai thin soy sauce

1/2 teaspoon granulated sugar

1/4 teaspoon ground black pepper

2 tablespoons water

BASTING LIQUIDS

A couple tablespoons Naam Man Hom Daeng (Fried-shallot oil), page 273, or Naam Man Krathiem (Fried-garlic oil), page 272

1/4 cup honey mixed well with 2 tablespoons hot water

RECOMMENDED DIPPING SAUCES

Naam Jim Kai (Sweet chile dipping sauce), page 276

Naam Jim Kai Yaang (Tamarind dipping sauce), page 277

BRINE THE BIRDS

Whisk the salt and sugar with the 10 cups of tepid water in a large mixing bowl or pot until the sugar and salt fully dissolve. Combine the garlic, peppercorns, ginger, and lemongrass in a mortar and lightly pound to bruise and slightly crush them. Add them along with the cilantro and green onions to the brine, then add the birds breast side down. If they float, weigh them down with a plate. If the birds still aren't completely submerged, choose a different container. Cover and refrigerate for at least 4 hours or, even better, overnight.

MAKE THE STUFFING AND STUFF THE BIRDS

Remove the birds, discarding the brine, and sit them ass down in a colander to drain.

Cut the lemongrass crosswise (tough parts, too) into rough 1/8-inch slices. Firmly pound it in a granite mortar until it's very fragrant, about 10 seconds. Add the garlic and pound to break it into small pieces (you're not making a paste), about 20 seconds. Add the salt and pepper, pound briefly, then add the cilantro stems and pound to bruise them, about 10 seconds more.

Divide the stuffing equally among the birds' cavities, set the birds breast side up on a plate (or even better, a rack set over a tray) so there's some space between them. Tuck each wing tip under the body. Put the birds in the fridge, uncovered, to dry out for at least 4 hours or up to 12 hours.

MARINATE THE BIRDS

Stir the fish sauce, soy sauce, sugar, and pepper in a small bowl along with the 2 tablespoons of water until the sugar is fully dissolved. Brush the birds with the marinade, then put them back, uncovered, into the fridge for about 2 hours.

COOK THE BIRDS

ON THE GRILL (HIGHLY RECOMMENDED): Prepare a charcoal grill to cook at 350°F to 375°F (see page 124). If your grill doesn't have a firebox, which allows for easy indirect cooking, push the coals to one side of the grill and form them into a mound. Add the birds, breasts up, to the grill rack opposite the charcoal, and cover the grill, opening the vents and rotating the grill cover if possible so the vents are directly over the birds. Positioning the open vents above the birds will pull the charcoal smoke toward them, giving them a little more smoky flavor. While you cook, you'll have to add more charcoal as necessary to maintain the temperature.

Cook for 25 minutes, flip the birds over to get some color on the other side, and after about 5 minutes more, flip the birds over again.

If you're not cooking on a grill with a firebox, carefully remove the birds and the grill grate. Spread out the coals so that instead of mound, they're lying in one or two layers, still on one side of the grill. Return the grate and the birds to the grill.

Continue cooking, covered, with the birds on the side opposite the coals. After 5 minutes, brush the birds all over with the shallot oil and re-cover. After 5 minutes more, brush the birds all over with the honey mixture and move them so they're directly over the coals. Keep cooking, covered, turning over and rotating the birds as necessary to achieve even browning and brushing occasionally with the honey mixture, until the skin is a slightly glossy golden brown with some dark patches and the juices of the thigh run clear, 5 to 10 minutes more, depending on the size of the bird.

IN THE OVEN: Move the oven rack to the bottom third of the oven, and preheat the oven to 350°F. Put the birds breast side up on a baking tray (or even better, a rack set over a tray or roasting pan).

Roast the birds for 30 minutes. Rotate the pan and brush the birds all over with the garlic oil. Cook for 5 minutes more, then brush the birds all over with the honey mixture. Crank up the heat to 400°F. Check on the birds every 5 minutes, brushing them with the honey mixture, until the skin is a slightly glossy golden brown with some darker patches and the juices run clear when you pierce the thickest part of the thigh, about 10 minutes more, depending on the size of the bird.

REST AND CARVE THE BIRDS

Let the birds rest for at least 10 minutes or up to 30 minutes. Serve them whole or carved—it's up to you—with the dipping sauces. At Pok Pok, we halve the birds lengthwise, then remove the hindquarters and separate them into drumsticks and thighs, remove the wings, and chop the breast portions through the bone into two or three pieces.

MR. LIT

Mr. Lit, my chicken mentor, was born in 1946, the eighth of ten kids, in a village deep in the forest at the foot of the mountains in Northern Thailand. His father kept a small orchard of longan and mango, and he sold the fruit to earn money. A good year meant a modest sum. A bad year meant nothing.

Each morning, his mother went to the village market before dawn. Mr. Lit often went along to help carry the baskets she brought full of items to sell—fruit from the orchard, herbs and leaves that grew in the forest. She'd use any money she made to shop at the market herself, buying ingredients to bring home. "That way," Mr. Lit told me, "we could have meat."

There was no electricity in the village, so candles and kerosene lamps lit their house. Without a refrigerator or icebox, his mother kept the meat on a rack over the stove, so the smoke from cooking could preserve leftovers. Storing fish was simpler. Either his brothers would catch river fish, with clever traps or sometimes with their bare hands, or his mother would buy live fish from the market. At home, they'd keep it, occasionally thrashing, in a tub of water.

Although the village was less than twenty miles from Chiang Mai, his family rarely made the journey. There were only two options: travel by foot or by bus (really, a modified truck with a pen in back where passengers sat). The bus ride took three hours on meandering, unpaved, pothole-pocked roads. The driver always kept a sturdy rope on hand, for the not-so-rare occasions that the bus got stuck. One day, a young Mr. Lit watched a black car drive past his village. "I thought to myself, *All I want for my future is a black automobile*," Mr. Lit told me.

Mr. Lit took his first trip to Chiang Mai when he was ten years old. It was the first time he saw electric light. He had come to continue his education, something his family could only afford by borrowing money from a rich neighbor. Most of his brothers and sisters had stopped after just four years of schooling. Mr. Lit studied in the city for six years, finishing tenth grade. By that time, Chiang Mai University had opened. Many of the friends he'd made went on to study there. Mr. Lit couldn't afford it. He moved to Bangkok to look for work, staying with a cousin and searching fruitlessly for work. He had no big dreams, he said. Because of his poor background and meager education, he didn't expect much of himself. He wanted to support himself, that's it.

Finally, he got a job as an office boy, where he earned 350 baht (about $11.50) a month for doing odd jobs ranging from typing to cleaning. In the evening, he studied English, the only subject he'd ever really liked. Eventually, he got a job at an agricultural behemoth where he stayed for twelve years, first as a salesman and later as a supervisor. His work took him all over Thailand, through the south and through the northeast, where he tasted Isaan's now-famous grilled chicken for the first time.

His company was responsible for, among other things, introducing to Thailand the broiler chicken, an especially meaty bird that was ready for slaughter much more quickly than the prevailing breed. The company,

Mr. Lit says, started a revolution in cheap, available chicken in Thailand. Later he rode the chicken wave, joining forces with a friend to establish a chicken slaughterhouse, which began with no chickens at all and was soon going through one thousand a day.

At twenty-nine, he married and wanted a change. With the urging of his friend from the slaughterhouse, who thought Mr. Lit should capitalize on the surging popularity of this chicken, he and his wife decided to move to Chiang Mai and open a restaurant. He would serve, Mr. Lit decided, Isaan food, which is known for *kai yaang*, grilled chicken. Of all of Thailand's regional cuisines, it was his favorite. At the time, Chiang Mai had a ton of Northern Thai restaurants but not many Isaan ones. (Today, Mr. Lit notes, the opposite is true.) He called the place SP Chicken—"SP" for his wife, Suleeporn.

There was only one problem. Mr. Lit didn't know how to cook Isaan food. He could cook only what he'd watched his mother make when he was a boy, and that was Northern Thai food. His wife, he said, didn't even know how to fry an egg. So they set out to learn. His wife spent day after day with a sister-in-law from Isaan, learning to make dishes like *laap*, *tom saep*, and *som tam*. She focused on learning to make everything but the chicken. That was Mr. Lit's job.

His friend from the slaughterhouse supplied rotisseries free of charge. He also told Mr. Lit that he had a client who owed him money and to pay off his debt, the client had agreed to give Mr. Lit a recipe for *kai yaang*. A really good recipe, presumably, because the debt was large. Mr. Lit insists that the recipe he eventually received was bogus. Not only that, over the next few years, the flim-flammer and his cousin both opened *kai yaang* restaurants nearby to compete with Mr. Lit. (That Mr. Lit has helped me so much despite this experience makes me even more grateful and in awe of his generosity.)

Mr. Lit, however, kept his head down. He pored over cookbooks. He experimented, constantly tweaking the brine and the stuffing. He dedicated himself to doing one thing well. After two years of obsessive fine-tuning, he was satisfied. The chicken hasn't changed since, he claims, and having eaten it again and again since the mid '90s, I'm inclined to believe him.

As Mr. Lit's business gradually caught on—first, the restaurant went through twenty chickens a day, then fifty, then seventy; now it does about one hundred—his two competitors closed shop. One day not so long ago, his two rivals came to SP Chicken to eat. The guy who originally passed the bum recipe even asked Mr. Lit if he'd share his formula for his chicken, either because the guy had forgotten what he'd done or because he had a lot of nerve. Mr. Lit told him, "I use the recipe you gave me, don't you remember?"

The pleasure of his underdog victory aside, his main source of satisfaction comes from what his business has provided for his family. He still doesn't have much money. Yet when he officially retired from the restaurant, he was able to transfer a debt-free business to his daughter. He didn't pass on mere property but rather a way for her to support her family. Oh, and he finally bought the car, a sedan, he once dreamed of owning. "Matter of fact, I have two automobiles," he told me. "Which might be one too many, because you can only drive one at a time."

Andy,

It's a great pleasure to have met you and your team.

I think this Thai-food project of yours is praiseworthy in that it will not only show the reader how to best prepare their Thai food at home, but will also explain the philosophy behind the various processes in a comprehensive way.

Having known you for nearly a decade, I can only say there are very few connoisseurs of Thai dishes; or even Thai chefs anywhere, who have an understanding of provincial Thai cuisine comparable to you.

For example, I was pleasantly surprised by your detailed explanation of the difference – both in the methods and the number of ingredients used – in preparing the "laab-muang" dishes between the people in the province of Nan and those who live in Chiang Mai.

Furthermore, we both share a common belief that the "old" way is the best way: that a chili paste from a mortar is much tastier than that from a grinder; and that meat grilled with charcoal smells far better than done any other way.

By making it a rule to travel to Thailand at least once a year in order to acquire deeper knowledge of the country's food and culture – you have thus become a Thai at heart.

In the name of all Thais, I wish to thank you for playing a part in upholding our cultural values.

Best wishes.

Chavalit Vannavichit

Chiang Mai, Thailand

August 25, 2012

Muu Sateh

PORK SATAY

THE PLAN

- Up to 1 week in advance: Make the peanut sauce
- Up to 1 day in advance: Make the cucumber relish and skewer the pork
- 1 hour before: Marinate the pork

SPECIAL EQUIPMENT

- 36 wood skewers (8 inches or so each), soaked in tepid water for 30 minutes
- A Thai granite mortar and pestle
- A charcoal grill (highly recommended), grates oiled

From its stranglehold on Thai menus in the US, you might assume that *sateh* occupies a place of eminence in Thailand. Sure, there are vendors who are renowned for their renditions, but really *sateh* is just a street snack, one among hundreds. Still, whoever was responsible for raising its profile among Americans is a genius. We honkies love this stuff. Tender meat soaked in a sweet coconut marinade—it's a no-brainer.

That's why I put it on Pok Pok's menu early on. Yet now, if I had my druthers, I'd take it off. It's not just that the slicing and skewering is time-consuming (not so much for the home cook, who doesn't have to produce several hundred per night). It's the reality that if the words "peanut sauce" appear on the menu, you get people who want to order peanut sauce by the liter to dump on rice. If I sound grumpy, it's because I'm tired of seeing people disrespect what I consider to be one of the greatest cuisines on earth. Everyone likes hollandaise sauce, too, but you don't get people requesting it and dumping it on top of every dish you order at a good French bistro.

But what are you going to do? Dishes like *sateh*, Kai Yaang (page 135), and Som Tam (page 35) get people in the door—don't get me wrong, they're delicious too—and my hope is that along with these sure things, a slightly more challenging plate of Laap Meuang (page 106) or Jin Hoom (page 154) finds its way into the mix.

Despite its near-omnipresence on Thai menus in the US, *sateh* (or "satay," in the common English spelling) is still a bit of a mystery. Its origins are, like so many dishes, lost to time, though David Thompson, a dogged researcher, has attempted to trace its spread through Southeast Asia, identifying Middle Eastern immigrants, primarily Muslims, as its likely source. To further complicate matters, in Thailand it almost goes without saying that *sateh* is made from pork (*muu*)—a no-no for Muslims and probably a surprise to anyone who's eaten *sateh* only in the States, where chicken breast rules the roost.

You'll find *sateh* on the streets where, even in Thailand-in-April levels of heat, vendors tend to vast rows of skewers grilling over a trough of glowing coals. I like to watch them turning the skewers with their fingers and sometimes using scissors to trim off blackened bits—a strange sight to any lover of char. The strips of meat on these skewers, by the way, tend to be twice as narrow and twice as short as those at Pok Pok. Making them as small as they are in Thailand is a major pain and would essentially double their labor cost. You'll see *sateh*, too, at restaurants that specialize in Khao Soi (page 214) or *khao man kai*, the Hainanese-Thai masterpiece of boiled chicken and rice. Typically, on the table alongside the skewers, you'll find the familiar cucumber relish and peanut sauce, plus the perhaps-not-so-familiar pieces of grilled white bread.

At Pok Pok, I figured that if we were going to do *muu sateh*, troublesome as it might be, we're going to do it well. Our version has been gradually changing since the beginning. All the recipes at Pok Pok begin with some skeletal grasp of a dish, which evolves as my understanding does. After one particularly intense *sateh*-sampling spree, from Bangkok to Chiang Mai to Lampang, I decided the version I'd been thrilled with for years was actually lacking something. I upped the sweetness and the galangal, I scaled back on coriander, I

{continued}

{Pork satay, continued}

tweaked and tweaked until I was incrementally happier. I'd guess that, in total, the marinade took two years of refining to achieve, the peanut sauce three. All that effort and I'm not sure anyone notices but me. And I still hear the same grumbles about how it's not spicy enough. Guess what? It's not supposed to be.

Flavor Profile SLIGHTLY SWEET AND UMAMI-RICH

Try It With Khao Soi Kai (Northern Thai curry noodle soup), page 214.

MAKES ABOUT 36 SKEWERS (SERVES 6 AS SNACK OR 6 TO 10 AS PART OF A MEAL)

MEAT

1 (6-ounce) piece pork back fat (highly recommended but optional)

2 pounds boneless pork loin, cut into strips that are approximately 3 inches long, 1 inch wide, and 1/4 inch thick

MARINADE

1 1/2 teaspoons coriander seeds

Very small pinch cumin seeds

1 teaspoon kosher salt, plus extra for seasoning the skewers

14 grams thinly sliced lemongrass (tender parts only), from about 2 large stalks

1 (14-gram) piece peeled fresh or frozen (not defrosted) galangal, thinly sliced against grain

1 (14-gram) piece peeled fresh or frozen (not defrosted) yellow turmeric root, thinly sliced against grain

2 tablespoons granulated sugar

6 tablespoons sweetened condensed milk, preferably Black & White or Longevity brand

1/2 teaspoon ground white pepper

1 cup unsweetened coconut milk (preferably boxed)

TO SERVE ALONGSIDE

About 1 1/2 cups Naam Jim Sateh (Peanut sauce), page 281

About 1 1/2 cups Ajaat (Cucumber relish), page 283

About 6 thick slices Pullman or other thick-cut white bread, lightly grilled or toasted, then quartered

MAKE THE SKEWERS

Put the fat in a small pot, add just enough water to cover, and set the pot over high heat. Bring the water to a rolling simmer, decrease the heat to maintain it, and cook until the opaque white fat has turned slightly translucent, about 5 minutes. Drain the fat, discarding the water, and cut it into approximately 3/4-inch squares that are about 1/4 inch thick.

Skewer one fat cube per skewer (discard any extras), pushing the cubes down to about 4 inches from the tip. Weave one skewer through the center of each strip of pork, exiting and entering several times, so the strip is fixed firmly to it and ends just below the tip of the skewer.

MAKE THE MARINADE

Combine the coriander and cumin in a small pan, set the pan over medium-low heat, and cook, stirring and tossing often, until the spices are very fragrant and the coriander seeds turn a shade or two darker, about 8 minutes. Let the spices cool slightly and pound them in a granite mortar (or grind them in a spice grinder) to

a coarse powder. Combine the spice powder, condensed milk, lemongrass, galangal, turmeric, sugar, salt, pepper, and all but a few tablespoons of the coconut milk in a blender. Blend until smooth, then pour the marinade into a container, preferably a deep, narrow one. Swish the remaining coconut milk in the blender and pour it into the container.

MARINATE THE PORK

Add the skewers to the container with the marinade so that the meat (not necessarily the fat) is submerged in the marinade. Let it sit for at least 30 minutes or up to 1 hour while you prepare the grill.

COOK THE PORK

Prepare a grill, preferably charcoal, to cook over medium-high to high heat (see page 124). Or preheat a lightly oiled, large flat griddle over medium-high heat. Remove the skewers from the marinade, letting any excess drip back into the container. Season both sides of the pork with salt and cook in batches, if necessary, turning the skewers over once and moving them around to contain flare-ups, until the pork is just cooked through and the outsides are as charred as you like them, 3 to 6 minutes total.

Serve them right away (or cover loosely with foil for up to 15 minutes after grilling) alongside the peanut sauce, cucumber relish, and bread.

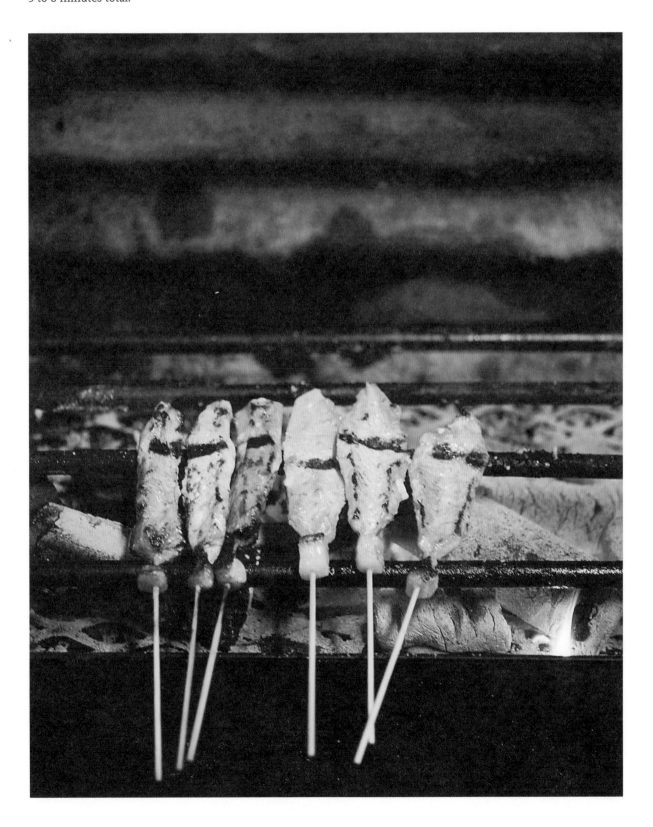

khong yaang

Khao Phot Ping

GRILLED CORN WITH SALTY COCONUT CREAM

SPECIAL EQUIPMENT

- **A charcoal grill (highly recommended), grates oiled**

When I decide to try to recreate a Thai dish in the States, I'm presented with a familiar problem. The ingredients here aren't quite as flavorful, pungent, or spicy, and I need to figure out a way to compensate. Then there are those rare occasions when the opposite is true. To my tastes, the corn in Thailand is, to be charitable, not awesome. But as soon as I tried this preparation from a vendor on the grounds of a Chiang Mai temple, I couldn't wait to try it back home. The combination of rich, salty coconut cream infused with pandan leaf and America's stunning sweet corn is so good it gives the mayo- and cheese-covered Mexican stuff a run for its money.

Flavor Profile SWEET, RICH, SALTY, SLIGHTLY SMOKY

Try It With Anything grilled, like Kai Yaang (Whole roasted young chicken), page 135, or Sii Khrong Muu Yaang (Thai-style pork ribs), page 128.

SERVES 6 TO 12 AS PART OF A MEAL OR AS A SNACK

6 large ears of corn, husked

COCONUT CREAM

1 cup unsweetened coconut cream (preferably boxed)

1 tablespoon granulated sugar

1 teaspoon kosher salt

1 fresh or frozen pandan leaf (optional), tied into a knot

TO SERVE ALONGSIDE

6 lime wedges (preferably from Key limes)

COOK THE CORN

Bring a large pot of water to a boil, add the corn, and cook until it's tender and no longer raw, about 8 minutes. Drain well. (You can boil the corn up to several hours before you plan to finish cooking it on the grill or even a few days in advance; just make sure to shock the corn in ice water as soon as the ears leave the boiling water.)

MAKE THE COCONUT CREAM

Combine the coconut cream, sugar, salt, and pandan leaf in a small pot. It's fine if the pandan leaf isn't completely submerged. Set the pot over high heat, bring the mixture to a simmer (don't let it boil), then decrease the heat to low. Cover and cook until the cream has thickened slightly and is infused with pandan flavor, about 10 minutes. Remove and discard the pandan leaf.

GRILL THE CORN

Prepare a grill, preferably charcoal, to cook over medium heat (see page 124). Or preheat a lightly oiled grill pan over medium heat on the stovetop.

Pour the cream mixture onto a large plate or platter. One or two at a time, add the corn, and rotate the ears to lightly coat them in the mixture. Grill the corn until it's lightly charred in spots, occasionally turning the ears and brushing the corn with the cream mixture (or transferring the corn to the plate with the cream mixture and rotating it again), 5 to 10 minutes.

Serve the corn with a drizzle of the remaining cream mixture and lime wedges for squeezing.

KAENG, TOM, & CO.
Curries and soups

This chapter contains a bunch of dishes that could be considered curries or soups. Within the world of Thai food, the distinction between the two is a fine one and, to an outsider like me, can occasionally seem arbitrary. As I understand it, a souplike dish becomes *kaeng* if it involves a paste of chiles and aromatics that is either dissolved in broth or fried, then diluted with liquids such as broth or coconut milk. Then, of course, my understanding is exploded by endless exceptions: Kaeng Jeut (page 149) often has no paste but is called *kaeng*; Yam Jin Kai (page 158) is made by dissolving paste in liquid but is nonetheless considered *tom* (a word essentially meaning "boiled" or "soup"). All this is further complicated by dialect and colloquialism: Jin Hoom (page 154) could very well be considered *kaeng*, yet the Northern word *hoom*, essentially meaning "to cook slowly," steps in.

The concept of curry deserves elaboration, because it looms so large in the American imagination. You'd be forgiven for thinking that Thai curries are all sweet, rich, and made with coconut milk. These soupy, pastel-colored dishes, on offer at every restaurant in America that deals in spring rolls and chicken in basil sauce, have become the face of Thai curries. When I first went to Thailand, I expected to eat their "authentic" equivalents, to get to know the real thing. But they were nowhere to be found at the restaurants my friends took me to. And we had plenty of curries. In Chiang Mai, I had a ruddy, brothy one with chunks of steamed blood spooned over noodles. In the South, I had fiercely spicy curry tinted yellow from turmeric and flavored with fish innards. In Bangkok, I saw trays and trays of curries—thick as gravy, thin as broth, and every texture in between— packed with all manner of vegetables. And I tasted so many distinguished by much more than mere color. Occasionally, I'd come across the familiar red and green coconut-rich versions, but they weren't nearly as common as their ubiquity back home would suggest.

The English word "curry," by the way, has no relation to the Thai word *kaeng*. Rather, it comes from the Tamil word *kàrìi*, meaning "sauce for rice." The Thai language employs the word *karii* to refer to *kaeng* with strong South Asian influence (*kaeng karii*, for example, a relatively mild yellow-tinted curry whose paste mostly contains dried spices associated with Indian cuisine) or dishes that contain curry powder (itself a British invention meant to approximate the spice mixtures common to Indian curries), such as Puu Phat Phong Karii (page 101).

Between *kaeng* and *tom* and the rest, the name game would be enough to drive you insane if the whole lot didn't taste so good.

Kaeng Jeut Wun Sen

"BLAND" SOUP WITH GLASS NOODLES

"This isn't spicy enough." I hear it all the time from people who think that all Thai food is a daredevil's endeavor, that each dish is a minefield of chiles waiting to blow your top off. The notion that everything should be fiery is misguided.

I think I understand the root of the spicier-is-better presumption. At first, Thai food came to us Americans defanged by restaurant owners forced to cook with a foreign pantry and appeal to foreign palates. Entire culinary subcategories have started this way—"chifa" in Peru, a Chinese-Peruvian hybrid, and Indo-Chinese fare (that is, Chinese food cooked for Indian customers), just to name a few. Thai cooks also employed this strategy, almost essential for anyone operating within another country's culinary parameters—and a successful one at that, given the packed dining rooms of rainbow curry-slingers around the US.

Yet gradually some diners came to want food that more closely resembled the stuff you'd find in Thailand. More than any other aspect of the cuisine, more than the funk of fermented fish and the pungency of herbs, the mouth-searing heat of chiles became an indication of authenticity, a mark of a dish's fidelity to the real thing. In some cases, that's true. If a Thai friend orders you Isaan-style *som tam*, you might find yourself gasping and searching frantically for a beer, especially if he asks for it *phet phet der*, which my friend Chanchao, a Dutch guy living in Chiang Mai whose online guides to food served me well back in the day, loosely translates as "prepare to die." Yet just as not every dish contains coconut milk, neither does every one aim to set your mouth on fire. There's a whole world of food, particularly in the North, that's barely to moderately spicy but still packed with vibrant flavor.

While any desire to eat something new is a good thing, the heat-seeker mentality has given rise to the mistaken impression that every dish without heat is deficient. Correcting this misconception is one of two reasons I want to introduce you to *kaeng jeut* or, roughly translated, "bland soup." The proper Thai meal comprises multiple dishes, each chosen to balance the others. A dinner that consists only of a giant bowl of red curry, for instance, as we often have here in the US, would be a meal out of whack. Thais call this soup "bland" not as an insult but to contrast its mild flavor with that of spicy, rich curries; fiery, tart salads; grilled meat or fish; and anything else it shares the table with. It's just one part of a harmonious meal. *Kaeng jeut* doesn't get nearly the props that coconut curries or spicy-tart salads do. But it is just as legit in the context of a Thai meal.

Which brings me to the second reason I want to introduce you to *kaeng jeut*: I love it. When it's on the table, I could sit there and eat it all meal long. I'm hooked on the mild broth, typically made from pork or chicken bones, that's complex thanks to aromatics like garlic, lemongrass, and cilantro. It's one of those dishes whose glory doesn't necessarily strike you at first slurp or even second. But once it does, you can't get enough. Just as there isn't just one kind of curry, there isn't just one type of *kaeng jeut*. One bowl might bring, for example, slick glass noodles, snappy wood ear mushrooms, and Chinese

{continued}

{"Bland" soup with glass noodles, continued}

spinach, while another might sport tofu, ground pork, and egg drizzled into the hot broth to make a sort of Thai equivalent of egg drop soup. This version contains balls of so-called bouncy pork balls (page 269), flavor-packed and dense, and a drizzle of garlic oil that provides another layer of aroma.

Flavor Profile UMAMI-RICH, AROMATIC, SLIGHTLY SALTY, SLIGHTLY PEPPERY

Try It With Yam Khai Dao (Fried egg salad), page 51, Plaa Neung Si Ew (Steamed whole fish with soy sauce, ginger, and vegetables), page 79, and Khao Hom Mali (Jasmine rice), page 31.

MAKES 1 LARGE BOWL (SERVES 2 TO 6 AS PART OF A MEAL); THE RECIPE IS EASILY DOUBLED

1 large or several small dried wood ear mushrooms (also called tree ear or black fungus) or small dried shiitake mushrooms

Scant 1 ounce dried glass noodles (also called bean thread or cellophane noodles)

1 tablespoon Thai thin soy sauce

1 tablespoon shredded salted radish, soaked in water for 10 minutes, then drained

Pinch ground white pepper

8 Muu Deng (Bouncy pork balls), page 269, at room temperature

1½ cups Sup Kraduuk Muu (Pork Stock), page 268

1 teaspoon Naam Man Krathiem (Fried-garlic oil), page 272

1 tablespoon Krathiem Jiaw (Fried garlic), page 272

A large pinch (about 1 tablespoon) coarsely chopped Chinese celery (thin stems and leaves)

A large pinch (about 1 tablespoon) thinly sliced green onions

A large pinch (about 1 tablespoon) coarsely chopped cilantro (thin stems and leaves)

Soak the mushrooms in enough boiling water to cover them by a few inches until they're fully soft, about 5 minutes for wood ear mushrooms and closer to 15 minutes for shiitakes. Drain well and slice enough of the mushroom into thin strips to give you 1 generous tablespoon.

Soak the noodles in lukewarm water until they're very pliable, about 10 minutes, then drain them well and snip them into approximately 3-inch lengths.

Combine the generous tablespoon of the sliced mushroom and the soaked noodles in a serving bowl along with the soy sauce, salted radish, pepper, and pork balls. Heat the stock in a small pot over medium-high heat until it just begins to boil, then immediately pour it into the bowl. The heat from the stock will finish cooking the noodles and warm up everything else.

Drizzle on the garlic oil, sprinkle on the fried garlic, Chinese celery, green onions, and cilantro, and season with more soy sauce if you want. Stir well before you eat it.

Jaw Phak Kat

NORTHERN THAI MUSTARD GREEN SOUP WITH TAMARIND AND PORK RIBS

THE PLAN

- Up to 1 week in advance: Make the paste and the tamarind water

- Up to 3 days or so in advance: Make the dish

- Up to 2 days in advance: Fry the shallots and the dried chiles

SPECIAL EQUIPMENT

- A Thai granite mortar and pestle

A rough Northern Thai translation of *jaw phak kat* is "mustard green soup," which makes it sound rather innocuous. But it's one of my favorites—an earthy, porky broth with a little tartness from tamarind, a perfect accompaniment to spicier fare like *laap*. This is Northern Thai comfort food—something grandma might make.

My guess is that the dish is an old one; it requires just a pot and a mortar. The fried-shallot garnish is likely a more modern addition. The grandma in question might begin with some water. In go pork ribs and a simple paste. As the ribs simmer—typically, vigorously because this is not a high-end French kitchen and grandma does not care if the broth is cloudy—they team up with the paste and some tamarind to flavor the soup. The pork, however, isn't the main event. As the Thai name for the soup suggests, the *phak kat* (a type of green vegetable we call *yu choy*) headlines the soup. As in a bowl of collard greens in the American South, the pork is implied. In Thailand, cooks season with toasted-then-pounded disks of fermented-then-dried soybean called *thua nao kap*. Here, we have to settle for Thai yellow bean sauce.

Flavor Profile EARTHY, VEGETAL, SOUR, SALTY

Try It With Phat Fak Thawng (Northern Thai-style stir-fried squash), page 94, or Laap Meuang (Northern Thai minced pork salad), page 106. Needs Khao Niaw (Sticky rice), page 33.

{continued}

{Northern Thai mustard green soup with tamarind and pork ribs, continued}

SERVES 6 TO 8 AS PART OF A MEAL

PASTE

2 grams dried Thai chiles (about 6)

1 teaspoon plus a pinch kosher salt

21 grams peeled garlic cloves, halved lengthwise

1 ounce peeled Asian shallots, thinly sliced against the grain

2 tablespoons Kapi Kung (Homemade shrimp paste), page 274

SOUP

2 pounds pork spareribs, cut lengthwise across the bone into 2-inch-wide racks by your butcher, then cut into individual ribs (most Asian butchers sell them already cut), rinsed well

8 cups water

Kosher salt

3/4 cup Naam Makham (Tamarind water), page 275

1 tablespoon Thai yellow bean sauce

1 pound yu choy (stems and leaves), bottoms trimmed, cut into 2-inch lengths

7 ounces peeled yellow onion, cut into approximately 1/2-inch-thick wedges

1 tablespoon Thai fish sauce

5 to 10 dried Thai chiles, fried (page 12)

2 tablespoons Hom Daeng Jiaw (Fried shallots), page 273

MAKE THE PASTE

Pound the chiles with a pinch of the salt in a granite mortar until you have a fairly fine powder (most of the seeds will still be visible), about 1 to 2 minutes. Add the garlic and pound to a fairly smooth paste, about 1 to 2 minutes, then add the shallots and do the same. Add the shrimp paste and pound just until it's incorporated, about 30 seconds. You'll have about a heaping 1/4 cup of paste. You can use it right away, or store the paste in an airtight container in the fridge for up to 1 week or in the freezer for up to 6 months.

MAKE THE SOUP

Put the ribs in a medium pot, and pour in the 8 cups of water. They should be submerged. Bring the water to a simmer over high heat, then immediately decrease the heat to maintain a gentle simmer, skimming off any gunk that rises to the surface. Add all of the paste, stir, then have a taste (don't worry, by the time all that water simmers, the ribs will no longer be raw). Stir in enough salt, about 1 teaspoon, to make it taste good and salty (the ribs will absorb some of this salt, and the tamarind you add later will help balance it).

Cover and cook at a steady simmer until the rib meat is tender but not so tender it's falling off bone, about 35 minutes. Stir in the tamarind water and yellow bean sauce, increase the heat to high, and bring the liquid to a full boil.

Add the yu choy and onions but don't stir. Cover the pot and wait until the yu choy wilts, about 5 minutes. Now uncover, give the pot a stir, and decrease the heat again to maintain a gentle simmer. Cook, uncovered, until the yu choy stems are very tender but not mushy, 10 to 15 minutes. The greens will be a dull green. The onions will fall apart. Stir in the fish sauce and turn off the heat.

Cooled and covered, it keeps in the fridge for up to 3 days and tastes even better after a day. Reheat gently in a covered pot.

Let it cool to warm, then taste and season with more fish sauce, if necessary. Right before you serve it, break the fried dried chiles in half (or leave them whole, as in the photo at right) and add them and the fried shallots. Bring the pot to the table along with small bowls and a ladle.

Jin Hoom Neua

{Pictured on page 156}

NORTHERN THAI STEWED BEEF SOUP

If you didn't know where to look, you wouldn't find restaurants like Krua Phech Doi Ngam. Even in Chiang Mai, the unofficial capital of Northern Thailand, it's getting harder to find places that do justice to the region's cuisine. It was at this restaurant that I first tasted *jin hoom*.

My Thai tutor took me there ten years or so ago. It was actually my second tutor. I had jettisoned the first for insisting on teaching me proper Thai, which completely failed me with the market sellers and street cooks that I wanted to talk to most. My second tutor understood my purpose, but was easily distracted by any talk of food, which is one reason why my knowledge of food words surpasses the rest of my vocabulary.

The menu at Krua Phech Doi Ngam is a what's-what of Northern Thai food. It is the place where I experienced many firsts. My first sip of water infused with pandan leaf. My first bite of Yam Samun Phrai (page 65), my first taste of curry paste–slathered fish steamed in bamboo. When I tried *jin hoom*, I did the eating equivalent of a double take: it's one of those dishes that you try and immediately meet your companion's eye, just to be sure you're not crazy and what you're tasting really is that good.

It would be many years before *jin hoom* (essentially, "slowly cooked meat" in the Northern Thai dialect) made it onto the menu at Pok Pok, which at this point hadn't even crossed my mind. But even then, I wondered why such a delicious thing never showed up in the US. It wasn't challenging, like some other Northern dishes—say, *kaeng khae kop*, frog hacked into large, bony chunks in a broth seasoned with handfuls of intense jungle herbs. To my Western palate, *jin hoom* was completely approachable, entirely comprehensible, but still different from anything I'd ever eaten, let alone what I expected from Thai food.

I had to eat it many times to figure it out. I had to consult with many Thai friends. I never found a particularly helpful recipe to work from. I had to try to make it and fail and try again. The dish, I now realize, is Northern Thai to the core. First, there's its cooking method. *Jin hoom* is sort of a stew made from a chile paste heavy on the turmeric and galangal. It's not made by frying the paste in fat and then diluting the mixture with liquid like coconut milk or stock. Instead, as is common in the North, the paste is simply dissolved in water; then the flavorful liquid, along with some lemongrass and galangal tossed in to steep, is used to slowly simmer beef. No wok necessary, just a mortar and a pot. In the old days, that pot would be made of clay and heated over a charcoal fire.

Then there's the turmeric (common in Southern and Northern food) and the last-minute addition of the region's trinity of fresh herbs (sawtooth, green onion, and cilantro). Taken together, these techniques and ingredients produce a flavor that strikes me as resolutely Northern Thai.

The beef is another giveaway. I've noticed that the Northern Thai people eat way more meat from cows, water buffalo, and oxen than Central Thais. They've long been using these animals to work the fields, and virtually anything with hooves eventually ends up in the pot. The meat you find in a pot of *jin hoom* often has a texture that resembles rubber bands. It's really tough, but really flavorful, too. When you cook the dish in the US, the beef will be more tender, though remember not to cook it until it falls apart. As Thai cooks have convinced me, chewiness is to be embraced, not feared.

Flavor Profile INTENSELY HERBACEOUS AND UMAMI-RICH, SPICY, SALTY

Try It With Yam Samun Phrai (Northern Thai-style herbal salad), page 65, or Het Paa Naam Tok (Isaan-style forest mushroom salad), page 70, and Khao Niaw (Sticky rice), page 33.

SERVES 4 TO 8 AS PART OF A MEAL

PASTE

1 ounce thinly sliced lemongrass (tender parts only), from about 4 large stalks

1 teaspoon kosher salt

1 (1¹/₂-ounce) piece peeled fresh or frozen (not defrosted) galangal, cut into thin slices against the grain

1 (1-ounce) piece peeled fresh or frozen (not defrosted) yellow turmeric root, cut into thin slices against the grain

14 grams stemmed dried Mexican puya chiles (about 8), soaked in hot tap water until fully soft, about 15 minutes

1¹/₂ ounces peeled garlic cloves, halved lengthwise

4¹/₂ ounces peeled Asian shallots, thinly sliced against the grain

1¹/₂ tablespoons Kapi Kung (Homemade shrimp paste), page 274

SOUP

6 tablespoons Thai thin soy sauce

3 tablespoons Phrik Phon Khua (Toasted-chile powder), page 270

8 cups water

2 pounds boneless beef shank or chuck, silver skin removed, cut against the grain into strips that are about 2 inches long, 1 inch wide, and ¹/₂ inch thick

6¹/₂ ounces peeled yellow onion, cut into approximately ¹/₂-inch-thick wedges

Kosher salt

12 fresh or frozen kaffir lime leaves

1¹/₂ teaspoons finely ground black pepper

¹/₄ cup coarsely chopped cilantro (thin stems and leaves), lightly packed

¹/₄ cup thinly sliced sawtooth herb, lightly packed

¹/₄ cup thinly sliced green onions, lightly packed

MAKE THE PASTE

Combine the lemongrass and salt in a granite mortar and pound until you have a fairly smooth, slightly fibrous paste, about 2 minutes. Add the galangal and pound, occasionally stopping to scrape down the sides of the mortar, until you have a fairly smooth paste, about 2 minutes. Do the same with the turmeric. Drain the chiles well, wrap them in paper towels, and gently squeeze them dry. Add them to the mortar and pound them, then the garlic, and then the shallots, fully pounding each ingredient before moving on to the next. Finally, pound in the shrimp paste until it's fully incorporated, about 1 minute.

You'll have about 1 cup of paste. You can use it right away, or store the paste in an airtight container in the fridge for up to 1 week or in the freezer for up to 6 months.

COOK THE SOUP

Combine all of the paste, soy sauce, and chile powder in a medium pot along with the 8 cups of water and stir well. (Add a tablespoon or two of the water to the mortar and stir to get as much of the paste as you can into the pot.)

Set the pot over high heat and bring the liquid to a strong simmer. Add the beef, let the liquid return to a full simmer, then cover the pot and immediately reduce the heat to maintain a gentle but steady simmer. Cook for 1 hour, then stir in the onions, and keep cooking, covered, until the beef is tender but not falling apart and the broth has thickened slightly, about 1 to 1¹/₂ hours more.

Season to taste with salt. Tear the lime leaves and add them to the pot along with the black pepper. Turn off the heat and let the dish cool slightly. Right before you serve it, sprinkle on the herbs and green onions.

Yam Jin Kai

{Pictured on page 157}

NORTHERN THAI CHICKEN SOUP

As a lowly cook in a *Kitchen Confidential*–esque past, I worked for several French-trained chefs who had me fastidiously straining stocks and making egg-white rafts to clarify consommé. Today I like a clear-as-glass broth as much as the next guy. But if I had the choice, I'd almost always pick *yam jin kai* instead.

I've had *yam jin kai*, which is very Northern Thai and very country at that, at roadside restaurants that are little more than concrete patches with lids. I've eaten it from pots plunked on tables at the houses of friends' grandmothers. I've ladled it from a vat in the modest village of Ban Pa Du, after waiting in line to see the local, pipe-smoking animist medium, who had been possessed by a spirit and was giving out blessings during Songkran, the Thai New Year. This soup is the opposite of refined. And slight cloudiness is the least of it. To get at the salty, spicy liquid, your spoon must dodge planks of galangal, chunks of lemongrass, and leaves of kaffir lime. In some versions, there are more inedible aromatics than there is chicken.

But the flavor more than makes up for the bit of work it takes to eat it. Besides those chunky aromatics, the soup gets its intensity from a paste made from chiles, dried spices, and two kinds of seafood subjected to controlled rot. The meatiness comes from flavorful yard birds, the scrawny, essentially wild chickens that wander and peck around villages. Although some staunchly traditional Northern Thai cooks would wince if they saw me do this, I like to add a few dashes of fish sauce to bump up the umami.

THE PLAN

- Up to 1 week in advance: Make the paste
- Up to 5 days in advance: Make the broth
- Up to 2 days in advance: Make the fried garlic

SPECIAL EQUIPMENT

- A Thai granite mortar and pestle

Flavor Profile HERBACEOUS, UMAMI-RICH, SALTY, MODERATELY SPICY, SLIGHTLY BITTER

Try It With Phat Fak Thawng (Northern Thai-style stir-fried squash), page 94, or Laap Meuang (Northern Thai minced pork salad), page 106. Needs Khao Niaw (Sticky rice), page 33.

PASTE

2 teaspoons coriander seeds

2 dried Indonesian long peppers (called pippali in Indian and Malay markets, dippli in Thai markets, and tiêu lốp in Vietnamese markets)

2 teaspoons makhwen (see NOTE, page 110), black Sichuan peppercorn, or 1 more Indonesian long pepper

4 pickled gouramy fish fillets

2 grams dried Thai chiles (about 6)

1 teaspoon kosher salt

2 teaspoons Kapi Kung (Homemade shrimp paste), page 274

BROTH

1 (2- to 3-pound) fresh or defrosted frozen lean stewing chicken (preferably head and feet on), gutted, offal reserved if you're into it

2 stalks lemongrass, outer layer removed, halved crosswise, and lightly smashed with a pestle, pan, or flat part of a knife blade

1 (2-ounce) piece unpeeled fresh or frozen (not defrosted) galangal, coarsely sliced

1 small bunch green onions, roots trimmed, tied into a bundle

14 grams cilantro roots, lightly smashed with a pestle, pan, or flat part of a knife blade, or 1 ounce coarsely chopped cilantro stems

2 tablespoons Kapi Kung (Homemade shrimp paste), page 274

SOUP

2 stalks lemongrass, outer layer removed

1 (1-ounce) piece unpeeled fresh or frozen (not defrosted) galangal, thinly sliced against the grain

2¹/₂ ounces peeled small Asian shallots or red pearl onions, halved lengthwise if larger (about ²/₃ cup)

14 grams peeled garlic (about 4 medium cloves), halved lengthwise then coarsely chopped

10 fresh or frozen kaffir lime leaves

Kosher salt to taste

2 tablespoons thinly sliced green onions, lightly packed

2 tablespoons thinly sliced sawtooth herb, lightly packed

2 tablespoons coarsely chopped cilantro (thin stems and leaves), lightly packed

2 tablespoons coarsely chopped dill fronds, lightly packed

2 tablespoons coarsely chopped Vietnamese mint, lightly packed

1 tablespoon Krathiem Jiaw (Fried garlic), page 272

SERVES 6 TO 8 AS PART OF A MEAL

MAKE THE PASTE

Combine the coriander seeds, long peppers, and makhwen in a small pan and set the pan over low heat. Cook, stirring and tossing often, until the spices are very fragrant and the coriander seeds turn a shade or two darker, about 8 minutes. Transfer the spices to a bowl.

Put the gouramy fillets on a double layer of foil or banana leaf and fold to make a package. Wipe the small pan that you used for the spices clean, heat it over medium heat (or better yet, grill over a low charcoal fire), add the foil package, and cook, turning it over occasionally, until you can smell the floral funk of the gouramy, about 15 minutes.

Open the gouramy package, discard any large bones and fins (don't try to remove the small bones), and transfer the gouramy to a granite mortar. Firmly pound it to a fine paste and until the bones have fully broken down, about 45 seconds. Scoop the paste into a bowl.

Combine the dried chiles and salt in the mortar and pound firmly, scraping the mortar and stirring the mixture once or twice, until you have a fairly fine powder, about 3 minutes. Add the spice mixture and pound to a coarse powder, about 1 minute. Pound in the shrimp paste and 2 teaspoons of the gouramy (reserving the rest for another purpose) just until they're fully incorporated and you have a coarse, dryish paste with visible flecks of spices, about 30 seconds.

You'll have about 3 tablespoons of the paste. You can use it right away, or store the paste in an airtight container in the fridge for up to 1 week or in the freezer for up to 6 months.

MAKE THE BROTH

Combine the chicken, offal, lemongrass, galangal, green onions, cilantro roots, and shrimp paste in a medium pot and add just enough water to cover the chicken.

Set the pot over high heat and bring the water to a strong simmer. Partially cover the pot, decrease the heat to maintain a steady simmer, and cook until the meat twists off easily from the bone and the legs and wings start to separate from the body, about 1¹/₂ hours.

Turn off the heat and transfer the chicken to a large plate or tray. Once it's cool enough to handle, pull the skin and meat (and, if you're Thai, the cartilage) from the bones into bite-size shreds. Cut the offal into bite-size pieces. Discard the bones.

Pour or strain the cooking liquid into a fresh pot, leaving the solids behind. You'll need 6 cups of broth for this recipe. You can store the broth and chicken together in an airtight container in the fridge for up to 5 days. You can freeze the rest for up to 3 months.

MAKE THE SOUP

Trim off and discard the bottom ¹/₂ inch and top 5 inches from the lemongrass. Lightly smash it with a pestle or pan, then cut it into ¹/₄-inch slices.

In a medium pot, combine all of the paste with the lemongrass, galangal, shallots, garlic, lime leaves, and 6 cups of the reserved broth. Set the pot over high heat, bring the liquid to a vigorous simmer, then decrease the heat to maintain a steady simmer.

Cook for 5 minutes to infuse the flavor of the aromatics into the broth, then add the chicken meat, skin, and offal, increase the heat again, bring it back to a simmer, and turn off the heat. Let the soup cool slightly and season to taste with salt.

Mix the remaining herbs and green onions in a small bowl, stir almost all of the herb mixture into the soup, then pour the soup into a big serving bowl. Sprinkle on the remaining herb mixture and the fried garlic, and serve.

Remember, this is a rustic soup, so you'll have to avoid the lemongrass, galangal, lime leaves, and other aromatics when you eat it, just like Thai people do.

Kaeng Khiaw Waan Luuk Chin Plaa

SPECIAL EQUIPMENT

- **A Thai granite mortar and pestle**

Of all the *kaeng* in this book, this curry will be perhaps the most recognizable to Americans. It's a green curry, made more or less in the Central Thai style, slightly sweet and rich from coconut milk and cream. Don't expect emerald green, however. The curry is named for the color of the fresh chile used to make it. I suspect any versions that do sport a vivid green color have seen food coloring—the proper color is closer to khaki. I strongly recommend that you use boxed coconut cream for this recipe. The fat and liquid in canned coconut cream don't separate as easily, and you need them to in order to properly fry the curry paste.

Flavor Profile RICH, SPICY, AROMATIC, SALTY, SLIGHTLY SWEET

Try It With Phat Phak Ruam Mit (Stir-fried mixed vegetables), page 98, or Yam Khai Dao (Fried-egg salad), page 51, and Khao Hom Mali (Jasmine rice), page 31. Or as a one-plate meal on Khanom Jiin (page 231) along with quartered Khai Tom (Eight-minute eggs), page 270, blanched bean sprouts, and sprigs of Thai basil.

SERVES 6 TO 8 AS PART OF A MEAL

CURRY PASTE

1½ teaspoons coriander seeds

¼ teaspoon cumin seeds

¼ teaspoon yellow mustard seeds

¼ teaspoon freshly ground black pepper

3 grams cilantro roots, thinly sliced

1 teaspoon kosher salt

14 grams thinly sliced lemongrass (tender parts only), from about 2 large stalks

1 (14-gram) piece peeled fresh or frozen (not defrosted) galangal, thinly sliced against the grain

1 teaspoon finely grated zest from fresh or frozen kaffir lime (if you must, you can skip the zest and add 2 extra kaffir lime leaves later on)

1¼ ounces fresh green Thai chiles or fresh green serrano chiles, thinly sliced

1 ounce peeled garlic cloves, halved lengthwise

1½ ounces peeled Asian shallots, thinly sliced against the grain

1 tablespoon Kapi Kung (Homemade shrimp paste), page 274

CURRY

2 cups unsweetened coconut cream (preferably boxed)

2 ounces palm sugar, coarsely chopped

4 cups unsweetened coconut milk (preferably boxed)

36 fresh or defrosted frozen fish balls

6 Thai apple eggplants (green and golf ball–size)

6 or so fresh or frozen kaffir lime leaves

2 leafy Thai basil sprigs

1 tablespoon plus 1 teaspoon Thai fish sauce

6 to 18 fresh green Thai chiles, halved lengthwise

MAKE THE PASTE

Combine the coriander, cumin, and mustard seeds in a small pan and set the pan over medium-low heat. Cook, stirring and tossing often, until the spices are very fragrant and the coriander seeds turn a shade or two darker, about 8 minutes. Let the spices cool slightly and pound them, along them with the pepper, in a granite mortar (or grind them in a spice grinder) to a fine powder. Scoop the powder into a bowl and set aside.

{continued}

Pound the cilantro roots and salt in a granite mortar to a fibrous paste, about 30 seconds. Add the lemongrass and pound to a fibrous paste, about 1 minute. Do the same with the galangal (1 minute), then the lime zest (1 minute), then the chiles (4 minutes), then the garlic (4 minutes), then the shallots (4 minutes), and finally, the shrimp paste (1 minute), fully pounding each ingredient before moving on to the next and stirring occasionally with a spoon. You'll have a smooth, slightly fibrous paste. Finally, pound the spice powder into the paste until it's well incorporated, about 30 seconds.

You'll have about 9 tablespoons of paste. You can use it right away, or store the paste in the fridge for up to 1 week or in the freezer for up to 6 months. You'll need about 6 tablespoons of paste for 6 portions of curry.

COOK THE CURRY

Pour 1/2 cup of the coconut cream into a medium pot or a wok and set it over high heat. Bring the cream to a boil, stirring often, then immediately decrease the heat to maintain a steady simmer. Cook, stirring occasionally, until the cream has reduced by about half and "breaks"—it'll look like curdled milk—anywhere from 3 to 10 minutes, depending on the brand of coconut cream. What you're doing as you simmer is cooking off the water in the cream so you're left with some whiteish solids but primarily the translucent fat, which you'll use to fry the curry paste. Patience is essential here. (If for some reason it doesn't crack after 10 minutes, add a tablespoon of vegetable oil, but know that the curry will be oilier than it should be.)

Decrease the heat to medium-low, add 6 tablespoons of the curry paste, and stir well. Take a careful sniff. You'll smell the raw shallots and garlic. Cook, stirring frequently, until garlic and shallots in the paste no longer smell raw and the paste has turned a shade or two darker, 6 to 8 minutes. Knowing when it's done takes experience, but as long as you're cooking it at a low sizzle, the curry will taste great.

Add the palm sugar and cook, stirring often and breaking up the sugar once it softens, until the sugar has more or less fully melted, about 2 minutes. Add the remaining coconut cream, the coconut milk, and the fish balls. You'll notice that the curry is not even close to emerald green but rather a khaki color. That's what it's supposed to look like. Have a taste and consider adding, gradually, more of the curry paste.

Increase the heat to high, bring the mixture to a simmer (don't let it boil), then decrease the heat to maintain a gentle simmer. Stem and quarter the eggplants, add them to the curry, and cook until they're tender but still crunchy, about 3 minutes.

Twist the lime leaves to bruise and break them slightly and add them to the curry with the Thai basil sprigs, fish sauce, and enough of the chiles to make the curry quite spicy. Stir well and turn off the heat.

Cover the pot and let the curry sit for at least 10 minutes or up to an hour (either way, remove the basil sprigs after 10 minutes). It tastes best served slightly warmer than room temperature. The oil that rises to the surface is a good sign, not a bad one.

Kaeng Som Kung

SOUR CURRY WITH SHRIMP

Kaeng som is a great example of curry that defies the rainbow-curry mold. Instead of sweetness and richness, it has sourness as its headlining flavor. The spicy curry (*kung* refers to the shrimp in this version) has all kinds of variations—it bubbles away in fish-shaped platters containing whole tilapia, it's embellished with an omelet flecked with the herb *cha-om*—but it needn't be any more elaborate than this one.

Flavor Profile SOUR, SPICY, SALTY, SLIGHTLY SWEET

Try It With Phak Buung Fai Daeng (Stir-fried water spinach), page 97, or Plaa Thawt Lat Phrik (Deep-fried whole fish with chile sauce), page 83, and Khao Hom Mali (Jasmine rice), page 31.

SERVES 4 TO 6 AS PART OF A MEAL

CURRY PASTE

6 grams stemmed dried Mexican puya chiles (about 4)

1 gram dried Thai chiles (about 4), optional

1 tablespoon kosher salt

14 grams fresh or frozen (not defrosted) whole krachai (wild ginger), unpeeled, washed especially well, and thinly sliced crosswise

1 ounce peeled garlic cloves, halved lengthwise

1¹/₂ ounces peeled Asian shallots, thinly sliced against the grain

2 teaspoons Thai shrimp paste (called gapi or kapi)

CURRY

8 ounces medium shrimp, shelled and deveined (about 16)

4¹/₂ cups water

¹/₂ cup Naam Makham (Tamarind water), page 275

1 ounce palm sugar, coarsely chopped

2 tablespoons Thai fish sauce

5 ounces pitted unpeeled chayote, or peeled and seeded firm cucumber, cut into bite-size ¹/₄-inch-thick half moons (about 1 cup)

4 ounces peeled daikon radish, peeled and cut into bite-size ¹/₂-inch-thick slices (about 1 cup)

4 ounces long beans or string beans, trimmed and cut into 2-inch lengths (about 2 cups)

4 ounces napa cabbage, outer leaves removed, cut into 1-inch chunks (about 1 cup)

MAKE THE PASTE

Combine the dried chiles in the mortar with the salt and pound firmly, scraping the mortar and stirring the mixture once or twice, until you have a fairly fine powder, about 3 to 5 minutes. Pound in the krachai, occasionally stopping to scrape down the sides of the mortar, until you have a fairly smooth, slightly fibrous paste, about 2 minutes. Do the same with the garlic, then the shallots, and then the shrimp paste, fully incorporating each ingredient before moving on to the next.

You'll have a generous ¹/₃ cup paste. You can use it right away, or store the paste in an airtight container in the fridge for up to 1 week or in the freezer for up to 6 months.

MAKE THE CURRY

Add three of the shrimp to the mortar with the paste and pound the shrimp until they are fully broken down and more or less disappear into the paste. Combine all of the paste with the 4¹/₂ cups of water in a medium pot, stir well, and set the pot over high heat. (Add a tablespoon or two of the water to the mortar and stir to get as much of the paste as you can into the pot.)

{continued}

{Sour curry with shrimp, continued}

Let the liquid come to a vigorous simmer, then decrease the heat to maintain it. After 5 minutes, add the tamarind water and increase the heat to return the mixture to a simmer. Add the palm sugar, fish sauce, and vegetables, and cook at a gentle simmer, stirring occasionally and breaking up the palm sugar as it softens, until the vegetables are tender but still have a little crunch, 10 to 12 minutes.

Turn off the heat, add the remaining shrimp, and stir. Once the shrimp are just cooked through from the heat of the broth, about 2 minutes depending on the size of the shrimp, ladle the curry into a large bowl. Let it cool slightly before serving. If the tamarind solids begin to separate from the broth, that's fine; just give it all a stir.

Kaeng Khanun

{Pictured on page 168}

NORTHERN THAI YOUNG JACKFRUIT CURRY

SPECIAL EQUIPMENT

• A Thai granite mortar and pestle

For many people in Thailand today, meat is a luxury. In the old days, it was even more so. Raising an animal takes time, effort, and a lot of feed. You can't kill a pig every week. Whole villages would chip in for the task, slaughtering a creature only for special occasions, like funerals and holidays. Before refrigeration was common, the meat was quickly grilled, stewed, hung over a charcoal fire, or otherwise preserved.

When my friend Sunny was a boy, he rarely ate meat. Before Sunny's mother went off to her day job, she would trek to the local market before dawn to sell what she grew, and with the money she earned, she'd occasionally bring home a small amount of meat. If his mother made *laap*, a meat-heavy and thus expensive dish, it would only be for an honored guest and they'd often add grilled, chopped eggplant to extend the minced pork.

Consider *kaeng khanun* in this context. Here you have a simple boiled curry, a classic Northern Thai dish that wrings flavor from pork bones. If you hadn't grown up in a world of butcher shops, twenty-four-pack hot dogs, and drive-thru burgers, what a treat it would be to suck those bones clean of flesh and gristle. But floating in the broth, red from dried chiles and aromatic from garlic and shrimp paste, are chunks of young jackfruit. In its immature form, jackfruit has an unmistakably meaty texture, akin to artichoke hearts. If you don't know better, or even if you do, you could easily imagine that these chunks are meat. (There's a reason jackfruit has a following among vegans, who dream up oxymoronic dishes like "jackfruit *carnitas*.") Whenever meat proved too expensive, you could grab a long stick and poke at a jackfruit until it fell to the ground. Money might not grow on trees, but meat can.

Anyone used to Thai food's caricature will be flummoxed by this dish, which has none of the expected sweet-tart flavors. Instead, get ready for a broth that's salty, earthy, and full of vegetal funk from betel leaf and *cha-om*.

Flavor Profile SALTY, EARTHY, HERBACEOUS, MEATY, SLIGHTLY TART

Try It With Yam Samun Phrai (Northern Thai-style herbal salad), page 65, or Yam Makheua Yao (Grilled eggplant salad), page 59. Needs Khao Niaw (Sticky rice), page 33.

CURRY PASTE

2 grams dried Thai chiles
(about 6)

1 teaspoon kosher salt

21 grams peeled garlic
cloves, halved lengthwise

1 ounce peeled Asian
shallots, thinly sliced against
the grain

2 tablespoons Kapi Kung
(Homemade shrimp paste),
page 274

CURRY

1 pound pork spareribs,
cut lengthwise across the
bone into 2-inch-wide racks
by your butcher (most Asian
butchers sell them already
cut), then cut into individual
ribs, rinsed well

1 teaspoon kosher salt

8 cups water

1 pound drained young
("green") jackfruit in brine
(from about two 20-ounce
cans), rinsed well, cut into
irregular 1- by 1/2- by 1/4-inch
chunks (about 4 cups)

2 1/2 ounces peeled small
Asian shallots or red pearl
onions, halved lengthwise
if larger than 1 inch in
diameter (about 2/3 cup)

6 ounces cherry tomatoes
(about 12), halved

2 1/2 ounces fresh cha-om,
thin stems and leaves
only (about 2 cups, lightly
packed), see NOTE

1 ounce fresh betel leaves
(about 1 cup, tightly packed)

NOTE: Look for fresh (not
frozen) cha-om, also called
acacia, at Southeast Asian
(but mostly at specifically
Thai) grocery stores, often in
the refrigerator. The flavor
and smell are funky; one
person's stinky is another's
heavenly. If you're lucky
enough to find it, beware
of the prickers on the thick
stems and use only the
delicate leaves and stems
from the top of the stalks,
picking them into small
sprigs before using for
this dish.

MAKE THE PASTE

Pound the chiles with the salt in a granite mortar until
you have a fairly fine powder (some of the seeds will
still be visible), about 1 to 2 minutes. Pound in the garlic
(about 2 minutes), then the shallots (about 3 minutes),
and then the shrimp paste (about 1 minute), fully incorporating each ingredient before moving on to the next.

You'll have about 5 tablespoons of paste. You can
use it right away, or store the paste in an airtight container the fridge for up to 1 week or in the freezer for
up to 6 months.

MAKE THE CURRY

Combine the ribs, all of the curry paste, salt, and 8 cups
of water in a medium pot. (Add a tablespoon or two of
the water to the mortar and stir to get as much of the
paste as you can into the pot.) Bring the water to a
steady simmer over high heat, skimming any scum
from the surface, then decrease the heat to maintain
a gentle simmer. Cook uncovered for 30 minutes.

Stir in the jackfruit, then increase the heat to bring
the liquid to a rolling simmer. Decrease it again to
maintain a gentle simmer, and cook until the jackfruit
starts to soften, about 15 minutes. Add the shallots,
cook for 5 minutes more, then stir in the tomatoes.

Keep cooking until the jackfruit is fully tender and
meaty (the texture you're looking for is similar to stewed
artichoke hearts), the pork is tender but still fairly
chewy, and the shallots and tomatoes are very soft but
still intact, about 15 minutes more. Canned jackfruit is
unpredictable, so this could take as long as 30 minutes.
That's fine. Taste and season with salt.

Add the cha-om and betel leaves, stir well, taste and
season with salt, then turn off the heat. Let the curry
cool slightly before you eat it. Bring the pot to the table
along with small bowls and a ladle.

Kaeng Hung Leh

{Pictured on page 169}

BURMESE-STYLE PORK BELLY CURRY

I have a photo of my friend Sunny holding a softball-size clump of sticky rice with one hand. In front of him, on the table, is a small bowl containing a few hunks of pork wading in a ruddy broth. What the photo doesn't show is that over the course of a leisurely dinner, Sunny used his other hand to pluck off ball after little ball from the big clump, dunk it into the broth, and continue until he'd gone through a kilo or so of rice. A little *kaeng hung leh* goes a long way.

Kaeng hung leh has iconic status in Chiang Mai. For tourists visiting from Bangkok, it's one of the first dishes on their eating agenda, just as New Yorkers might hit Austin, Texas, and head straight for barbecued brisket. As a foreigner in Chiang Mai, you'll find that locals will steer you toward *kaeng hung leh*. Listen to them—they've got your palates nailed. They know you'll love the tender pork shoulder and belly, the broth in which the tang from tamarind and pickled garlic tugs against the sweetness of palm sugar. Actually, the curry occupies an unusual place within the litany of Northern Thai food, because of this sweetness and the richness from pork fat. Locals refer to it as Burmese curry, and odds are the dish has its origins in Burma, one of Thailand's neighbors to the north. Chiang Mai was under Burmese control for centuries until the late 1700s.

The specifics of the broth, as usual, depend on the cook. I've seen it every which way from soupy and golden to deep red and gravylike to dark brown and thick. As far as I can tell, when you see peanuts in the bowl, you're eating a more modern version. (If you'd like, swap 1/4 cup skinless unsalted roasted peanuts for the long beans in this recipe.) When you're handed a bowl with just belly, and no shoulder or ribs, it's an old-school rendition.

As you can imagine, eating a meal of just *kaeng hung leh* would be overkill. A bowl of it is meant to share the table with other food—perhaps a chile relish, a bunch of herbs and vegetables, and lots of sticky rice. Because it's awkward to cook a very small batch, this recipe makes enough to leave you plenty of leftovers for another day. In the nine-to-five modern world, time-consuming *kaeng hung leh* is an increasingly rare sight on home stoves. You're more likely to find it at restaurants and markets that sell to-go food to be spooned into a plastic bag and tied up for the ride home. Perhaps because it's so rich, there are often leftovers that home cooks mix with glass noodles and herbs for a next-day treat called *kaeng hok*. It's the Hamburger Helper of Thai food, though it tastes so much better.

THE PLAN

- **Up to 1 week in advance: Make the curry paste and the tamarind water**

- **Up to a few days in advance: Make the curry**

- **Up to 2 days in advance: Make the fried shallots**

SPECIAL EQUIPMENT

- **A Thai granite mortar and pestle**

Flavor Profile RICH, COMPLEX, SWEET, TANGY, AND SLIGHTLY SALTY

Try It With Kaeng Khanun (Northern Thai young jackfruit curry), page 166, or Yam Samun Phrai (Northern Thai-style herbal salad), page 65. Needs Khao Niaw (Sticky rice), page 33.

SERVES 6 TO 8 AS PART OF A MEAL

CURRY PASTE

1 ounce thinly sliced lemongrass (tender parts only), from about 4 stalks

1 teaspoon kosher salt

1 (14-gram) piece peeled fresh or frozen (not defrosted) galangal, thinly sliced against the grain

7 grams stemmed dried Mexican puya chiles (about 4), soaked in hot tap water until fully soft, about 15 minutes

1½ ounces peeled Asian shallots, thinly sliced against the grain

1½ teaspoons Kapi Kung (Homemade shrimp paste), page 274

CURRY

2 tablespoons vegetable oil

1 ounce peeled Asian shallots, thinly sliced with the grain (about ¼ cup)

1½ teaspoons mild Indian curry powder

½ teaspoon turmeric powder

1 pound skinless pork belly, cut into approximately 1½-inch chunks

1 pound boneless pork shoulder, cut into approximately 1½-inch chunks

3 tablespoons Thai fish sauce

2 tablespoons Thai black soy sauce

1½ tablespoons liquid from Thai pickled garlic (straight from the jar)

1½ ounces palm sugar, coarsely chopped

6 tablespoons Naam Makham (Tamarind water), page 274

2 cups water

1 (1-ounce) piece peeled ginger, cut into long (about 1½-inch), thin (about ⅛-inch) matchsticks (about ¼ cup)

1½ ounces separated and peeled pickled garlic cloves (about 30 small cloves)

4 ounces long beans, trimmed and cut into 1½-inch lengths (about 2 cups)

6 tablespoons Hom Daeng Jiaw (Fried shallots), page 273

MAKE THE PASTE

Combine the lemongrass in the mortar with the salt and pound firmly until you have a fairly smooth, slightly fibrous paste, about 2 minutes. Add the galangal and pound until you have a smooth, slightly fibrous paste, about 2 minutes. Drain the chiles well, wrap them in paper towels, and gently squeeze them dry. Add them to the mortar and pound them, then add the shallots, and then the shrimp paste, fully pounding each ingredient before moving on to the next.

You'll have about ½ cup of paste. You can use it right away, or store the paste in the fridge for up to 1 week or in the freezer for up to 6 months.

MAKE THE CURRY

Heat the oil in a medium pot over medium-low heat until it shimmers. Add all of the paste, breaking it up slightly and stirring occasionally, until it's fragrant and turns a slightly duller shade of red, 2 to 3 minutes.

Stir in the shallots and cook until they soften slightly, about 3 minutes, then add the curry powder and turmeric powder and stir frequently for a minute or so to bring out their fragrance. Add the pork belly and shoulder, stir to coat the pork, and cook for a few minutes, so the pork has a chance to absorb a little of the flavor of the paste. You're not trying to brown the meat; crowding the pot is fine.

Stir in the fish sauce, black soy sauce, and pickled garlic liquid, then add the palm sugar. Increase the heat slightly to bring the liquid to a simmer, cook until the palm sugar has more or less completely dissolved, then stir in the tamarind water along with the 2 cups of water. Increase the heat to high, let the liquid come to a strong simmer, then immediately decrease the heat to low and cover (or partially cover, if your lid doesn't let any steam escape), adjusting the heat to maintain a steady simmer. Cook for 45 minutes, stir in the ginger, then remove the lid and cook at a steady simmer until the pork shoulder is very tender but not falling apart and the liquid has thickened slightly, about 45 minutes more. The curry should still be fairly soupy (not gravylike and dry) with a layer of reddish liquid fat near the surface. You want some of this fat, but depending on the pork's fattiness, you might have too much; use your discretion and spoon off as much as you'd like.

Stir in the pickled garlic cloves, cook for 10 minutes, then stir in the long beans and cook until they're just tender but still slightly crunchy, about 5 minutes more. Let the curry cool to warm (it'll taste even better after half an hour), then taste it. There should be a balance between sweet, salty, and sour flavors, with sweetness taking the lead. If necessary, season with more palm sugar, tamarind water, and fish sauce.

At this point, the curry will keep in the fridge for up to 5 days (it actually tastes better the day after you make it).

Before serving, gently reheat the curry. Just before serving, top with the fried shallots.

NAAM PHRIK

Chile dips

My first trip to Chiang Mai, way back in the early '90s, was only a week long, but it was probably the most formative time in my culinary life. I didn't intend for the trip to be anything but a visit with Chris, an old friend, and his wife, Lakhana. Yet this was Thailand, after all, so food was big on the agenda. They took me around the city, to restaurants, to markets, and to homes of her family members, introducing me to the food of Northern Thailand and to people who would eventually become my mentors, teachers, and friends.

One of our first meals together came from plastic bags that we lugged home from Talaat Ton Phayom, a small covered market within walking distance from their house on the hillside behind Chiang Mai University, where Lakhana taught. Many of the vendors here have spent decades plying their wares made from recipes handed down through generations. We sat on a reed mat on their floor, laid out our provisions, and ate with our hands (a first for me), as is the custom in Northern Thailand. Along with sticky rice, grilled sausage, steamed vegetables, and herbs, there was a pulpy green mash called *naam phrik num*.

For me, a meat-minded Westerner, I assumed the sausage would be the star of the meal. Instead, the *naam phrik* stole the show. I watched Chris and Lak eat. A nugget of sticky rice in hand, they used it to snatch a bite-size chunk of sausage, then dunked it into the chile relish. Sometimes they used a length of long bean or crunchy curl of pork skin to scoop. The relish was powerful, with mouth-filling flavor driven but not dominated by chile heat.

Thailand has a vast array of *naam phrik*—the family of foodstuff often translated as chile pastes, dips, or relishes made with everything from fresh prawns to pork to shrimp paste to preserved fish. At their most basic, they provide a window into ancient eating, into an era when a meal meant a few ingredients pounded together and eaten with rice.

Despite the diversity of textures, colors, flavors, levels of complexity, and quirks, *naam phrik* play a similar role. They make an intensely flavored part of a balanced Thai meal eaten with rice; vegetables (often steamed), and perhaps meat, such as crunchy fried pork skins.

The recipes in this chapter by no means represent the wide range of *naam phrik*; they're simply the four I know best.

Naam Phrik Num

Attempting to make this quintessential Northern Thai dish in Portland provided me with one of Pok Pok's prototypically infuriating challenges. In Thailand, making it is a cinch: grill a few ingredients, mash them up, season, and you're done. To make matters even simpler, just as market vendors in Bangkok sell kaffir lime leaves, galangal, and lemongrass conveniently portioned and bundled for making *tom yam*, many in the North sell the main components of *naam phrik num*—fresh green chiles, shallots, and garlic—already grilled.

The problem is, the type of chile you need doesn't exist in the US. At first I thought this was no big deal. After all, we've got jalapeño and serrano chiles out of our ears. But my early attempts just tasted wrong, like guacamole made with habaneros. Sometimes those of us who don't come from chile-rich culinary cultures can forget that chiles are not just heat givers, that each type has its own distinctive flavor, aroma, and texture. The primary flavor of this relish comes from its namesake *phrik num*, a long, moderately spicy green chile that, after much trial and error, I figured out could be reasonably replicated with Anaheim, Hungarian wax, or goat horn chiles, plus some serrano chile, if necessary, for extra heat.

At Pok Pok, we always pair *naam phrik num* with Sai Ua Samun Phrai (page 132), in part because a plate of steamed vegetables served with a vegetable-based dip is a tough sell for American eaters and in part because the two often share the table in Thailand.

Flavor Profile SPICY, VEGETAL, SALTY, SLIGHTLY FUNKY

Try It With Sai Ua Samun Phrai (Northern Thai-style herbal sausage), page 132, and Khao Niaw (Sticky rice), page 33.

2 ounces unpeeled Asian shallots	8 ounces small whole green Anaheim, Hungarian wax, or goat horn chiles	TO SERVE ALONGSIDE
1 ounce unpeeled garlic cloves	3 pickled gouramy fish fillets	Raw cucumber, unseasoned pork cracklings, and assorted steamed mixed vegetables (such as long beans, cabbage, chayote, or winter squash), for dipping
Several fresh green Thai or serrano chiles (in case the other chiles are too mild)	4 grams cilantro roots, thinly sliced	
	1 teaspoon Thai fish sauce	

MAKES ABOUT 1 CUP, ENOUGH FOR 4 TO 8 PEOPLE AS PART OF A MEAL

Prepare a grill, preferably charcoal so you have an area of high heat and another area of medium heat (see page 124). Alternatively, you can heat two heavy pans on the stovetop, one over medium heat and one over high heat.

If you're grilling, skewer the shallots, garlic, and Thai or serrano chiles (if you're using them) separately. There's no need to skewer the larger chiles. Put the

gouramy fillets on a double layer of foil or banana leaf and fold to make a package.

Grill the chiles on the high heat area of the grill and the shallots, garlic, and foil package on the medium heat area, transferring the items to a plate as they're finished. Cook the chiles, turning them over frequently and occassionally pressing them so they cook evenly,

{continued}

Khaep muu
(pork cracklings)

Khao Niaw
(page 33)

Naam Phrik Ong
(page 179)

Sai Ua Samun Phrai
(page 132)

Naam Phrik Num
(page 174)

Cucumbers and
Thai apple eggplant

Naam Phrik Kha
(page 180)

Naam Phrik
Plaa Thuu
(page 177)

Thai basil (center), steamed mixed vegetables
(kabocha squash, white cabbage, knotted long beans,
oyster mushrooms, baby Asian eggplant)

{Green chile dip, continued}

until they're completely blistered and almost completely blackened all over and the flesh is fully soft but not mushy, 5 to 8 minutes for the smaller chiles and 15 to 25 minutes for the larger ones. Cook the foil package, turning it over occasionally, just until you can smell the floral funk of the gouramy, about 15 minutes. Cook the garlic and shallots, turning them occasionally, until the skin is charred in spots and they're fully soft but still hold their shape, 15 to 20 minutes. Let the grilled chiles, shallots, and garlic cool to room temperature.

Meanwhile, open the foil package, discard any large bones and fins (don't try to remove the small bones), and transfer the gouramy to a granite mortar. Firmly pound it to a fine paste and until the bones have fully broken down, about 45 seconds. Remove all but 1 teaspoon of the gouramy paste from the mortar, reserving it for another purpose.

Add the cilantro roots to the mortar with the 1 teaspoon of gouramy and pound to a coarse paste, about 30 seconds. Peel the shallots and garlic (but don't be obsessive about it). Add the garlic to the mortar and pound to a thick, fairly fine sludge, about 1 minute, then do the same with the shallots, about 2 minutes.

The finished naam phrik should be quite spicy, but of course, everyone has a different perception of what that means. So taste the cooked Anaheim or goat horn chiles. If the heat level is too high, remove some or all of their seeds. If the heat level is too low, gradually supplement the larger chiles with a few Thai or serrano chiles.

Use your fingers or a small knife to stem and peel the chiles. Add the chiles to the mortar and pound until they break down into long, thin strands (don't mash it to a fine paste), 1 to 2 minutes. Add the fish sauce, then pound gently and briefly to incorporate it.

You can store the naam phrik in an airtight container in the fridge for up to 3 days. Let it come to room temperature before serving.

Naam Phrik Plaa Thuu

{Pictured on page 175}

GRILLED-FISH DIP

Less fiery and chile focused than its cousin *naam phrik num*, this relish has a different headlining ingredient: grilled *plaa thuu*, a type of mackerel that's a common sight in markets, with its arresting, silly-looking crooked jaw. Atlantic mackerel or even sardines make a solid substitute for its slightly oily flesh.

Flavor Profile MILDLY FISHY, SLIGHTLY VEGETAL, SPICY

Try It With Aep Plaa (Curried fish grilled in banana leaves), page 85, or Phat Fak Thawng (Northern Thai-style stir-fried squash), page 94, and Khao Niaw (Sticky rice), page 33.

SPECIAL EQUIPMENT

- A charcoal grill (highly recommended), grates oiled
- 2 or 3 wood skewers (but only if you're grilling), soaked in tepid water for 30 minutes
- A Thai granite mortar and pestle or clay mortar and wooden pestle

MAKES ABOUT 1 CUP; ENOUGH FOR 2 TO 6 AS PART OF A MEAL

1 ounce unpeeled Asian shallots

14 grams unpeeled garlic cloves

Several fresh green Thai or serrano chiles (in case the chiles below are too mild)

4 ounces small whole green Anaheim, Hungarian wax, or goat horn chiles

1 (1-pound) whole Atlantic mackerel, or 1 1/2 pounds large fresh sardines, scaled, gutted, and cleaned

1/4 teaspoon kosher salt

1/4 teaspoon naam plaa raa (fermented fish sauce)

About 1 teaspoon lime juice (preferably from a Key lime or spiked with a small squeeze of Meyer lemon juice)

1 tablespoon coarsely chopped cilantro (thin stems and leaves), lightly packed

1 tablespoon thinly sliced green onions, lightly packed

TO SERVE ALONGSIDE

Raw cucumber, unseasoned pork cracklings, and assorted steamed mixed vegetables (such as long beans, cabbage, chayote, or winter squash), for dipping

Prepare a grill, preferably charcoal, so you have an area of high heat and another area of medium heat (see page 124). Alternatively, you can heat two heavy pans on the stovetop, one over medium heat and one over high heat.

If you're grilling, skewer the shallots, garlic, and Thai or serrano chiles (if you're using them) separately. There's no need to skewer the larger chiles. Cook the chiles on the high heat area and the garlic, shallots, and fish on the medium heat area. Transfer the grilled items to a plate as they're finished.

Cook the chiles, turning them over frequently and occasionally pressing them so they cook evenly, until they're completely blistered and almost completely blackened all over and the flesh is fully soft but not mushy, 5 to 8 minutes for the smaller chiles and 15 to 20 minutes for the larger ones. Cook the garlic and shallots, occasionally turning them over, until the skin is charred in spots and they're fully soft but still hold their shape, 15 to 20 minutes. Cook the fish (adding a

splash of oil to the pan if you're cooking on a stovetop), turning it over once, until the skin is blistered with dark brown spots on both sides and the fish is fully cooked, about 10 minutes total for the mackerel and 5 minutes total for sardines. Let the grilled ingredients cool to room temperature.

Peel the shallots and garlic (but don't be obsessive about it). Pound the garlic with the salt in a granite or clay mortar (either one will do for this recipe) to a thick, fairly fine sludge, about 45 seconds, then do the same with the shallots, about 90 seconds.

The finished naam phrik should be moderately spicy, but of course, everyone has a different perception of what that means. So taste the cooked Anaheim or goat horn chiles. If the heat level is too high, remove some or all of their seeds. If the heat level is too low, gradually supplement the larger chiles with a few Thai or serrano chiles.

{continued}

{Grilled-fish dip, continued}

Use your fingers or a small knife to stem and peel the chiles. Add the chiles to the mortar and pound to a coarse paste, about 45 seconds.

Peel off as much skin from the fish as you can, then use a fork to pull the flesh from the bones. Remove the bloodline, pull the flesh into large pieces, and pick them over for stray bones. Measure 1 cup, lightly packed, of the fish and reserve any extra for another purpose. Lightly pound the fish in the mortar, stirring with a spoon if necessary to evenly distribute the chile mixture, to a coarse mash, about 30 seconds. (At this point, you can store the naam phrik in an airtight container in the fridge for up to 3 days. Let it come to room temperature before proceeding.)

Add the fermented fish sauce and just enough lime juice so the naam phrik tastes bright without being tart, then pound briefly to incorporate them. Gently stir in the cilantro and green onion.

Naam Phrik Ong

{Pictured on page 175}

NORTHERN THAI PORK AND TOMATO DIP

I've given this Northern Thai relish a nickname: *naam phrik* Bolognese. The liquidy concoction made from ground pork and tomatoes does indeed resemble an Italian ragu, especially when it's served over spaghetti-like strands of *khanom jiin*. The funky undercurrent of fermented shrimp and soybeans, however, reminds you that you're definitely not in Italy.

Flavor Profile UMAMI-RICH, SLIGHTLY TART, FUNKY, SLIGHTLY SALTY, SPICY

Try It With Naam Phrik Num (Green chile dip), page 174, and/or Sai Ua Samun Phrai (Northern Thai-style herbal sausage), page 132, and Khao Niaw (Sticky rice), page 33, or on top of Khanom Jiin (page 231).

SPECIAL EQUIPMENT

- A Thai granite mortar and pestle

MAKES ABOUT 3 CUPS, ENOUGH FOR 4 TO 6 AS PART OF A MEAL

PASTE

2 grams dried Thai chiles (about 6)

Scant 1¹/₂ teaspoons kosher salt

5 grams cilantro roots, thinly sliced

1 ounce peeled garlic cloves, halved lengthwise

21 grams peeled Asian shallots, thinly sliced against the grain

2 tablespoons Kapi Kung (Homemade shrimp paste), page 274, plus more if necessary

NAAM PHRIK

2 tablespoons Naam Man Krathiem (Fried-garlic oil), page 272, or Naam Man Hom Daeng (Fried-shallot oil), page 273

1 pound ground pork (not lean)

1 pound cherry tomatoes (about 24), halved

1 teaspoon Thai yellow bean sauce

1 tablespoon Hom Daeng Jiaw (Fried shallots), page 273

TO SERVE ALONGSIDE

Raw cucumber, unseasoned pork cracklings, and assorted steamed mixed vegetables (such as long beans, cabbage, chayote, or winter squash), for dipping

---

MAKE THE PASTE

Combine the dried chiles and salt in the mortar and pound firmly, scraping the mortar and stirring the mixture once or twice, until you have a fairly fine powder, about 3 minutes. Pound in the cilantro roots, occasionally stopping to scrape down the sides of the mortar, until you have a fairly smooth paste, about 1 minute. Do the same with the garlic, then the shallots. Pound in the shrimp paste until it's fully incorporated, about 30 seconds. You'll have a generous 1/4 cup of paste.

MAKE THE NAAM PHRIK

Heat the oil in a medium pot over medium-low heat until the oil shimmers. Add all of the paste and cook, stirring frequently, until the paste is very fragrant and loses the smell of raw garlic and shallots, about 5 minutes.

Add the pork, increase the heat to high, and cook, stirring constantly, until about half of the meat is cooked (you're not trying to brown it), about 1 minute. Add the tomatoes and cook, stirring and breaking up the meat as it cooks, for another minute. Cover the pot, decrease the heat, and cook, stirring occasionally to break up any meat clumps, until the flavors have had a chance to develop and meld, about 30 minutes. As they cook, the tomatoes and meat will give off liquid; adjust the heat as necessary to maintain a steady simmer. The mixture should look like a Bolognese sauce, very moist but not watery. (If it's watery, remove the lid and cook off some of the liquid.)

Let the naam phrik cool to room temperature and season with more shrimp paste, keeping in mind that the naam phrik is a highly seasoned dip. Sprinkle on the fried shallots and serve.

Naam Phrik Kha

{Pictured on page 175}

DRY-FRIED GALANGAL-CHILE DIP

SPECIAL EQUIPMENT

- **A Thai granite mortar and pestle**
- **A wok (nonstick highly recommended)**
- **A wooden wok spatula (if using a nonstick wok) or a metal wok spatula**

Even in Thailand, where restaurants often don't resemble restaurants, Pa Daeng Jin Tup doesn't initially look like a place where you'd want to eat.

This dirt patch on the side of the road, about 15 minutes northeast of Chiang Mai, is scattered with tables covered with oilcloth, folding chairs, and benches haphazardly nailed together. Tarps, blankets, and overhanging trees form an improvised roof. There are no less than five stray cats slinking between the tables, looking for scraps.

Diners here hang out in T-shirts in front of tall bottles of beer and ice-filled glasses, leisurely emptying pastel-colored plastic plates filled with fatty slabs of charred pig teat and sour fermented pork sausage served beside tiny garlic cloves and alarmingly tiny fresh green chiles. There are banana leaf packages of custardlike, curry paste–slathered pig brain, and, of course, baskets of sticky rice and local herbs.

This is *aahaan kap klaem*, or Thai drinking food, which tends toward the charred, chewy, and funky. It's awesome stuff, and I devoted the menu at Whiskey Soda Lounge, in Portland, to its pleasures. Specifically, Pa Daeng specializes in the Northern subset of this genre.

I've been coming here since my friend Sunny absent-mindedly pointed it out on a drive to Chiang Mai. I love to watch the cooks work in the outdoor kitchen, if you can call it a kitchen. It amounts to a few pots and a couple of grills fashioned from oil drums. There's an old fan perched on a stool stoking the coals. The cooks operate a crude pulley system, raising and lowering a meat-strewn rack over the embers.

On my first visit, a sustained banging caught my attention. A woman was using a mallet to attack a piece of beef on a thick wood slab. Our waitress and Sunny both looked entertained by my bemusement. Sunny let loose a string of Northern Thai, the dialect still common in these parts and virtually unintelligible to me, that I thought would never end. He was ordering. Soon our table was filled with pink, blue, yellow, and green plastic plates.

Of all the wonderful foods that appeared, one of my favorites was the least conspicuous: a few tablespoons of coarse powder fragrant with chiles and citrusy, almost soapy galangal. I watched Sunny as he grabbed a small hunk of meat, swiped it through, and ate it. I tried it, too. It was awesome.

Two hours later, I was busy with two things—polishing off another round of fermented sausage and trying to figure out what was in this incredible powder. As soon as Sunny told me its name, *naam phrik kha*, I could place it in the family of relishes called *naam phrik*, which are typically eaten as a sort of dip for vegetables and meat. Yet unlike those I'd encountered before, this one was not a wet paste. It was not moist. It was completely dry. After a boisterous conversation with Pa Daeng herself, Sunny explained that they pound massive amounts of the *naam phrik* in a massive mortar, then they cook the fibrous paste in batches in a dry heavy wok set over a charcoal fire until all the moisture is gone. My best guess is that this preserves it, though they burn through so much of it here that I doubt leftover *naam phrik* stays around for long.

This stuff is salty and intense, so the 1/2 cup this recipe makes goes a long way. In Thailand, you often see it served with steamed beef or steamed mushrooms. Typically, I'm disappointed that the younger, more delicate galangal you see in Thailand is so tough to find in the US, but for this recipe, there's good news: it's meant to be made with the older, more fragrant stuff.

Flavor Profile SALTY, HIGHLY AROMATIC, SPICY

Try It With Sii Khrong Muu Yaang (Thai-style pork ribs), page 128, or other grilled meat and Khao Niaw (Sticky rice), page 33.

MAKES ABOUT 1/2 CUP, ENOUGH FOR 4 TO 6 AS PART OF A MEAL

14 grams stemmed dried Mexican puya chiles (about 8)

1 teaspoon kosher salt

14 grams thinly sliced lemongrass (tender parts only), from about 2 large stalks

2 1/4 ounces peeled fresh or frozen (not defrosted) galangal, thinly sliced against the grain

1 1/4 ounces peeled garlic cloves, halved lengthwise

TO SERVE ALONGSIDE

Assorted steamed mixed vegetables (such as oyster mushrooms, long beans, cabbage, chayote, or winter squash), for dipping

---

Combine the dried chiles in the mortar with the salt and pound firmly, scraping the mortar and stirring the mixture once or twice, until you have a fairly fine powder, about 5 minutes. Pound in the lemongrass, occasionally stopping to scrape down the sides of the mortar, until you have a fairly smooth, fibrous paste, about 2 minutes. Do the same with the galangal (about 4 minutes), then the garlic (about 3 minutes), fully pounding each ingredient before moving on to the next. You'll have about 1/3 cup of paste.

Next, you're going to slowly cook the paste in a dry wok until all the moisture has evaporated and you're left with a completely dry, coarse powder. The trick is using very low heat (if you can't get your heat low enough, try occasionally removing the wok from the burner) and, in this case, a nonstick surface. A wooden wok spatula will allow you to scrape the pan without scratching it.

Preheat a wok over very low heat. Add all of the paste and cook—stirring constantly, breaking up even small clumps where moisture might be lurking, and scraping the pan often to make sure the paste doesn't clump or burn—until the paste has transformed into a very coarse, completely dry mixture, 30 to 50 minutes.

Transfer the mixture to a shallow bowl or plate. Let it cool completely and use it right away or store it, covered, at room temperature for up to a month.

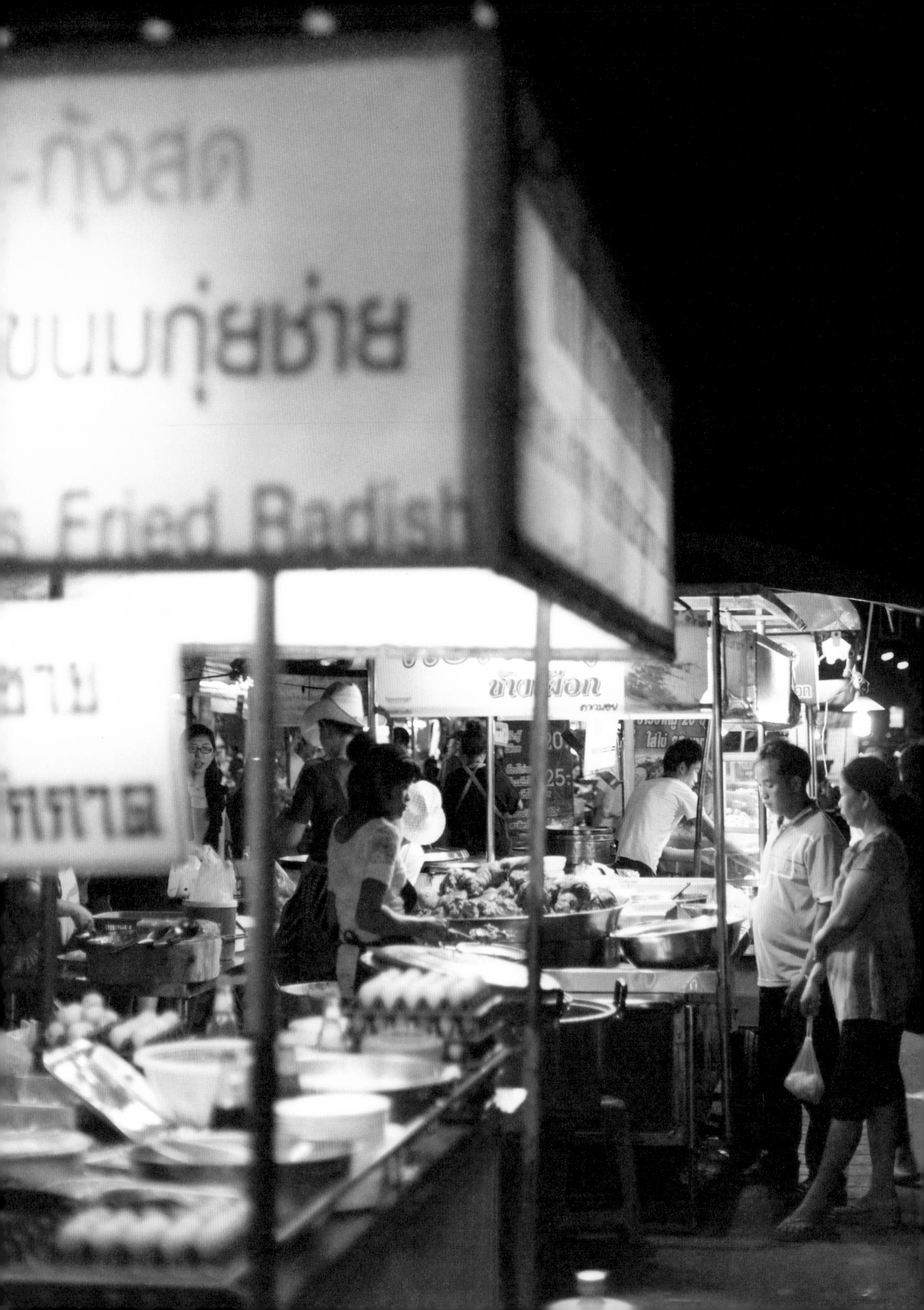
กุ้งสด
ขนมกุ่ยช่าย
Fried Radish

AAHAAN JAAN DIAW

The one-plate meal

In Thailand, the one-plate meal is a quick one, for those times when eating is just a task to be checked off your list. It is the pizza slice, the turkey sandwich, of Thai food. (And like those two items, it can be incredibly delicious.) You get your *aahaan jaan diaw*, devour it, and get back to work or fuck off to a bar with friends. This category includes a wide variety of dishes, from noodle soups and stir-fries (which tend to serve as one-plate meals) to dishes meant to be served over rice.

You'll notice that some of them make one portion, rather than the typical-cookbook-requisite four or six. That's because they're typically made one portion at a time in a wok. And you just can't cram four portions into the wok. If you want to make two or more portions, scale up the ingredients you'll need and make each portion, one at a time.

KHAO (RICE)

Read on for several one-plate meals that make use of Thailand's staple cereal grain. Depending on the dish, rice either is a foil for flavorful accompaniments like papaya salad or stir-fried meat, or it becomes the dish, whether it's drowned in pork stock for rice soup or stir-fried for fried rice.

Khao Kha Muu

PORK SHANK STEWED WITH FIVE SPICE

SPECIAL
EQUIPMENT

• A Thai granite mortar
and pestle

• A very large (about
8-quart) pot

A lady in a cowboy hat is standing beside a pile of pig knuckles.

I'm at Talaat Chang Pheuak, a small roadside night market in Chiang Mai. I've come here for those pig knuckles ("shanks" on this side of the pond), stewed with soy and spices until they're impossibly tender, then hacked up and piled on rice. The dish is *khao kha muu*, and hers is the best version I've ever tasted.

Two young girls in aprons, probably her daughters, help take orders and plate, while she wields a heavy cleaver. Her fans convene here nightly, lining up on the street in front of her, standing and either nabbing orange plastic stools under blue umbrellas or, in typical Thai fashion, not even bothering to get off their motorbikes. Wobbly metal tables fill with plates, everyone eating the same thing and often neglecting the other vendors who share space in this concrete lot. Unlike many other purveyors of *khao kha muu*, she doesn't stew the hard-boiled eggs in the porky liquid. She keeps them pristine on a plate and splits them with each order, revealing a perfectly creamy yolk. I always add a spoonful of the mild, vinegary chile sauce that's offered, which is the same electric yellow-orange as the yolk.

Khao kha muu is not a Northern Thai dish, even though my favorite vendor plies her trade in the North's capital city. You see it all over Thailand, yet another dish that's Chinese in origin but now resolutely Thai. In Bangkok, it's as ubiquitous as traffic. In markets and street stalls, you'll spot pots of stewed pork nearly submerged in murky broth, often bobbing with eggs. For something like 30 baht, about $1, you get a small mound of meat and slick, creamy skin on rice along with small handful of stewed pickled mustard greens and a hard-boiled egg.

The pork, infused with the flavor of five spice and pandan leaf, almost always makes a fine meal, but the best vendors take the dish beyond merely tasty. Many use some of rich, slightly sweet cooking liquid to cook the next day's knuckle. Done day after day, year after year, this process produces a sort of master sauce that survives, purportedly, for generations, like the starter for sourdough breads. The proprietress with the ten-gallon hat has yet another secret. She spikes her cooking liquid with Milo, a sort of Ovaltine-like powder. In homage, I do, too.

Flavor Profile MEATY AND UMAMI-RICH, SLIGHTLY SALTY AND SWEET

{continued}

{Pork shank stewed with five spice, continued}

SERVES 6 AS A ONE-PLATE MEAL

PASTE

1 ounce cilantro roots, thinly sliced

1 (1-ounce) piece peeled fresh or frozen (not defrosted) galangal, cut into thin slices against the grain

1 tablespoon white peppercorns

1¼ ounces peeled garlic cloves, halved lengthwise

¼ cup Thai five-spice powder (look for Thai characters or the words pha lo or pae lo)

PORK

¼ cup vegetable oil

2 skin-on, bone-in pork shanks (about 4 to 5 pounds)

1¼ cups Thai thin soy sauce

½ cup Thai black soy sauce

¾ cup Thai oyster sauce

⅓ cup Shaoxing wine

4½ ounces palm sugar

2 tablespoons Milo powder

1 (1½-ounce) piece fresh or frozen (not defrosted) galangal (unpeeled), sliced against the grain

5 or 6 cilantro roots with 3 or so inches of stem attached

About 6 pandan leaves, tied into a small bundle

1 medium yellow onion, quartered

1 whole unpeeled garlic head

5 quarts water

6 Khai Tom (Eight-minute eggs), page 270

3 cups drained coarsely chopped pickled mustard green (leaves and thinly sliced stems), soaked in water for 10 minutes and drained well

About ½ cup very coarsely chopped cilantro (thin stems and leaves), lightly packed

TO SERVE ALONGSIDE

Khao Hom Mali (Jasmine rice), page 31

Phrik Naam Som (Sour chile dipping sauce), page 279

MAKE THE PASTE

Pound the cilantro roots in a granite mortar to a coarse, fibrous paste, about 1 minute. Add the galangal and pound to a fairly smooth, fibrous paste, about 1 minute. Do the same with the peppercorns, then the garlic, then the five-spice powder, fully pounding each ingredient before moving on to the next.

You'll have a firmly packed ½ cup of paste. You can use it right away, or store the paste in the fridge for up to 1 week or in the freezer for up to 6 months.

COOK THE PORK

Heat the oil in a large pan over medium-high heat until the oil shimmers. One by one, cook the shanks in the oil, carefully turning them over occasionally, until they're mostly a very light golden brown color (not even close to the fully deep brown color common in Western cooking), about 5 minutes per shank. Transfer the shanks to a plate and reserve 2 tablespoons of the oil.

Add the 2 tablespoons of reserved oil to a large pot, and set the pot over medium-low heat. When the oil is hot, add all of the paste and cook, breaking it up and stirring often, until it's a couple of shades darker and very fragrant, about 10 minutes.

Add the pork shanks, soy sauces, oyster sauce, Shaoxing wine, palm sugar, Milo powder, galangal, cilantro roots, pandan leaves, onion, and garlic, and the 5 quarts of water. Bring the liquid to a simmer over high heat, cover the pot, and decrease the heat to maintain a steady simmer. Cook until the pork is so tender that it begins to fall apart, about 4 hours.

Spoon off the layer of fat on the surface. Once the pork and liquid cool to warm, add the eggs and let them soak for at least 30 minutes or even better, overnight. You can store the pork in its stewing liquid in the fridge for up to a day or two (if you do, wait until the liquid is cold to skim off the solid fat). Reheat the pork very gently in the stewing liquid and scoop out the eggs as soon as the broth is liquid again.

FINISH THE DISH

Put the mustard greens in a medium pot, ladle in enough pork stewing liquid to cover them, bring the liquid to a rolling simmer, and cook until they're tender and have taken on some of the flavor of the liquid, about 30 minutes.

Halve the eggs lengthwise. Divide the rice, eggs, and mustard greens among the plates. Pull the pork off the bone (don't neglect the skin) and chop it into approximately ½-inch-thick slices. Put the pork on top of the rice, ladle ¼ cup or so of the stewing liquid overtop, and sprinkle on the cilantro. Serve with the dipping sauce alongside.

NOTE: This is not a Western braise or stew. In Thailand, it's made in vats with the pork knuckles submerged in a sea of dark brown bobbing with eggs. So when you make it at home, you'll have a lot of extra stewing liquid. My suggestion: strain the liquid and use it for your next braise or as the base for noodle soup. It freezes well.

KHA MUU THAWT
(Deep-fried stewed pork shank)

At Pok Pok, we serve a variation of this dish called *kha muu thawt*. I love dropping this joint of deep-fried meat onto the table, like something out of the Flintstones, and watching people get cross-eyed. I like to think how confused they'd be if I served it with its common accompaniment in Thailand—mashed potatoes.

This seemingly incongruous Thai dish is actually a fine example of sanctioned fusion food. Germans have been coming to Thailand for many years. Thais love to drink beer—matter of fact, much of the beer in Thailand is based on German brew—and to eat food outside. So the German beer garden concept has really taken hold there.

And German food, too. There's a guy in the middle of nowhere near Chiang Mai who makes German-style sausages, and his lot is always packed with cars, mostly Thais who have come from as far away as Bangkok. At Tawandang, now a multilocation operation (one of their Bangkok locations seats two thousand), you can order *tom yam*, steamed squid with chile and lime juice, or a plate of grilled *wurst* with sauerkraut—and wash it down with a stein of Dunkel.

The beer halls themselves have been thoroughly Thai-ified, with live Thai music blaring from a stage and the room populated with the requisite beer girls, scantily clad women hired by beer companies like Chang or Singha. It's no shocker, then, that the food has been Thai-ified as well. Deep-fried pork knuckle takes no great stretch of the Thai culinary imagination. Since knuckle stewed with soy and spices is already part of the repertoire, and frying pig parts is basically a national pastime, why not drop that tasty bundle of tender flesh, sticky cartilage, and bones into bubbling fat?

What the stewed-then-fried shank, crispy on the outside and tender within, comes with varies by restaurant and intended audience. It might be potatoes and cabbage. Perhaps a handful of the pickled mustard greens that go with *khao kha muu* and a dip of green chiles, lime, and fish sauce.

I don't recommend trying it at home, or at least that's what I feel obligated to say. The truth is, it's not easy to get up the nerve to drop the thing in a pot of hot oil. But any deep-fried-turkey hounds out there will want to try it. If you do, be careful.

- Get a deep pot and a splatter screen, or a turkey deep-fryer.

- Cook the pork as instructed, but omit the black soy sauce (which could burn in the hot fat) and cook until it's very tender but still intact, 3 to 3½ hours rather than the full 4 hours.

- Pat the shank dry and let it sit uncovered, preferably in front of a fan, until the skin is as dry as possible. If you're making the pork in advance, reheat the shank in a low oven just until the center is warm. It'll cook in the oil for only a few minutes.

- Heat enough oil to submerge the shank to 400°F. Cross your fingers, add the knuckle, and quickly stand back. Cook just until the skin is brown, crispy, and hopefully slightly puffy, about 5 minutes. Transfer it to paper towels to drain.

Kai Kaphrao Khai Dao

STIR-FRIED CHICKEN WITH HOT BASIL

SPECIAL EQUIPMENT

- A Thai granite mortar and pestle
- A wok and wok spatula

It's morning in Bangkok. Motorcycles zig-zag treacherously through the lines of cars clogging the streets. You're walking along grand boulevards and down narrow side streets. Overhead, great masses of electric wires snake through the city and skyscrapers gleam in the skyline. You're hungry, searching for something to eat. But you don't have to try hard to find food, because in Bangkok, food usually finds you.

You can't go far without passing a cluster of umbrella-covered stands, selling mammoth pink segments of pomelo or skewers of meat or noodle soups. Finally, you stop at a vendor set up beside an alley, a woman presiding over more than a dozen aluminum trays, each piled with dish you can't for the life of you identify. Still, you want to eat them all.

It's in this type of restaurant, called *raan khao kaeng* (roughly, curry-over-rice shops), where many visitors to Thailand, not just to Bangkok, come across *kai kaphrao*, a stir-fry of pork or chicken seasoned aggressively with garlic, chiles, fish sauce, soy sauce, and a touch of sugar. It's a common morning food (Thais don't eat breakfast the way we do), but it's also lunch, it's a late-afternoon snack, it's whatever you want it to be. Served beside a heap of jasmine rice and perhaps a crisp-edged fried egg, it is a fine example of *aahaan jaan diaw*, what Thais call a one-plate meal.

The dish is defined by a last-minute dose of *kaphrao* (holy or hot basil), an ingredient so essential that the dish is named for it. For short, people often order it as *phat kaphrao*, literally "stir-fried holy basil." In the US, we'd never give top billing to an herb. Dill salad? No, it's egg salad. Grilled rosemary? No, it's a charred steak—so what if it happens to be perfumed by a few sprigs?

The herb has a very particular flavor, to be sure, a distinctive peppery heat, but in Thailand, it's prized for its powerful aroma. The notion of aroma eclipsing flavor can sometime confound us Westerners. Ask a Thai person to describe holy basil and the first thing they'll say is *hom*, or "smells good." You'll notice that versions that people have cooked for themselves and their families, compared to those sold by street vendors, contain even more holy basil, which is relatively pricey in Thailand. That's one benefit of making it yourself—you control the size of the handful. The other is being above the hot pan when you add that handful, the pleasure of being in a room overtaken by its scent.

Flavor Profile AROMATIC, SALTY, SPICY, SWEET

{continued}

{Stir-fried chicken with hot basil, continued}

SERVES 1 AS A ONE-PLATE MEAL (TO MAKE MORE, DOUBLE OR QUADRUPLE THE INGREDIENTS, BUT COOK EACH BATCH SEPARATELY)

2 tablespoons vegetable oil

1 large egg, at room temperature

1 tablespoon Thai fish sauce

2 teaspoons Thai black soy sauce

1 teaspoon granulated sugar

11 grams peeled garlic cloves, halved lengthwise and lightly crushed into small pieces in a mortar (about 1 tablespoon)

5 ounces ground chicken (preferably thigh meat) or pork

1 ounce long beans, cut crosswise into 1/8-inch slices (about 1/4 cup)

1 1/2 ounces peeled yellow onion, thinly sliced with the grain (about 1/4 cup)

6 grams fresh Thai chiles (about 4), preferably red, thinly sliced

3 or 4 dried Thai chiles, fried (page 12) and very coarsely crumbled

6 grams hot basil leaves (about 1 cup), see NOTE

TO SERVE ALONGSIDE

1 to 1 1/2 cups Khao Hom Mali (Jasmine rice), page 31

Phrik Naam Plaa (Fish sauce–soaked chiles), page 286, optional

NOTE: Holy or hot basil (bai kaphrao in Thai) is a variety of basil with a peppery flavor and distinctive aroma. To find it, your best bet is a Thai-focused market, though you might get lucky at Indian grocery stores (where the herb might be called tulsi) or farmers' markets. Beware of inaccurate labeling: I've seen "Holy basil" used to refer to purple-stemmed Thai or sweet basil.

COOK THE EGG

Heat a wok over very high heat, add the oil, and swirl it in the wok to coat the sides. When it begins to smoke lightly, crack in the egg and cook for about 5 seconds. It should spit and sizzle violently and the whites should bubble and puff. Decrease the heat to medium and cook the egg, frequently tipping the pan slightly and basting the egg with the oil, just until the white has set and turned golden at the edges and the yolk is cooked the way you like it (I prefer my yolk slightly runny), about 1 minute. Turn off the heat. Transfer the egg to paper towels to drain, leaving the oil in the wok.

STIR-FRY AND SERVE THE DISH

Combine the fish sauce, soy sauce, and sugar in a small bowl and stir well.

Heat the wok again over very high heat. When the oil smokes lightly, add the garlic, take the wok off the heat, and let the garlic sizzle, stirring often, until it turns light golden brown, about 30 seconds. Put the wok back on the heat, then add the chicken, long beans, onions, and fresh chiles. Stir-fry (constantly stirring, scooping, and flipping the ingredients) and break up the chicken as you do until the meat is just barely cooked through, about 1 minute.

Add the dried chiles and the fish sauce mixture (add a splash of water, if necessary, to make sure nothing's left behind in the bowl), and stir-fry until the liquid has been absorbed by the meat, 30 seconds to 1 minute more. Turn off the heat.

Just before you're ready to serve, turn the heat back to high, and once the meat is heated through, add the basil, and stir just until it is wilted and very fragrant, 15 seconds or so.

Serve with the jasmine rice, fried egg, and fish sauce–soaked chiles.

Khao Phat Muu

THAI-STYLE FRIED RICE WITH PORK

SPECIAL
EQUIPMENT

- A Thai granite mortar
and pestle
- A wok and wok spatula

Well before I opened Pok Pok, I'd get home after a day of knocking down walls in someone's condo or painting a four-thousand-square-footer, and I'd be starving. For months and months, I'd have the same craving: fried rice. Even today, it's still one of my go-to dishes for a quick, spirited meal.

Raised on the tasty but forgettable takeout version, I didn't think I'd ever be captivated by such a basic dish. Yet one day many years ago, hunger made me pull my motorbike off the highway in the middle-of-nowhere Thailand and stop beside a roadside shack situated at the corner of a field. I asked the vendor what he was selling and was disappointed when he said, *"Khao phat."* Anything else? I asked. Nope. So I gave it a shot. There were no bells or whistles. There were certainly no basil, bell peppers, or baby corn. The rendition represented Thai food at its most elemental, the fish sauce and lime distinguishing it from its Chinese sibling. It was a stroke of brilliance that resurrects leftover rice and makes it into something that tastes like much more than the sum of its parts.

Just about any protein can replace the sliced pork: ground meat, sliced chicken, squid, shrimp, or beef. For instance, sometimes I like to make fried rice with 2 ounces of lump crabmeat instead of the pork listed here. In that case, add the crab right after you add the fish sauce, granulated sugar, etc., and stir-fry just until the crab is warm through.

Flavor Profile SALTY AND UMAMI-RICH

SERVES 1 AS A ONE-PLATE MEAL (TO MAKE MORE, DOUBLE OR QUADRUPLE THE INGREDIENTS, BUT COOK EACH BATCH SEPARATELY)

1 tablespoon Thai fish sauce

1 teaspoon Thai thin soy sauce

1 teaspoon granulated sugar

Pinch ground white pepper

2 tablespoons vegetable oil

1 large egg, at room temperature

1 ounce peeled small shallots, preferably Asian, or very small red onions, halved lengthwise and thinly sliced with the grain (about 1/4 cup)

11 grams peeled garlic cloves, halved lengthwise and lightly crushed into small pieces in a mortar (about 1 tablespoon)

4 ounces boneless pork shoulder, sliced against the grain into approximately 1/8-inch-thick bite-size pieces

2 cups Khao Hom Mali (Jasmine rice), page 31, preferably day-old

2 tablespoons thinly sliced green onions, lightly packed, plus a pinch for finishing

1 tablespoon coarsely chopped cilantro (thin stems and leaves), lightly packed

TO SERVE ALONGSIDE

8 or so 1/4-inch-thick slices firm cucumber, peeled if thick-skinned

1 lime wedge (preferably from a Key lime)

Phrik Naam Plaa (Fish sauce–soaked chiles), page 286, optional

Combine the fish sauce, soy sauce, sugar, and pepper in a small bowl and stir well.

Heat a wok over very high heat, add the oil, and swirl it in the wok to coat the sides. When it begins to smoke, crack in the egg (it should spit and sizzle violently and the whites should bubble and puff) and cook without messing with it until all but the center of the whites have set, about 15 seconds. Flip the egg (it's fine if the yolk breaks) and push it to one side of the wok (up the wall of the wok is fine). Add the shallots and garlic and

{continued}

{Thai-style fried rice with pork, continued}

cook, stirring them (but not the egg) often, until they've lightly browned, about 1 minute.

Add the pork, stir everything together well, and stir-fry (constantly stirring, scooping, and flipping the ingredients) until the pork is no longer pink on the outside, about 30 seconds.

Add the rice and stir-fry, breaking up the egg a bit, for 30 seconds. Add the fish sauce mixture (add a splash of water, if necessary, to make sure nothing's left behind in the bowl) and continue to stir-fry until the pork is just cooked through and the flavors have permeated the rice, a minute or so more.

Turn off the heat, stir in the 2 tablespoons of green onions, and transfer the rice to a plate. Top with the cilantro and remaining green onions, and serve with the cucumber slices on the edge of the plate, the lime wedge for squeezing, and the fish sauce–soaked chiles in a small bowl to spoon on top.

Khao Man Som Tam

PAPAYA SALAD WITH COCONUT RICE AND SWEET PORK

As best as I can tell, this one-plate meal is a remnant of high-society fare in the days before *som tam* had completed its journey from Laos and Isaan to the far corners of Thailand and beyond. Writing about the growth in popularity of Isaan food for *The Bangkok Post*, the longtime ex-pat and Thai food vet Bob Halliday refers to days long ago when papaya salad was not an omnipresent street-corner staple but a rarefied dish eaten by moneyed Bangkok women. Back then, suggests Halliday, it was heavy on the sugar and served alongside not the sticky rice of Isaan but jasmine rice subtly perfumed with coconut cream.

Whenever I've eaten the two together, they've come with a few sticky slivers of sweet pork (*muu waan*). These are just supposed to be a garnish, a flavor enhancer, a teaser for the dish's two stars. But customers would look at me funny if they got the portion you'd get in Thailand, so we go a little heavier on the pork. Pok Pok regulars call the stuff "pork candy," and they're on to something. Just four ingredients and slow cooking turn hunks of pork shoulder into this addictively sticky offspring of pulled pork, which is so good that I'm sure many readers will make a batch and forgo the papaya salad and rice altogether.

Flavor Profile NEARLY EQUAL PARTS SWEET, SOUR, SPICY, AND SALTY (PAPAYA SALAD), RICH AND AROMATIC (COCONUT RICE), SWEET AND SALTY (PORK)

SERVES 4 AS A ONE-PLATE MEAL

MUU WAAN (SWEET PORK)	COCONUT RICE	DISH
1 (2-pound) piece boneless pork shoulder, gristle and large pockets of fat trimmed	2 cups uncooked jasmine rice	A double batch of Som Tam Thai (Central Thai–style papaya salad), page 38, made just before serving
1/4 cup plus 1 tablespoon Thai sweet soy sauce	1/2 cup unsweetened coconut cream (preferably boxed)	1/4 cup Hom Daeng Jiaw (Fried shallots), page 273
1/4 cup plus 1 tablespoon Thai thin soy sauce	1 1/2 tablespoons superfine sugar	A few large pinches torn cilantro leaves
2 1/2 ounces palm sugar, very coarsely chopped	1/2 teaspoon kosher salt	
1 teaspoon ground white pepper	1 3/4 cups water	

MAKE THE MUU WAAN (SWEET PORK)

Cut the pork, with (not against) the grain of the meat, into approximately 5-inch-long slabs that are about 3/4 inch thick.

Combine the pork, both soy sauces, palm sugar, and white pepper in a heavy-bottomed pot and stir to coat the pork. Set the pot over medium-high heat, bring the liquid to a strong simmer (make sure it never boils or it'll burn), then cover the pot and decrease the heat to maintain a steady simmer. Cook until the pork is so tender that it breaks easily into shreds when you prod it, about 1 1/2 hours.

{continued}

{Papaya salad with coconut rice and sweet pork, continued}

With the pot still on the heat, use a sturdy whisk or large spoon to mash the pork until it's all in small shreds. Increase the heat, bring the liquid to a steady simmer, and cook, uncovered, until the liquid has evaporated and the shreds glisten and look sticky, like candy, 5 to 20 minutes, depending on how much liquid the pork gave off during cooking. You'll have about 3 1/2 cups of shredded pork.

If you're planning to eat it right away, let it cool slightly. Otherwise, let it fully cool, and store it in a covered container in the fridge for up to a week. Reheat it in the microwave or in a pot over very low heat.

MAKE THE COCONUT RICE

Put the rice in a fine-mesh strainer set inside a large bowl and fill the bowl with enough cool tap water to cover the rice by an inch or two. Use your fingers to gently stir the rice, then lift the strainer to drain. The water in the bowl will be white and cloudy. Empty the water, set the strainer in the bowl again, and repeat the process until the water that covers the rice is, more or less, clear. You'll probably have to change the water two or three times. Drain the rice, gently shaking it occasionally, until it is fully dry to the touch, about 15 minutes.

Combine the rice, coconut cream, sugar, salt, and the 1 3/4 cups of water in a rice cooker. Mix well with your hands, then cover, press the button, and let the cooker do its thing.

Once it's done, let the rice sit in the rice cooker on the "Warm" setting with the cover on for about 20 minutes. Fluff the rice: Use a fork to gently rake the top few layers of rice to separate the grains, and gradually rake the next few layers and so on, working your way toward the bottom. Try your best not to break or smash the grains. You might see brown flecks of caramelized coconut cream at the bottom—congratulations.

The coconut rice will stay warm in the rice cooker for several hours.

FINISH THE DISH

Put a packed 3/4 cup of coconut rice (or as much as you'd like) on each of 4 plates. Top the rice with a packed 1/2 cup of pork (or as much as you'd like). Divide the papaya salad among the plates next to the rice. Top each portion of pork with a tablespoon of fried shallots and a sprinkle of cilantro, and serve.

Khao Tom

Talaat Meuang Mai is the big wholesale market in central Chiang Mai. It's sprawling and loud even at midnight, when the trucks filled with heaps of pineapples, cabbage, and garlic start to crowd in. The market opens to the public before dawn, when customers stock up for their restaurants, street stalls, village market stands, and the rest. In the morning, I like to spend a good hour window shopping, ogling baskets of fermented rice noodles, crates of young tamarind and mangosteens, and heaps of greens or herbs, some of which I still can't identify. Afterward, I wend my way through, dodging guys pushing fifteen-foot-long wheelbarrows piled with pumpkins or motorcycles squeezing past the shoppers crammed into the narrow aisles, toward my favorite rice soup joint.

Other than the Steelcase desks repurposed as tables, the spot looks like most market food hawkers'—walls plastered with calendars, advertisements, and placards displaying wise words from the Buddha, rickety wood benches and plastic stools for sitting. (This style of no-design-at-all design inspired the aesthetic at all of my restaurants.) On my last visit, the owners had set up several small shrines at the rear and laid out abundant offerings. They explained that they were giving thanks, because a lottery ticket had paid out.

There are a few prepared food items on offer. Laid out on wax paper are slices of white bread brushed with scarily yellow margarine. Occasionally, I'll have a slice topped with a coddled egg (*khai luak*), but the thing to order here is what's warming in a cheap pot balanced precariously on a portable burner. This is *khao tom*, pork broth kitted out with springy pork meatballs, slivers of ginger and green onion, and yesterday's rice. If you wish, the counterman will deposit one of those coddled eggs into your bowl—the white not quite set, the yolk just warmed through. I like muffins and bagels as much as the next guy, but I'll take rice soup over these any day. This is morning-time fare in Thailand, but it eats good anytime.

Flavor Profile UMAMI-RICH, AROMATIC, SALTY

SERVES 1 AS A ONE-PLATE MEAL

1 large egg, at room temperature

2 cups Sup Kraduuk Muu (Pork stock), page 268

8 Muu Deng (Bouncy pork balls), page 269

Scant 2 tablespoons shredded salted radish, soaked in water 10 minutes then drained

1 tablespoon Thai thin soy sauce

1 tablespoon Thai fish sauce

Pinch ground white pepper

1 cup cooked Khao Hom Mali (Jasmine rice), page 31, preferably day-old

1 (7-gram) piece peeled ginger, cut into long (about 1 1/2-inch), very thin (about 1/16-inch) matchsticks (about 1 tablespoon

1 tablespoon Krathiem Jiaw (Fried garlic), page 272

1 tablespoon coarsely chopped Chinese celery (thin stems and leaves), lightly packed

1 tablespoon thinly sliced green onion, lightly packed

1 tablespoon coarsely chopped cilantro (thin stems and leaves), lightly packed

Bring a small pot of water to a boil. Put the egg in a narrow heat-proof container (like a measuring cup or an empty aluminum can) that holds about two cups by volume. Pour in enough boiling water to cover the egg by a few inches and let it sit for 10 to 15 minutes, depending on how cooked you like your eggs. Remove the egg from the water and set it aside.

Pour the remaining water out of the pot and add the stock, pork balls, salted radish, soy sauce, fish sauce, and pepper. Bring the liquid to a boil over high heat, immediately add the rice, let the liquid come back to a boil, then pour the soup into a serving bowl.

Crack the egg into the bowl and add the remaining ingredients. Stir well before you eat it.

KUAYTIAW (NOODLES)

Thai food has become known for noodles, even though most noodles and the dishes made from them have Chinese origins. For the cuisine's deserved reputation, we have to thank the country's significant population of Thai nationals who are ethnically Chinese for helping to popularize them in the first place and its ingenious cooks for integrating noodles so thoroughly into the Thai culinary canon. In this section, you'll find a handful of my favorite noodle dishes, including soups and stir-fries. In addition to noodle dishes of Chinese origin, you'll find a few that make use of (a replica of) *khanom jiin*, Thailand's only indigenous noodle.

The customizability common to many Thai foods assembled at the last minute (think papaya salad) is a feature of noodle dishes as well, and virtually no component is off limits. You can even order your favorite noodle soup *khruk khrik* (with just a little broth) or *haeng* ("dry," without any). While most dishes have a preferred noodle type (thin, flat rice noodles for Kuaytiaw Reua, page 204; thin, round wheat noodles for Ba Mii Tom Yam Muu Haeng, page 207), the customer typically makes the final call (and as a cook, you can too, though I've made noodle recommendations). Some people even order noodle soups without noodles.

On the table at shops selling noodles, you'll typically find four little jars containing *khruang phrung*, the "four flavors" with which you're meant to season your dish. The common foursome is sugar, fish sauce with chopped Thai chiles, chile powder, and mild green chiles soaked in vinegar. Soups in particular arrive mildly seasoned, with the understanding that the punter will apply these four flavors to his liking. As always, the particulars vary. For boat noodles, for instance, and other soups with dark, intense broths, the chile powder is made with dried chiles that have been toasted for an even longer time than usual, until they're almost black in color and smoky, almost tobaccolike in flavor. For *khao soi*, which walks the line between curry and noodle soup, the chile comes in the form of a slightly oily paste. At many shops selling stir-fried noodles, you typically won't see all four (for *phat thai*, the common accompaniments are just fish sauce, sugar, and chile powder). Whatever the dish, the injection is almost always the same: serve the *khruang phrung* alongside and use them if you want to.

Finally, when you read the instructions for the first three noodle dishes in this section, you'll notice that I ask you to set up a sort of assembly line and cook each batch of noodles and finish each bowl one at a time. It would be nice, perhaps, to figure out some way to present the bowls to your guests at the same moment, to engineer the at-home equivalent of the high-end restaurant flourish where four waiters simultaneously raise silver domes to reveal four perfectly roasted quails. But preparing them the way I instruct is how they taste best. After all, they're not restaurant dishes; rather, they're sold from stalls and other makeshift operations. This is casual eating. And they taste incredible enough that no one will mind that one friend has had a go before another gets her bowl.

Kuaytiaw Pet Tuun

{Pictured on page 202}

STEWED DUCK NOODLE SOUP

THE PLAN

- Up to 5 days in advance: Make the broth and the toasted-chile powder

- Up to 3 days in advance: Make the sour chile dipping sauce

- Up to 2 days in advance: Make the fried garlic and fried-garlic oil

SPECIAL EQUIPMENT

- A long-handled noodle basket (or even better, two of them)

If some therapist ever asks me to name my "safe place," I'll choose a stool at a Thai noodle shop. The hub of many of these operations is a metal counter crowded with stacks of plastic bowls. A glass case displays various shapes and sizes of noodle and cuts and forms of meat. Behind the counter, there's usually a woman wielding a giant ladle next to a substantial pot of murky broth. If the operation is a busy one, there will be another pot around back that's so large it comes up to her shoulders.

I've sat under many a sun-shielding umbrella, sweating over steaming bowls of pinkish *yen ta fo* (fermented tofu providing the color and funky flavor), clear soups strewn with eggy wheat noodles and slices of red-hued roasted pork or fish balls the size of marbles, and stewed beef parts floating in brown broth with thin rice noodles. I love them all. But my heart beats especially quickly for *kuaytiaw pet tuun* with its coffee-colored, ducky broth boldly flavored with star anise, cinnamon, and soy and sweetened with rock candy.

Because the broth is so good, we serve this in various incarnations at Pok Pok, sometimes skipping the noodles altogether and offering the duck leg in its braising liquid with stewed pickled mustard greens to be eaten with jasmine rice, similar to Khao Kha Muu (page 185). Nothing beats this version, though.

Flavor Profile MEATY AND UMAMI-RICH, AROMATIC, SLIGHTLY SALTY AND SWEET

MAKES 4 BOWLS (EACH A ONE-PLATE MEAL)

BROTH

1 (1-ounce) piece fresh or frozen (not defrosted) galangal (unpeeled), thinly sliced against the grain

4 large stalks lemongrass (outer layer, bottom 1/2 inch, and top 4 inches removed), thinly sliced

10 grams cilantro roots (about 10 large), lightly smashed with a pestle, pan, or flat part of a knife blade

2 fresh or frozen pandan leaves, tied into a knot

1 ounce Chinese celery, cut into approximately 3-inch lengths (about 2 cups, lightly packed)

1 cup Thai thin soy sauce

Scant 1/3 cup Thai black soy sauce

2 ounces rock sugar

3 grams (about one 1 1/2-inch piece) Ceylon or Mexican cinnamon

2 star anise

4 medium dried bay leaves (preferably from an Asian market)

1 tablespoon black peppercorns

4 relatively lean duck legs (about 2 pounds), rinsed in cold water

25 grams dried whole shiitake mushrooms (about 2 cups), soaked in a generous 2 cups of hot water until fully soft, about 1 hour (soaking liquid reserved)

5 cups water

NOODLE SOUP

1¹/₂ pounds fresh wide (about 1¹/₂-inch), flat rice noodles (see Wide Rice Noodles, page 19), or fresh or defrosted frozen uncooked thin, round Chinese wheat noodles (sometimes called wonton noodles)

Generous ¹/₄ cup coarsely chopped Chinese celery (thin stems and leaves), lightly packed

Generous ¹/₄ cup coarsely chopped cilantro (thin stems and leaves), lightly packed

Generous ¹/₄ cup Krathiem Jiaw (Fried garlic), page 272

Generous ¹/₄ cup Naam Man Krathiem (Fried-garlic oil), page 272

TO SERVE ALONGSIDE

Phrik Naam Som (Sour chile dipping sauce), page 279, optional

Fish sauce

Granulated sugar

Phrik Naam Som (Vinegar-soaked chiles), page 286

Phrik Phon Khua (Toasted-chile powder), page 270

MAKE THE BROTH

Combine all the broth ingredients in a medium pot along with the reserved mushroom soaking liquid and the 5 cups of water. Set the pot over high heat, bring the liquid to a simmer, cover the pot, and decrease the heat to maintain a steady simmer until the meat comes off the bone very easily with a tug of tongs but isn't dry or falling from the bone, about 2 hours.

Spoon off most of the fat from the surface. (This is even easier when broth is chilled and the fat solidifies.) Either fish out the duck legs and mushrooms, then strain the broth, discarding the solids, or do it as you serve the soups, avoiding the aromatics as you ladle out the broth. You can store the duck, mushrooms, and broth in an airtight container in the fridge for up to 5 days. You'll need 4 cups of the broth for the 4 bowls. Freeze the rest for another purpose. Bring the broth (with the duck and mushroom in it) to a bare simmer over medium-low heat right before you're ready to serve the soup.

BUILD EACH BOWL

When you're ready to finish the dish, bring a large pot of water to a rolling boil.

Cut off and discard the mushroom stems, if necessary, and cut any very large mushrooms into large bite-size pieces.

If you're using rice noodles, carefully separate them. Unless you've found freshly made noodles, either microwave them briefly or dunk them in the boiling water for a few seconds just until they're pliable enough to separate without crumbling. Drain them well, and separate them into four 6-ounce portions. Keep the water at a boil.

Set up an assembly line: Ready the four portions of noodles and the broth and duck legs. Put the Chinese celery, cilantro, fried garlic, and garlic oil in four separate containers. Make one bowl at a time (or two at a time if you have two noodle baskets).

Put one portion of noodles and a quarter of the mushrooms in a long-handled noodle basket and put the basket in the water. Cook, gently shaking the basket frequently to move the ingredients around, just until the rice noodles are hot through, about 20 seconds. (If you're using wheat noodles, boil until they're cooked but still slightly chewy, about 2 minutes.) Firmly shake the basket to drain the noodles and mushrooms well. Add the noodles and mushrooms to a bowl, top them with a duck leg, then spoon on ¹/₂ to 1 cup of the broth. Add a large pinch of the cilantro and Chinese celery. Spoon on fried garlic and oil.

Get to work on the next bowls.

Serve alongside the chile dipping sauce, fish sauce, sugar, vinegar-soaked chiles, and chile powder. Season to taste and stir well before you dig in.

Kuaytiaw Reua

{Pictured on page 203}

{Pictured on page 203}

THE PLAN

- **Up to 2 weeks in advance: Make the toasted-chile powder**
- **Up to 5 days in advance: Make the broth and the chile vinegar**
- **Up to 2 days in advance: Make the fried garlic and fried-garlic oil**

SPECIAL EQUIPMENT

- **A long-handled noodle basket (or even better, two of them)**

It's hard to walk fifty feet in a Thai city and not run into a noodle shop, either a proper brick-and-mortar operation or a smattering of colorful tables on the sidewalk. You become accustomed to it, passing by almost without noticing. But it's hard to ignore a man slinging bowls of rice noodles in dark broth while seated in a boat—parked on dry land, mind you. These are boat noodles, and they're not to be missed.

Back in the day, merchants would travel by boat from the city of Ayutthaya, seat of the old Thai kingdom, more than a hundred miles down the Chao Phraya River and through a network of *khlong* (canals) to Bangkok. Just as vendors now line city streets, floating hawkers once crowded the banks of these busy waterways. Ayutthaya's vendors, now mostly parked on dry land, still make the finest boat noodles I've eaten.

Today you can identify a shop that specializes in *kuaytiaw reua* even if you don't read Thai, which I don't, by the presence of a boat—a boat-shaped emblem on signs and storefronts, a boat-shaped counter, and yes, even an actual boat serving as kitchen work station. Most places in Thailand serve prudent portions, not the bathtub-size bowls we get in the States. You might have just one bowl as a snack. You might order another.

At first, I figured that a dish named for a boat would be made with fish. Instead, boat noodles rely on beef or pork broth, infused with the flavor of galangal, star anise, and pandan leaf and enriched with a spoonful of blood. You customize your bowl, choosing among beef or pork parts and products. For our purposes, I call for pork and omit the typical cartilage and other odd bits.

Besides the meaty array, there's usually water spinach and *kuaytiaw* (rice noodles), either wide strips or skinny strands. Alongside most noodle soups is *phrik phon khua*, toasted and ground chiles, but boat noodles deserve a particularly dark version, slowly toasted until the chiles are almost black. The good places make it themselves, and a small spoonful or two adds an inimitable depth and character to the broth.

NOTE ON MEATBALLS

The meatballs floating in bowls of boat noodles have spawned an evocative Thai-ified English word to describe their texture. To transliterate phonetically: rubber-*REE*. These dense spheres have a snappy texture that Westerners occasionally struggle to embrace, though I have to point out that the same people who balk at a beef ball will down a hot dog without blinking. A common addition to many noodle soups, these balls are made from a mixture of, in ascending order of firmness, fish, pork, or beef, plenty of fat, and flour that's ground repeatedly then slapped again and again against a mixing bowl to activate the flour's gluten. They take skill, finesse, and time to make. Do yourself a favor and buy premade ones.

Flavor Profile UMAMI-RICH, SPICY, SLIGHTLY SWEET, SLIGHTLY TART

MAKES 4 BOWLS
(EACH A ONE-PLATE
MEAL) AND ENOUGH
LEFTOVER BROTH AND
STEWED PORK FOR
ABOUT 8 MORE
(MAKING LESS OR
MORE IS EASY; JUST
PAY ATTENTION TO
THE AMOUNTS IN THE
"BUILD EACH BOWL"
SECTION BELOW)

BROTH

2 1/2 pounds boneless pork shoulder, rinsed and cut into approximately 2-inch-long, 1-inch-wide, 1/4-inch-thick strips

1 (1-ounce) piece fresh or frozen (not defrosted) galangal (unpeeled), thinly sliced against the grain

3 large stalks lemongrass (outer layer, bottom 1/2 inch, and top 4 inches removed), thinly sliced

10 grams cilantro roots (about 10 large), lightly smashed with a pestle, pan, or flat part of a knife blade

2 fresh or frozen pandan leaves, folded and tied into a knot

1 ounce Chinese celery, cut into approximately 3-inch lengths (about 2 cups, lightly packed)

3/4 cup Thai thin soy sauce

1 tablespoon Thai black soy sauce

2 ounces rock sugar

3 grams (about one 1 1/2-inch piece) Ceylon or Mexican cinnamon

4 medium dried bay leaves (preferably from an Asian market)

1 tablespoon black peppercorns

2 star anise

12 cups water or Sup Kraduuk Muu (Pork stock), page 268

NOODLE SOUP

1/4 cup Thai fish sauce

1/4 cup Phrik Tam Naam Som (Grilled-chile vinegar), page 285

1/4 cup granulated sugar

2 tablespoons Naam Man Krathiem (Fried-garlic oil), page 272

2 tablespoons Krathiem Jiaw (Fried garlic), page 272

1 tablespoon plus 1 teaspoon Phrik Phon Khua (Toasted-chile powder), page 270

1 tablespoon plus 1 teaspoon fresh or defrosted frozen raw pork blood (optional)

8 ounces boneless pork shoulder, sliced against the grain into 1/8-inch-thick bite-size strips

16 fresh or defrosted frozen pork balls

10 ounces semi-dried thin, flat (linguine-shaped) rice noodles (about 5 cups, tightly packed), soaked in lukewarm water until fully pliable but not fully soft, about 15 minutes, then drained well

2 ounces water spinach, leaves and thin stems only, cut into 2-inch lengths (about 2 1/2 cups, lightly packed)

4 ounces bean sprouts (about 2 cups, lightly packed)

Generous 1/4 cup coarsely chopped Chinese celery (thin stems and leaves), lightly packed

Generous 1/4 cup coarsely chopped cilantro (thin stems and leaves), lightly packed

Generous 1/4 cup thinly sliced sawtooth herb, lightly packed

TO SERVE ALONGSIDE

Phrik Naam Plaa (Fish sauce–soaked chiles), page 286

Granulated sugar

Phrik Naam Som (Vinegar-soaked chiles), page 286

Phrik Phon Khua (Toasted-chile powder), page 270

MAKE THE BROTH

Add all the broth ingredients to a large pot along with 12 cups of water (if you have pork stock, substitute it for some or all of the water). Bring the liquid to a simmer over high heat, then immediately decrease the heat to low, cover the pot, and tweak the heat to maintain a steady simmer. Cook, covered, until the pork is very tender but still holds its shape, about 1 hour. You'll have about 12 to 14 cups of broth. Do not strain it. Reserve a generous 4 cups of the broth and a generous 1 cup of the stewed pork for the 4 bowls. Store the leftover broth and pork in the fridge for up to 5 days or the freezer for up to 6 months.

Bring the broth to a bare simmer over medium-low heat right before you're ready to serve the soup.

BUILD EACH BOWL

When you're ready to finish the dish, bring a large pot of water to a rolling boil. Ready 4 large soup bowls. To each bowl, add 1 tablespoon of the fish sauce, 1 table-spoon of the chile vinegar, 1 tablespoon of the sugar, 1 1/2 teaspoons of the garlic oil, 1 1/2 teaspoons of the fried garlic, 1 teaspoon of the chile powder, and 1 teaspoon of the blood, if you're using it.

Set up an assembly line: In each of 4 containers, combine 2 ounces of the raw pork shoulder, 4 of the pork balls, 2 1/2 ounces of the noodles, 1/2 cup or so of the water spinach, and 1/2 cup of the bean sprouts. Measure the ingredients at first, then eyeball once you get the hang of it. Put the remaining ingredients in separate containers.

{continued}

{Boat noodles, continued}

Make one bowl at a time (or two if you have two noodle baskets). Add one portion of the noodle mixture to a long-handled noodle basket and put the basket in the water. Cook, using a spoon to stir the ingredients once or twice, just until the pork shoulder is cooked through, about 1 minute. Firmly shake the basket to drain the ingredients well. Add the contents of the basket to the bowl, add a few pieces of the stewed pork (about ¼ cup), and ladle in 1 cup of the broth, leaving behind the aromatics. Add a large pinch of each of the herbs and get to work on the next bowl.

Serve alongside the fish sauce–soaked chiles, sugar, vinegar-soaked chiles, and chile powder. Season to taste and stir well before you dig in.

Ba Mii Tom Yam Muu Haeng

SPICY, SWEET, TART NOODLES WITH PORK, PEANUTS, AND HERBS

THE PLAN

- **Up to 2 weeks in advance:** Make the toasted-chile powder

- **Up to 5 days in advance:** Make the pork stock and chile vinegar

- **Up to 2 days in advance:** Cook the ground pork, and make the fried garlic and fried-garlic oil

SPECIAL EQUIPMENT

- **A long-handled noodle basket (or even better, two of them)**

If you had a glance at the Thai title, you probably noticed the words "tom yam," recognizable to most of us as the name of a soup found in almost every Thai joint in the American universe. But these days, the phrase doesn't denote a particular dish so much as a certain irresistible flavor profile, loosely defined by the elements of that soup. *Tom* means "boiled" and refers to the liquid base. The flavor profile is similar to that found in *yam*, a category of spicy, sweet, and sour jumbles that we often translate, because we lack a better word, as "salads." This noodle dish embodies all those lovable flavors.

If your head is spinning, welcome to my world. I'm constantly trying to piece together bits of information to make sense of what I'm hearing and eating. To make it spin even faster, I've learned that my preferred way to enjoy this noodle soup is *haeng* or "dry"—without broth. Yep, you read that right, dry soup. In the version below, there's a little broth on the side for lapping up or for adding to your bowl.

The portions of this recipe are roughly double what you'd get in Thailand or about the size of a *phiseht* order, the Thai version of supersize. That's because when I get a diminutive bowl of *ba mii tom yam* at a shop in Thailand, I almost always order a second when I'm halfway through the first.

Flavor Profile SWEET AND SOUR, SPICY, AROMATIC, UMAMI-RICH

MAKES 4 BOWLS (EACH A ONE-PLATE MEAL); MAKING LESS OR MORE IS EASY (JUST PAY ATTENTION TO THE AMOUNTS IN THE "BUILD EACH BOWL" SECTION BELOW)

GROUND PORK

1 teaspoon vegetable oil

7 ounces ground pork

A few dashes Thai fish sauce

TO DISTRIBUTE AMONG BOWLS

1/2 cup coarsely chopped unsalted roasted peanuts

1/4 cup plus 2 tablespoons Thai fish sauce

1/4 cup granulated sugar

1/4 cup Phrik Tam Naam Som (Grilled-chile vinegar), page 285

1/4 cup shredded salted radish, soaked in water 10 minutes then drained

2 tablespoons Krathiem Jiaw (Fried garlic), page 272, or Hom Daeng Jiaw (Fried shallots), page 273

2 tablespoons Naam Man Krathiem (Fried-garlic oil), page 272, or Naam Man Hom Daeng (Fried-shallot oil), page 273

4 teaspoons Phrik Phon Khua (Toasted-chile powder), page 270

{ingredients continued on page 209}

COOK THE PORK

Heat the oil in a medium pan over medium-high heat until it shimmers, add the pork, and cook (stirring, breaking up the meat, and about halfway through, adding the fish sauce) just until it's cooked through, about 5 minutes.

BUILD EACH BOWL

I encourage you to serve the bowls as you make them, rather than letting the first one sit while you make the rest. Remember, this is street food, not formal dining.

Bring a large pot of water to a rolling boil. Ready 4 large bowls. To each bowl, add 2 tablespoons of the peanuts, 1 1/2 tablespoons of the fish sauce, 1 tablespoon

{continued}

TO FINISH THE NOODLES

$3^{1}/_{2}$ ounces long beans, thinly sliced on the diagonal into $^{3}/_{4}$-inch-long pieces (about 1 cup)

4 ounces bean sprouts (about 2 cups, lightly packed)

9 ounces fresh or defrosted frozen uncooked thin, round Chinese wheat noodles (sometimes called wonton noodles)

16 fresh or defrosted frozen pork balls

8 ounces boneless pork shoulder, sliced against the grain into $^{1}/_{8}$-inch-thick bite-size strips

$^{1}/_{4}$ cup very coarsely chopped (about $^{1}/_{4}$-inch pieces) unseasoned pork cracklings, preferably with some meat attached

Generous $^{1}/_{4}$ cup thinly sliced green onions, lightly packed, plus a few pinches

Generous $^{1}/_{4}$ cup coarsely chopped cilantro (thin stems and leaves), lightly packed

Generous $^{1}/_{4}$ cup thinly sliced sawtooth herb, lightly packed

4 fresh square, "thick" wonton wrappers, halved diagonally, briefly deep-fried until golden brown, and drained on paper towels (optional)

TO SERVE ALONGSIDE

2 cups Sup Kraduuk Muu (Pork stock), page 268, warmed in a small pot

1 tablespoon plus 1 teaspoon Thai fish sauce

4 pinches ground white pepper

4 small lime wedges (preferably from Key limes)

of the sugar, 1 tablespoon of the chile vinegar, 1 generous tablespoon of the salted radish, $1^{1}/_{2}$ teaspoons of the fried garlic or shallots, $1^{1}/_{2}$ teaspoons of the fried garlic or shallot oil, and 1 teaspoon of the chile powder.

Set up an assembly line: In each of 4 containers, combine $^{1}/_{4}$ cup of the long beans, $^{1}/_{2}$ cup of the bean sprouts, $2^{1}/_{4}$ ounces of the noodles, 4 of the pork balls, 2 ounces of the pork shoulder, and $^{1}/_{4}$ cup of the ground pork. Measure the ingredients at first, then eyeball once you get the hang of it. Put the cracklings, green onions, cilantro, and sawtooth herb in separate containers.

Make one bowl at a time (or two if you have two noodle baskets). Add one portion of the noodle mixture to each long-handled noodle basket and put the basket in the water. Cook, using a spoon to stir the ingredients once or twice, just until the pork shoulder is cooked through and the noodles are fully cooked but still slightly chewy, about 2 minutes. Firmly shake the basket to drain the ingredients well. Add the contents of the basket to one of the bowls and toss well.

Add about 1 tablespoon of the cracklings, a large pinch of the green onions and each of the herbs, and 2 pieces of the fried wonton skin, if you're using it. Get to work on the next bowl.

Season the warm stock with the fish sauce and pepper, add a few pinches of green onions, and divide the stock between 4 small bowls. Serve the bowls of noodles with a lime wedge for squeezing onto the noodles and the broth alongside for slurping between bites of the intensely flavored noodles. Stir well before you dig in.

Kung Op Wun Sen

SHRIMP AND GLASS NOODLES BAKED IN A CLAY POT

SPECIAL EQUIPMENT

- A Thai granite mortar and pestle
- A 1½- to 2-quart Chinese clay pot (soaked in water for an hour, then drained before the first use)
- A charcoal tao (highly recommended but optional)

I hauled the *kung op wun sen* to the table and removed the lid of the clay pot. Chef Chew, Pok Pok's second ever employee, took a sniff. Chef Chew was not impressed.

I'd eaten this dish again and again in Chinese restaurants throughout Thailand, in places known for mastering it, and thought I'd cracked the code. Chef Chew (the "chef" title was just me razzing him; he'd never worked in a restaurant before) clearly disagreed. What he said after I lifted the lid was, "*Mai hom phrik thai, mai hom keun chai.*" Basically, "I don't smell pepper, I don't smell Chinese celery."

Before I launched Pok Pok proper, I was tending to the take-out shack, building out the space next door, and sleeping on the floor. In what little spare time I had, I was developing the new menu and testing prospective dishes. And who better to weigh in than Chew, a Chinese-Thai guy from an upper-middle-class family. In other words, exactly the kind of person who would have eaten a ton of top-notch *kung op wun sen*—or approximately "shrimp baked with glass noodles." This is not a street-stall dish, but one served at Chinese seafood restaurants in Bangkok and cities near the sea.

While Chinese in origin, this dish, like nearly any foreign food Thai cooks come across, has been tailored over the years to satisfy the Thai palate. The clay pot it's traditionally cooked in, the noodles, the combination of seafood and pork—all very Chinese. Yet the cilantro root–garlic mixture that joins forces with Chinese aromatics like ginger—distinctly Thai.

Chef Chew's reaction was a lesson for me on the significance of aroma in Thai food. For us Westerners, it's important, sure—if something is delicious, it's nice if it smells great, too—but in Thai food, the importance of aroma approaches that of flavor. In my conversations about food with Thai friends, I've heard them praise the smell of a dish as often as I hear them talk up the flavor. As Westerners, we don't primarily, if at all, think of ingredients like black pepper and Chinese celery in terms of smell, which in the case of the latter is really too bad, because its smell is much more exciting than the flavor. In restaurants throughout Thailand and at Pok Pok, a pot of *kung op wun sen* arrives at the table covered. Then, right in front of the diners, the lid is lifted and BLAMMO! You get hit with that aroma.

A less practiced eater of *kung op wun sen* than Chew might not have been so harsh, but really, this isn't an easy dish to fuck up. In fact, its method embodies the alchemy of simple cooking. You tile the bottom of a pot with slices of pork belly, then add a layer of aromatics, one of shrimp, and one of cellophane noodles. Finally, you pour sauce over the top. As it all cooks in the covered vessel, the pork starts to caramelize and absorb the sauce, the shrimp slowly steam and imbibe the flavor from the aromatics, and a flavorful liquid bubbles up and coats the noodles. Sometimes green onions stand in for Chinese celery and Sichuan peppercorns for black. Some cooks use crab instead of shrimp or prawns with roe, which gives the noodles an orange hue.

{continued}

{Shrimp and glass noodles baked in a clay pot, continued}

In the best versions, the clay pot rests on a charcoal grill called a *tao*—in contrast to the common aluminum pot set over a gas burner. The flames creep up the sides of the pot (that's why you need flame, either gas or charcoal, for this dish; a typical grill and electric range won't do) and the smoke sneaks in through the porous vessel, infusing the dish with its flavor. The word "op" in the title means "baked," because the heat from the grill envelops the pot, so the effect is similar to baking, even though technically the main source of heat comes from beneath.

Flavor Profile AROMATIC, UMAMI-RICH, SALTY, PEPPERY

Try It With Phat Phak Ruam Mit (Stir-fried mixed vegetables), page 98, and Plaa Neung Si Ew (Steamed whole fish with soy sauce, ginger, and vegetables), page 79, or Puu Phat Phong Karii (Crab stir-fried with curry powder), page 101.

SERVES 1 AS A ONE-PLATE MEAL (OR 2 TO 6 AS PART OF A MEAL)

9 grams cilantro roots, thinly sliced

1/2 teaspoon whole black peppercorns, plus 1/4 teaspoon coarsely cracked black peppercorns

1/4 teaspoon kosher salt

1 tablespoon plus 1 teaspoon vegetable oil

4 ounces peeled yellow onion, thinly sliced with the grain (about 1 cup)

1/4 cup coarsely chopped thin Chinese celery stems (cut into approximately 11/2-inch lengths), plus 2 tablespoons very coarsely chopped Chinese celery leaves

1 (14-gram) piece peeled ginger, cut into long (11/2-inch), thin (1/8-inch) matchsticks (about 2 tablespoons)

2 ounces skinless pork belly, cut into 1/8-inch-thick, 21/2-inch long slabs

6 ounces large shell-on shrimp (about 4), preferably head-on

31/2 ounces dried glass noodles (also called bean thread or cellophane noodles), soaked in lukewarm water until very pliable, about 30 minutes, drained well and snipped into approximately 4-inch lengths

1/2 teaspoon Thai black soy sauce

1 tablespoon Thai thin soy sauce

11/2 teaspoons Thai oyster sauce

11/2 teaspoons Thai seasoning sauce

11/2 teaspoons Shaoxing wine

11/2 teaspoons granulated sugar

1/2 teaspoon Asian sesame oil (look for brands that are 100 percent sesame oil)

11/2 teaspoons water

TO SERVE ALONGSIDE

Naam Jim Seafood (Spicy, tart dipping sauce for seafood), page 280, optional

---

ASSEMBLE THE DISH

Pound the cilantro roots, whole peppercorns, and salt to a coarse paste in a granite mortar, about 15 seconds. Heat 1 tablespoon of the vegetable oil in a wok or frying pan over medium-high heat until it shimmers, decrease the heat to medium, and add the onion, Chinese celery stems, ginger, and the cilantro-root paste. Cook, stirring frequently, until the onion has wilted slightly, about 90 seconds. Turn off the heat.

Pour the remaining 1 teaspoon of vegetable oil into the clay pot and rub to coat the bottom and sides. Line the bottom of the pot with one layer of the pork

belly, then add the onion mixture in an even layer. Use kitchen shears to snip off any pointy feelers from the shrimp, then snip through the shell on the back of the shrimp and barely into the flesh to expose the vein. Discard the veins and add the shrimp to the pot in one layer. Sprinkle on the cracked black pepper.

In a medium mixing bowl, toss the noodles with the black soy sauce until the noodles are an even amber color, then add the noodles to the pot in an even layer. You can stop here and cook the dish up to an hour later or cover and keep the pot in the fridge overnight. Let it come to room temperature before cooking.

COOK THE DISH

In a small bowl, stir together the thin soy sauce, oyster sauce, seasoning sauce, Shaoxing wine, sugar, sesame oil, and the 1½ teaspoons of water. Measure 3 tablespoons of this mixture and drizzle it over the noodles. Top with the Chinese celery leaves.

This dish tastes best cooked on a charcoal tao. (You can get away with cooking it on a gas stovetop rack.) Prepare the tao, as you would a charcoal grill, to cook over medium heat (see page 124).

Cover the pot with the lid and cook until the noodles and the shrimp are completely cooked, 9 to 12 minutes, resisting the temptation to check under the lid until at least 9 minutes have passed. You won't be able to tell until you stir, but the pork belly should be slightly caramelized. If it's not, then use a slightly higher heat the next time you make the dish.

Stir well before serving. If you've made it, serve the dipping sauce alongside and occasionally dunk a shrimp.

Khao Soi Kai

NORTHERN THAI CURRY NOODLE SOUP WITH CHICKEN

My first taste of *khao soi* came a few days after May 17, 1992. I remember the date not only because of my great affection for this noodle dish, but because it was on the eve of Black May, when a government crackdown on protestors in Bangkok led to thousands arrested and dozens dead. This began my enduring habit of traveling to Thailand right when the shit hits the fan: protests, riots, coups, you name it. Even in Chiang Mai, where I was staying with my friends Chris and Lakhana, the mood was dark. Yet commerce in Thailand, I've noticed, never stops. Noodle shops were open and doing cracking business. Chris and Lakhana welcomed me home, I put down my bags, and we went in search of a bowl of *khao soi*, probably the most famous of all Northern Thai dishes and the most popular with the many foreigners who pass through the North's cultural center, Chiang Mai.

Khao soi, I soon learned, is essentially just a bowl of noodles, which is a bit like saying the *banh mi* is just a sandwich. Tender wheat noodles and bone-in chicken swim in an orange-tinged coconut milk curry that's incredibly rich and aromatic. On top, there's a crown of those same wheat noodles, but they're crunchy from a dunk in hot oil. On the side comes an assortment of embellishments that you use to season your one-bowl meal: a dark, tobacco-y paste of fried chiles, pickled mustard greens, hunks of raw shallot, and wedges of lime.

Yet for all the flavors in the dish that we Westerners recognize as "Thai," the dish actually has its roots in, depending on who you talk to, either Burmese or Muslim Chinese cooking. Chiang Mai, having been a stop on ancient spice routes and under Burmese control for two centuries, is home to several such examples of glorious fusion. Along with typical Thai ingredients like lemongrass and galangal, the curry paste contains Chinese aromatics and spices (ginger and black cardamom) as well as those better associated with Burmese cooking (curry powder, coriander seeds, turmeric). It has long struck me as strange that such an iconic Northern Thai dish would contain coconut milk, a relatively modern induction into the region's cuisine. It's probably a Burmese thing, too.

As with so many Thai dishes, every restaurant serves its own rendition. I've eaten many dozens, all of which riff on the basic blueprint. The curry paste, amount of coconut milk and cream, sweetness, noodle style, and proteins vary widely. I've even eaten outliers, like one made with fish and another that paired cow's milk with coconut. "Healthy," the waiter said as he told us about the dairy addition.

There's no shortage of *khao soi* revelations to be had in Chiang Mai. The version we serve at Pok Pok is a sort of composite of my favorites. One is the version at Khao Soi Lam Duan on Fa Ham Road. The owners claim that the seventy-plus-year-old shop is the oldest *khao soi* slinger in the city. The cluttered kitchen is out front, comprising a round wood butcher block with a cleaver, heaps of homemade noodles, and two vats of bubbling broth, one of beef and another of pork and chicken. (Regulars, I've heard, will come late in the day, when the broth has concentrated.) Young women assemble the dish, one grabbing melamine bowls from a precarious stack and adding a tangle of

r ladling in broth and pieces of bone-in chicken, and another
wl with fried noodles and a small ladle of coconut cream.
othing tops the decades-old Khao Soi Prince, where I had my
The place is rarely open—at least, it's rarely open when I show
t's closed for an Islamic holiday; most times, though, the rea-
is has become a running joke among my friends in Chiang
o go to Khao Soi Prince. We might as well choose someplace else.
ar headscarves and the sign sports a star and crescent. The
s burgers and pizza. I do not recommend either. Instead,
ake dish. You get a deep bowl of pale, oil-slicked broth
us and bland, but it is not. The curry is subtly spiced, its
lor betraying the cook's judicious hand with curry powder
t is slightly sweet from coconut milk and cream, rich but
hey make their own noodles, in this case an eggless wheat
s deftly cooked.
at home takes a bit of work. There's a paste to pound, a curry
to fry and to boil. The good news is that the paste can be
d so can the curry itself. And because *khao soi* is an example
a one-plate meal, you don't have to cook anything else to
or dinner that tastes straight out of Chiang Mai.

Flavor Profile RICH AND COMPLEX, SLIGHTLY SWEET, SLIGHTLY SPICY AND SALTY

MAKES 6 BOWLS (EACH A ONE-PLATE MEAL)

CURRY PASTE

1 pod black cardamom (often labeled cha koh, tsao-ko or thao qua)

1¹/₂ tablespoons coriander seeds

¹/₂ teaspoon cumin seeds

14 grams dried Mexican puya chiles (about 8), slit open, seeded, and deveined

1 teaspoon kosher salt

7 grams thinly sliced lemongrass (tender parts only), from about 1 large stalk

1 (7-gram) piece peeled fresh or frozen (not defrosted) galangal, thinly sliced against the grain

1 (14-gram) piece peeled ginger, thinly sliced against the grain

1 ounce peeled garlic cloves, halved lengthwise

4 ounces peeled Asian shallots, thinly sliced against the grain

1 tablespoon Kapi Kung (Homemade shrimp paste), page 274

CURRY

2 tablespoons vegetable oil

1 tablespoon turmeric powder

¹/₂ teaspoon mild Indian curry powder

¹/₄ cup Thai fish sauce

2 tablespoons Thai thin soy sauce

3 ounces palm sugar, coarsely chopped

1¹/₂ teaspoons kosher salt

6 small skin-on chicken legs (about 2¹/₂ pounds), separated into thighs and drumsticks

5 cups unsweetened coconut milk (preferably boxed)

TO FINISH THE DISH

Vegetable oil for deep frying

1 pound fresh or defrosted frozen uncooked thin, flat Chinese wheat noodles (sometimes called wonton noodles)

1¹/₂ cups unsweetened coconut cream (preferably boxed), gently warmed

{ingredients continued on page 217}

MAKE THE CURRY PASTE

Use a pestle or heavy pan to lightly whack the cardamom pod to break the shell. Pry it open, take out the
seeds, and discard the shell. Combine the cardamom
seeds in a small pan with the coriander and cumin, set
the pan over low heat, and cook, stirring and tossing
often, until the spices are very fragrant and the coriander seeds turn a shade or two darker, about 8 minutes.
Let the spices cool slightly and pound them in a granite

{continued}

aahaan jaan diaw

TO SERVE ALONGSIDE

About 1 cup drained, chopped (into bite-size pieces) Thai pickled mustard greens (stems preferred for their crunch), soaked in water for 10 minutes and drained well

About 1 cup small (about 1/4-inch) wedges of peeled shallots, preferably Asian

6 small lime wedges (preferably from Key limes)

About 1 cup very coarsely chopped cilantro (thin stems and leaves), lightly packed

Naam Phrik Phao (Roasted chile paste), page 287

Thai fish sauce

---

mortar (or grind them in a spice grinder) to a coarse powder. Scoop the powder into a bowl and set aside.

Combine the dried chiles in the mortar with the salt and pound firmly, scraping the mortar and stirring the mixture after about 3 minutes, until you have a fairly fine powder, about 5 minutes. Add the lemongrass and pound until you have a fairly smooth, slightly fibrous paste, about 2 minutes. Do the same with the galangal, then the ginger, then the garlic, and then half of the shallots, fully pounding each ingredient before moving on to the next. Pound in the dried spice mixture, then the rest of the shallots. Finally, pound in the shrimp paste until it's fully incorporated, about 1 minute.

You'll have about 10 tablespoons of paste. You can use it right away, or store in an airtight container in the fridge for up to 1 week or in the freezer for up to 6 months. You'll need 5 tablespoons of paste for 6 bowls of khao soi.

MAKE THE CURRY

Heat the oil over medium-low heat in a large, heavy-bottomed pot until it shimmers, add 5 tablespoons of the curry paste and the turmeric powder and curry powder, and cook, breaking up the paste, then stirring frequently, until the paste smells very fragrant and loses the smell of raw garlic and shallots, about 8 minutes. Knowing when it's done takes experience, but as long as you're cooking at a low sizzle, the curry will taste great. Some of the paste might brown and stick to the pot, so occasionally scrape it to make sure it doesn't burn.

Add the fish sauce, soy sauce, palm sugar, and salt to the pot, increase the heat to medium-low, and cook, stirring often and breaking up the sugar once it softens, until the sugar has more or less fully melted, about 2 minutes. Add the chicken, tossing to coat the meat in the liquid. Cook for about 2 minutes so the chicken can absorb the flavors a bit, then stir in the coconut milk.

Increase the heat to medium high. Bring the liquid to a simmer (don't let it boil), then decrease the heat to maintain a gentle simmer. Cook, uncovered, stirring occasionally, until the meat comes easily from the bone but isn't falling off, about 45 minutes. You'll see droplets or even a layer of red oil on the surface. This is good. The broth will taste fairly salty and intense. Keep in mind that it will dilute slightly after you add the coconut cream later. You can keep the curry warm on the stove for up to 3 hours or in the fridge for up to 3 days. (It'll get even better as the flavors meld and the meat soaks up some of the curry.) Bring it to a very gentle simmer right before serving to make sure the chicken is heated through.

FINISH THE DISH

Pour enough oil into a wide medium pot to reach a depth of 2 inches and set the pot over medium-high heat. Heat the oil to 350°F (or test the temperature by dropping a piece of noodle into the oil; it should turn golden brown in about 20 seconds). Put 3 ounces of the noodles on a plate and gently toss them so there are no clumps. Fry them in 6 portions, turning over the nest of noodles once, just until the noodles are golden brown and crunchy, 20 to 45 seconds per batch. Transfer them to paper towels to drain. You can let them cool and store them for a day or two in an airtight container kept in a dry, cool place (not in the fridge).

When you're nearly ready to serve the curry, bring a large pot of water to a rolling boil. Add the remaining noodles and cook, stirring occasionally, just until the noodles are fully tender (you're not going for al dente here, but not mushy either), 2 to 3 minutes. Drain them well and divide them equally among 6 bowls.

To each bowl, add a thigh and drumstick, ladle on about 1 cup of the curry, spoon on 1/4 cup of the warm coconut cream, and top with a nest of fried noodles. Serve the bowls with a plate of pickled mustard greens, shallots, lime wedges, and cilantro; a bowl of the chile paste; and a bottle of fish sauce. Season your bowl and stir well before you dig in.

Phat Si Ew

STIR-FRIED RICE NOODLES WITH PORK, CHINESE BROCCOLI, AND SOY SAUCE

SPECIAL EQUIPMENT

- A Thai granite mortar and pestle
- A wok and wok spatula

I have American friends who swear by *phat si ew*. Because it's on the menu at every last Thai restaurant in the US, and no matter the quality of the place, they maintain, the dish is always pretty good. I do have fond memories of sitting down to a heap of thick rice noodles stir-fried with broccoli (if you're lucky, *Chinese* broccoli), egg, and sliced chicken breast, slicked with oil and tinted brown with sweet sauce. But I have to admit that I haven't for a long time eaten this stir-fry outside of Thailand. Not since my first time at Yok Far Pochana.

I was riding by puttering motorbike through Chiang Mai when I hit Ratchapakinai Road and spotted a fire. A giant wok rested on a jet engine of a portable burner, the screaming flames more effective for me than a billboard ad. I had to stop. I had to eat what was coming out of that wok. I placed my order and, minutes later, was presented with a small, spare portion of noodles, strips of pork, and thin-stemmed Chinese broccoli. It was essentially sauceless, barely sweet, and incredibly smoky. "Why is this so good?" I wondered, as I polished off the last curd of charred egg. Finding out, I discovered, was as easy as watching.

I looked on as the man presiding over the wok made *phat si ew* over and over. I must have stood there for an hour. Every order initiated the same brief process, which seemed to repeat itself infinitely. Into the wok went a little oil (barely any, I remember thinking). The main ingredients seemed never to stop moving, as the cook deftly tumbled them with two wok spatulas. A little sugar, a little soy sauce, and onto the plate. That was it—no obscure ingredients, no complicated pastes, just a handful of ingredients transmogrified by the wok.

This was one of my first inklings that despite its reputation for elaborate curries, Thai food could be remarkably simple. There was no magic, no secrets, no inscrutable ingredients. And it got me thinking, *Why couldn't someone do this in the US?*

Phat si ew turns out great in a wok on the stove set as high as it can go. But the ambitious among you should consider recreating the street vendor technique by employing the *tao* (see Using a Tao, page 90). A quick cook in a screaming-hot wok—what I now recognize to be the Chinese stir-fry technique—this is the key to achieving the smoky, charred flavor common to the best versions of the dish. My suggestion: Follow this recipe, which is calibrated for the stovetop, a few times before you attempt it on the *tao*. The cooking times will change, of course, and you'll have to rely on intuition, which comes with a little practice.

A NOTE ON Chinese Broccoli: The ideal Chinese broccoli for phat si ew is the young, thin-stemmed kind that's sometimes called gai lan miew (essentially, "little Chinese broccoli") or gai lan "tips" and occasionally labeled choy sum. (The term choy sum essentially means "small shoots" and is used to refer to many different vegetables in their young form.) If you can't find this type, you can make do with the thick-stemmed version.

Flavor Profile UMAMI-RICH, SMOKY, SALTY, AND A LITTLE SWEET

{continued}

{Stir-fried rice noodles with pork, Chinese broccoli, and soy sauce, continued}

PORK

1½ teaspoons vegetable oil

2 grams peeled garlic (about 1 small clove), lightly crushed into small pieces in a mortar

Scant 4 ounces boneless pork loin or lean shoulder, thinly sliced against the grain into bite-size (approximately ⅛-inch-thick) strips

½ teaspoon Thai fish sauce

¼ teaspoon granulated sugar

SERVES 1 AS A ONE-PLATE MEAL (TO MAKE MORE, DOUBLE OR QUADRUPLE THE INGREDIENTS, BUT COOK EACH BATCH SEPARATELY)

NOODLES

6 ounces fresh wide (about 1½-inch), flat rice noodles (see Wide Rice Noodles, page 19)

1 tablespoon Thai thin soy sauce

1 teaspoon Thai black soy sauce

1 teaspoon granulated sugar

Small pinch ground white pepper

1 tablespoon Naam Man Krathiem (Fried-garlic oil), page 272, or Naam Man Hom Daeng (Fried-shallot oil), page 273

1 large egg, at room temperature

11 grams peeled garlic cloves, halved lengthwise and lightly crushed into small pieces in a mortar (about 1 tablespoon)

2 ounces baby Chinese broccoli (see NOTE, page 218), stems trimmed to 1 or 2 inches and clusters separated, or regular Chinese broccoli, leaves coarsely chopped and stems thinly sliced

TO SERVE

Phrik Naam Plaa (Fish sauce–soaked chiles), page 286

Granulated sugar

Phrik Naam Som (Vinegar-soaked chiles), page 286

Phrik Phon Khua (Toasted-chile powder), page 270

COOK THE PORK

Heat a wok over very high heat, add the oil, and swirl it in the wok to coat the sides. When it begins to smoke lightly, add the garlic, take the wok off the heat, and let the garlic sizzle, stirring often, until it's fragrant but not colored, about 15 seconds.

Put the wok back on the heat, add the pork, and stir well. Then add the fish sauce and sugar and stir-fry (constantly stirring, scooping, and flipping the ingredients) until the pork is just cooked through, about 1 minute. Transfer the pork to a bowl. You can cover and refrigerate it for up to 2 days.

PREPARE THE NOODLES

Carefully separate the noodles. Unless you've found freshly made noodles, either microwave them briefly or briefly dunk them in boiling water (for a few seconds) just until they're pliable enough to separate without crumbling. Drain them well before proceeding.

STIR-FRY AND SERVE THE DISH

Combine the thin and black soy sauces, sugar, and pepper in a small bowl and stir well.

Wipe out the wok, if necessary, then heat it over very high heat, add the garlic oil, and swirl it in the wok to coat the sides. When the oil begins to smoke lightly, crack in the egg. It should spit and sizzle violently and the whites should bubble and puff. Cook without messing with it until the egg turns light golden brown at the edges, about 30 seconds. Flip the egg (it's fine if the yolk breaks), push it to one side of the wok (up the wall of the wok is fine).

Add the noodles and cook for 15 seconds or so, prodding and stirring them lightly them so they spread out a bit and don't clump together. Add the garlic and cook for 15 seconds or so, stirring to mix and to break up the noodles and egg slightly. Add the Chinese broccoli and stir-fry (constantly stirring, scooping, and flipping the ingredients) until the leaves just begin to wilt, about 15 seconds.

Add the pork, then the soy sauce mixture (add a splash of water, if necessary, to make sure nothing's left behind in the bowl), and stir-fry, letting the egg break up as you do, until the pork is heated through and the noodles have had a chance to absorb the liquids, about 1 minute. Transfer it to a plate and season to taste with the fish sauce, sugar, vinegar-soaked chiles, and chile powder.

̶'IR-FRIED RICE NOODLES WITH SHRIMP, TOFU, AND PEANUTS

had eaten a lot of *phat thai* before December 5, 1999. I'd devoured it at Thai Me Up, Appe-Thai-zing, and other pun-happy restaurants from Portland, Oregon, to Burlington, Vermont. I'd eaten it in backpacker ghettos throughout Thailand. I don't remember any of those versions, just a blur of sweet-tart noodles.

That December day, when truly remarkable *phat thai* came into focus, was King Bhumibol Adulyadej's birthday. Like a good tourist, I went down to the palace in Bangkok to see the pageantry. Soon after I did, I decamped from the main plaza to escape the heat and the crowds. And to look for lunch. That was when I came upon a place that specialized in *phat thai*. Now, at the time, that seemed strange. *Phat thai* didn't seem to me like a dish worth devotion. As usual, I had a reckoning coming.

Phat thai has become perhaps Thailand's best-known export (culinary and otherwise), vaulting past mere restaurant-menu ubiquity into microwavable-dinner territory. Yet the dish as it exists in Thailand outside of the tourist enclaves remains just one tasty snack among many. Which is why its origin stories—many of them apocryphal, I'm sure—might come as letdowns. I defer on the matter to chef-scholar David Thompson, whose book *Thai Street Food* points to a national contest promoted by former Field Marshall Phibun in the late 1930s and early '40s. Befitting the jingoistic mood of the day, Thompson explains, the goal was to create a noodle dish (most of which were Chinese in origin and spirit) that was distinctly Thai. And so the winning dish won the now-familiar name, which literally means "Thai stir-fry."

Sometimes a Thai dish will impress you because it has *more* funk or heat or some other quality that tourist versions typically tone down. My first taste of good *phat thai* stayed with me for the opposite reason: It was *less* spicy, sweet, and tangy than those I'd eaten previously—and it was better for it. This minimalism binds all of my favorite versions. Of course, variations abound, because, in case you haven't tired of me saying it, there is no authentic example that all others aspire to. I've had *phat thai* made with fresh shrimp, with pork, and with crab. I've had it made with glass noodles. I've had it stir-fried, then wrapped like a present in a thin omelet. Besides the sugar, chile powder, fish sauce, and lime wedges offered alongside so you can season your portion, you'll often find tannic slices of banana blossom or the herb pennywort. *Phat thai* is rich, and a bite of this or that between bites is refreshing.

Years of watching vendors make the dish, peppering them with awkward questions, and eating small pile after pile off of plates, banana leaves, and even newspaper yielded a basic understanding of how to make *phat thai*. I noted the little details that marked the renditions I liked best, like the rendered pork fat with which old-school vendors insist on stir-frying, and the slower, more gentle cooking in a flat pan many vendors prefer to a brief trip in a hot wok.

Still, for a long time I was reluctant to serve it at my restaurants. I didn't want to give in to cliché. Soon I was sneaking it onto the late-night menu at Whiskey Soda Lounge. Then I opened a storefront on Manhattan's Lower East Side devoted to it. Go figure.

{continued}

aahaan jaan diaw

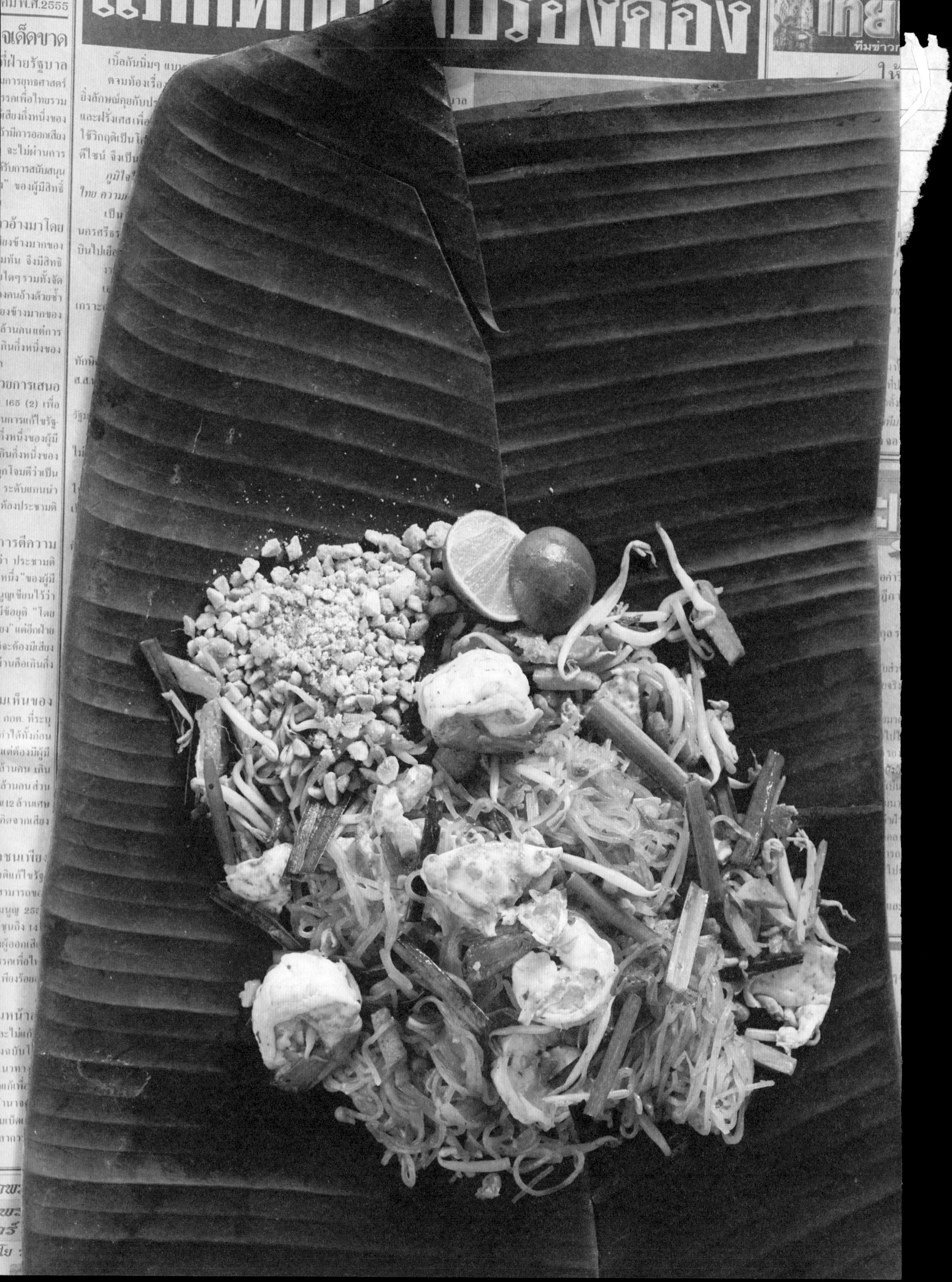

Flavor Profile SLIGHTLY SWEET, SLIGHTLY TART, AND UMAMI-RICH

SERVES 1 AS A ONE-PLATE MEAL (TO MAKE MORE, DOUBLE OR QUADRUPLE THE INGREDIENTS, BUT COOK EACH BATCH SEPARATELY)

SHRIMP AND SAUCE

1 tablespoon medium-size dried shrimp, rinsed and patted dry

3 tablespoons Naam Makham (Tamarind water), page 275

2 tablespoons plus 3/4 teaspoon Naam Cheuam Naam Taan Piip (Palm sugar simple syrup), page 275

1 1/2 tablespoons Thai fish sauce

STIR-FRY

4 ounces (about 2 cups, tightly packed) semi-dried thin, flat rice noodles (sometimes labeled "phat thai"), see NOTE

2 tablespoons rendered pork fat or vegetable oil

1 large egg, at room temperature

1 1/4 ounces unflavored pressed tofu (firmer than "extra firm"), cut into small pieces (about 1 inch long, 1/2 inch wide, and 1/4 inch thick), about 1/4 cup

1 tablespoon shredded salted radish, soaked in water 10 minutes then drained

2 ounces bean sprouts (about 1 cup, lightly packed)

2 ounces medium shrimp, (about 4), shelled and deveined

1/4 cup very coarsely chopped (about 1-inch lengths) garlic chives, plus a pinch or two for finishing

2 generous tablespoons coarsely chopped unsalted roasted peanuts

TO SERVE ALONGSIDE

2 small lime wedges (preferably from a Key lime)

Fish sauce

Granulated sugar

Phrik Naam Som (Vinegar-soaked chiles), page 286

Phrik Phon Khua (Toasted-chile powder), page 270

NOTE: Semi-dried noodles (fairly pliable rather than brittle, like fully dried) are widely available in the refrigerated sections of Asian markets. If you can't find semi-dried noodles, you can substitute 2 1/4 ounces of fully dried "phat thai" noodles soaked in lukewarm water for about 10 extra minutes (to approximate the texture of semi-dried noodles).

TOAST THE SHRIMP AND MAKE THE SAUCE

Heat a small dry pan or wok over medium heat, add the dried shrimp, and cook, stirring frequently, until they're dry all the way through and slightly crispy, about 5 minutes. Set them aside in a small bowl. Covered at room temperature, they'll keep for up to 1 week.

Combine the tamarind water, simple syrup, and fish sauce in a small bowl and stir well. Measure 1/4 cup plus 2 tablespoons, discarding the rest.

SOAK THE NOODLES AND STIR-FRY THE DISH

Soak the noodles in lukewarm water until they're very pliable but not fully soft, about 20 minutes. Dain them well and snip them into approximately 8-inch lengths just before stir-frying.

Heat a large, heavy skillet over medium-high heat (or a wok over very high heat), add the pork fat, and swirl it to coat the sides. When it begins to smoke lightly, crack the egg into the center of the pan (it should spit and sizzle violently and the whites should bubble and puff). Add the tofu, radish, and dried shrimp beside the egg. If you're using a skillet, decrease the heat to medium; if you're using a wok, keep the heat very high.

Cook, stirring everything but the egg, until the edges of the egg are light golden brown, about 1 minute, then flip the egg (it's fine if the yolk breaks), break the egg into several pieces with the spatula, and stir everything together well.

Add the noodles and bean sprouts, and stir-fry (constantly stirring, scooping, and flipping) until the noodles and bean sprouts have softened slightly, about 1 minute.

Add the shrimp, then stir the tamarind mixture once more and add it to the pan. Stir-fry, making sure the shrimp get plenty of time on the hot surface, until they are cooked through, just about all the liquid has evaporated, and the noodles are fully tender and no longer look gloppy or clumpy, 2 to 4 minutes.

Add the chives and 1 tablespoon of the peanuts. Stir-fry briefly, then transfer it all to a plate, sprinkle on the remaining peanuts and chives, and serve with the lime wedges. Season to taste with the fish sauce, sugar, vinegar-soaked chiles, and chile powder.

Hoi Thawt

BROKEN CREPE WITH MUSSELS

This is a one-plate meal that you don't eat with rice and that doesn't contain noodles. Why is it here, then? Since it didn't fit neatly into any of the requisite cookbook chapters, I present it here, right after *phat thai*, which is often cooked in the same vessel (a slightly concave slab of steel), using some of the same ingredients (egg, bean sprouts, and garlic chives), and by the same vendors.

My first bite came in Hua Hin, a town on the Gulf of Thailand, a quintessential Thai beach resort. Although in the West, resorts suggest long stretches of white-sand beach dotted with sunbathers, here it means a rocky shore, brisk winds, ruddy sand, and a shitload of tables, chairs, and hawker stands every twenty feet—selling not hot dogs and funnel cake, but full-blown food. For Thais, diversion means eating, and eating near the sea typically means seafood, even if there's not a fishing fleet in sight.

Hua Hin is a seafood center, and a town known for good food. At night, when the sun sets, a street filled with strolling vacationers transforms into a vast hive of commerce—stalls selling produce and trinkets and T-shirts and, of course, dinner. Vendors roll out full kitchens. It's like a massive pop-up restaurant that serves thousands of people every night. Much of the food sold here is *aahaan tham sang*, or "food made to order." Vegetables, herbs, and seafood are laid out on ice. Cooks employ woks, steamers, and grills to make virtually whatever you request.

One night I sidled up to a particularly busy stall, and the response to my eager look was an insistent offer in intelligible English: "Oyster omelet?" Typically, rule number one as a whitey trolling a market is to not accept the first offer, because it's often something tailored to Western tastes and not worth the stomach space. But I accepted, and watched as the woman ladled a loose batter into the hot oil pooling in her barely concave pan, scattered on a handful of fat oysters, and cracked on an egg. Once the bubbling oil had browned and crisped the thin crepelike pancake, she added bean sprouts and garlic chives. Then she used what looked like a long-handled shovel to tear the crepe into pieces. A toss, a stir, and she transferred it to a flimsy plastic plate.

I didn't know it at the time, but I was eating *hoi thawt*, a common sight on streets and in night markets all over the country. Mediocre versions abound, but a really good version, like the one I stumbled upon in Hua Hin, is an incredible thing—a pile of broken crepe, some of it crispy, some chewy and soft, as messy as it is tasty. I could spend all day watching vendors make this dish, each with his or her own technique, including my favorite to observe: the flinging of the batter sideways onto the pan so it scatters.

At Pok Pok, we use Prince Edward Island mussels rather than the fingertip-sized mussels or the large, plump, rather unbriny oysters they use in Thailand. We use thin rolled-steel pans to approximate the typical market vessels, though you can get by with a frying pan, cast-iron skillet, or large griddle. You need plenty of oil to make this dish work. *Thawt* means deep-fried, though the pancake is never submerged in fat, but instead drifts like a raft on a river of oil. Even the good versions are a bit greasy.

{continued}

{Broken crepe with mussels, continued}

NOTE ON SRIRACHA: In Thailand, there's a town called Sri Racha that's famous for its eponymous hot sauce. This sauce, not the Sriracha made by the California-based Vietnamese-American company Huy Fong Foods that has conquered America, is what you want for this dish. The "rooster brand" sauce has its virtues, but it's too harsh for hoi thawt. Look for the Shark brand and, if that fails, another Thai brand, and welcome a different Sriracha into your pantry.

Flavor Profile RICH, SALTY, SLIGHTLY FISHY

SERVES 1 AS A ONE-PLATE MEAL (OR 2 TO 4 AS PART OF A MEAL)

1 cup plus 1 tablespoon water

8 ounces Prince Edward Island mussels, scrubbed and debearded

1/2 cup ounces bánh xèo mix, preferably Vinh Thuan brand (see NOTE)

2 tablespoons tempura batter mix (preferably Gogi brand)

1/4 cup very coarsely chopped garlic chives (about 1-inch lengths), plus a large pinch for finishing

Pinch ground white pepper

1/2 teaspoon Thai fish sauce, plus a few dashes

Vegetable oil (enough for a 1/8-inch-deep layer in your skillet)

1 large egg, at room temperature

2 ounces bean sprouts (about 1 cup, lightly packed)

Thai Sriracha sauce, such as Shark brand (*not* the rooster brand or any other American-made versions)

NOTE: In Thailand, you'd buy a bagged mixture made specifically for hoi thawt. In the US, your best bet is to buy bánh xèo mix, which is similar but meant for the eponymous Vietnamese crepe, and augment it with tempura flour, as I recommend. Look for the product in Asian markets, particularly those with a Southeast Asian focus.

STEAM THE MUSSELS

Pour 1/2 cup of the water in a medium pot, set it over high heat, and bring it to a boil. Add the mussels, cover the pot, and decrease the heat to medium. Cook, gently shaking the pot occasionally, until the mussels pop open, about 3 minutes, transferring them to a bowl as they open and discarding any that haven't opened after 6 minutes. Let the cooked mussels cool slightly, then remove the meat and discard the shells.

MAKE THE CREPE

Combine the banh xeo mix, tempura flour, and the remaining 1/2 cup plus 1 tablespoon of water in a mixing bowl and whisk until you have a very smooth, thin batter. In another mixing bowl, combine the shucked mussels, the 1/4 cup of garlic chives, the pepper, 1/2 teaspoon of the fish sauce, and 1/2 cup of the batter and stir well.

Pour enough oil into a large (at least 12 inches wide) frying pan or skillet—preferably steel or cast-iron, though nonstick will do—to reach a depth of 1/8 inch, and set the pan over high heat. When the oil smokes lightly, stir the mussel mixture and add it to the pan. (It should spread in the pan to form a rough circle with a thickness halfway between that of a crepe and a pancake; if need be, coax it with the spatula.) Decrease the heat to maintain a steady sizzle.

Crack the egg into the middle of the circle of batter, and prod the yolk so it breaks. Try to keep the egg from spilling onto the pan. Wait about a minute without doing a thing, then slip the spatula under the edges of the circle to loosen them and cook, using the spatula to turn the circle around a few times to make sure it's cooking evenly, until the edges look crispy and light golden brown, about 2 minutes.

Use the spatula to push the circle to one side of the pan, add the bean sprouts to the other, and sprinkle a few dashes of fish sauce on the bean sprouts. Carefully flip the circle onto the bean sprouts. Lift the pan from the stove, steady the crepe with the spatula, and pour off as much oil as you can.

Return the pan to the heat and cook until the crepe is fully cooked through but still soft in the middle, about 30 seconds. Use the spatula to break the crepe into roughly 2-inch pieces.

Transfer it to a plate, leaving any remaining oil behind. Add the remaining garlic chives, and serve with a small bowl of the Sriracha sauce.

Kuaytiaw Khua Kai

STIR-FRIED NOODLES WITH CHICKEN, EGG, AND CUTTLEFISH ON LETTUCE

To Americans, this might sound like a culinary experiment gone wrong. Yet one night, my friend Austin Bush, an ex-pat and voracious photographer, traveler, and eater, led me through Yaowarat, Bangkok's Chinatown. I followed him along the hectic main drag, clogged with traffic and bright-lit signage. We passed countless outdoor restaurants, their plastic chairs monopolizing the sidewalks. Austin nodded in the direction of a few other vendors who made this unusual dish, but he was taking me to the man who did it best.

We slid down an alley where kids dodged stray dogs and where a man with a boxer's nose presided over a charcoal fire and brass wok, as he's been doing for more than forty years. Austin ordered, and I looked on as the man briskly prodded and stirred our noodles with a metal spoon. He added egg, sliced chicken, and brown hunks of preserved cuttlefish, stir-fried some more, then dumped the jumble into two small bowls lined with lettuce leaves. We ate at an old wood table in the alley, which Austin likes to call the dining room. Now I know the dish is not strange at all. Chinese noodle dishes often mix meat and seafood, and lettuce ends up in stir-fries and even noodle soups.

This dish is nothing if not straightforward. The seasoning is spare. But little details—a little rendered pork fat, a wok hot enough to slightly char and crisp the noodles—made this stir-fry a revelation. At Pok Pok Phat Thai, in Manhattan, we stay true to the original, except for the crunchy preserved cuttlefish (an acquired taste). In its place, we use fresh cuttlefish, which has a meaty texture, though at home you can use the easier-to-find fresh squid instead.

Like so many noodle dishes, this one comes mildly seasoned. Everyone's meant to add fish sauce, sugar, and season to his or her taste.

Flavor Profile SALTY, UMAMI-RICH, AND SLIGHTLY SMOKY

SERVES 1 AS A ONE-PLATE MEAL (TO MAKE MORE, DOUBLE OR QUADRUPLE THE INGREDIENTS, BUT COOK EACH BATCH SEPARATELY)

6 ounces fresh wide (about 1½-inch), flat rice noodles (see Wide Rice Noodles, page 19)

1 large egg, at room temperature

1 tablespoon Thai oyster sauce

1 tablespoon Thai fish sauce

1 teaspoon granulated sugar

Pinch ground white pepper

10 or so 2-inch pieces torn green leaf lettuce

2 tablespoons rendered pork fat, Naam Man Krathiem (Fried-garlic oil), page 272, or vegetable oil

4 ounces boneless, skinless chicken breast, thinly sliced into bite-size pieces

¼ cup sliced green onions (about ¼-inch lengths), plus a little extra for finishing

2 ounces fresh raw cuttlefish or squid bodies, cut into bite-size pieces

TO SERVE ALONGSIDE

Phrik Naam Plaa (Fish sauce–soaked chiles), page 286

Granulated sugar

Phrik Naam Som (Vinegar-soaked chiles), page 286

Phrik Phon Khua (Toasted-chile powder), page 270

PREPARE THE NOODLES

Carefully separate the noodles. Unless you've found freshly made noodles, either microwave them briefly or briefly dunk them in boiling water (for a few seconds) just until they're pliable enough to separate without crumbling. Drain them well before proceeding.

{continued}

{Stir-fried noodles with chicken, egg, and cuttlefish on lettuce, continued}

STIR-FRY AND SERVE THE DISH

Combine the egg, oyster sauce, fish sauce, sugar, and pepper in a small bowl and beat together well. Line a large shallow serving bowl with the lettuce.

Heat a wok over very high heat, add the fat, and swirl it in the wok to coat the sides. When it begins to lightly smoke, add the chicken and stir-fry (constantly stirring, scooping, and flipping the ingredients) until the slices are barely cooked through, about 1 minute.

Add the cuttlefish, stir-fry briefly, then push the chicken and cuttlefish to one side of the wok. Add the noodles to the center, prodding and stirring them lightly so they don't clump together. Decrease the heat to medium-high, scoop the chicken and cuttlefish on top of the noodles, and cook them, undisturbed, for

20 seconds or so. Ideally, the noodles will bubble and blister at the edges.

Stir the egg mixture once more, pour it directly onto the noodles, then sprinkle on 1/4 cup of the green onions. Use the wok spatula to flip over the noodle-egg bundle onto the chicken and cuttlefish and cook undisturbed for about 1 minute.

Use the wok spatula to break up the bundle and stir-fry until the cuttlefish is completely cooked, about 1 minute more.

Transfer the noodles to the lettuce leaves, and sprinkle on the extra green onions. Season to taste with the fish sauce, sugar, vinegar-soaked chiles, and chile powder.

Khanom Jiin

THREE WAYS WITH THAILAND'S INDIGENOUS NOODLE

When the evening comes, Talaat San Paa Khoi transforms from a typical market selling produce and meat into a sort of cafeteria for Chiang Mai's *khanom jiin* cognoscenti. Cheap, colorful tablecloths are thrown over the tables that once held bushels of water hyacinth and clusters of *long gong*. You roll up to a vendor standing before huge pots containing curries, one brick-red, another orange, another pale green. You watch her ladle one into a bowl and hand it to a customer. Even many accomplished curry eaters might wonder, "Where's the rice?"

But look closer. At the bottom of the bowl are three small coils of noodles, and not just any noodles. They're *khanom jiin*, which have the distinction, according to mega-scholar David Thompson, of being Thailand's only indigenous noodle.

For centuries, the laborious process required to make these thin strands of fermented rice dough consigned them to religious ceremonies and other special occasions. But less than a century ago, says Thompson, machines made it easy and *khanom jiin* became a common sight. Bundles of them are on display at markets, piled up like skeins of yarn and sold fresh by the kilo. Or they're sold topped with all manner of soupy currylike dishes at dedicated food stalls, especially during the morning. You'll find these stalls everywhere from markets to truck stops to barbershops—or at least one barbershop that I stumbled upon. The barber's wife was a good cook, so why not?

The curries that follow can sit for hours after they're made. In fact, they're better after they rest and best eaten at just above room temperature.

REPLICATING KHANOM JIIN

The thin, fermented rice noodles are close to impossible to find in the US. To approximate them at home, do as we do at Pok Pok and buy Vietnamese or Thai dried rice vermicelli, then follow these steps: Bring a large pot of water to a boil and cook the noodles, stirring often, according to the package instructions, because different brands might require different cooking times. You do not want al dente noodles. They should be fully soft, but not cooked so long that they turn to mush.

Meanwhile, prepare a large bowl of cold water filled with ice cubes and a large bowl of lukewarm water. Drain the noodles in a large colander, then rinse them well under lukewarm running water for about 1 minute to wash off the starch. Shake the colander to drain the noodles, then transfer the colander with the noodles to the ice water, gently stirring the noodles with your hand. When the noodles have fully cooled, transfer the noodles to the bowl of lukewarm water to hold them as you make the coils. Each recipe calls for a little more than you'll actually use, because some noodles will inevitably break or be otherwise unfit for forming the coils.

Set a wire cooling rack or a similar perforated surface over a tray or platter. Grab about 2 ounces of noodles (weigh it the first time, then eyeball thereafter) with one hand. Wrap them around the middle three fingers of your other hand, starting at your fingertips and working toward your palm. (If instead you start at the base of your fingers, the coil will unravel later.)

Transfer the coil to the rack, letting it slide off your fingers. Repeat with the remaining noodles, overlapping or stacking the coils if necessary. Let them drain at room temperature until they're dry, at least 20 minutes or up to several hours. (Don't store them in the fridge.)

Ideally, you'd serve them at what I like to think of as Thai room temperature, which is a bit higher (let's call it 90°F) than the typical room temperature in the US. Transfer them to shallow serving bowls and microwave on low, just until they reach this temperature, no more than 30 seconds.

Khanom Jiin Naam Yaa

THAI RICE NOODLES WITH FISH-AND-KRACHAI CURRY

THE PLAN

- **Up to several months in advance:** Make the shrimp paste

- **Up to 1 week in advance:** Toast the dried chiles

- **A few hours in advance:** Prepare the rice vermicelli, make the curry, and cook the eggs

SPECIAL EQUIPMENT

- A Thai granite mortar and pestle

SERVES 6 AS A ONE-PLATE MEAL

This version of the curry requires no laborious pounding of ingredients in the mortar and pestle, although I'm pretty sure it did in the days before blenders. Heavy on the *krachai*, a spindly relative of ginger, and thickened with pureed fish, the distinctive curry is an eye-opener for anyone raised on the standard red curry with chicken.

Flavor Profile EARTHY, RICH, MODERATELY SPICY, SLIGHTLY FISHY, SALTY

CURRY

5 ounces peeled Asian shallots, halved (quartered if large)

1 ounce peeled garlic cloves, coarsely chopped into approximately 1/2-inch pieces

9 grams peeled fresh or frozen (not defrosted) galangal, thinly sliced against the grain

14 grams thinly sliced lemongrass (tender parts only), from about 2 large stalks

1 1/4 ounces fresh or frozen (not defrosted) whole krachai (wild ginger), unpeeled, washed especially well, and thinly sliced crosswise

7 grams stemmed dried Mexican puya chiles (about 4)

1 tablespoon Kapi Kung (Homemade shrimp paste), page 274

6 pickled gouramy fish fillets

1 1/2 pounds fresh or defrosted frozen basa fillets (also known as swai or pangasius), or fillets from another mild, firm white-fleshed freshwater fish, any straggling bones removed and flesh cut into 2-inch chunks

1 tablespoon kosher salt

2 cups unsweetened coconut milk (preferably boxed)

1/4 cup Thai fish sauce or more to taste

12 ounces Vietnamese or Thai dried rice vermicelli, prepared according to the instructions on page 231

ACCOMPANIMENTS (PICK A FEW)

3 Khai Tom (Eight-minute eggs), page 270, quartered

Dried Thai chiles, toasted (page 12)

Drained Thai pickled mustard greens, soaked in water for 10 minutes, drained again, then chopped into small bite-size pieces

Bean sprouts, dunked in boiling water, shocked in ice water, and drained well

Finely shredded white cabbage

Sprigs of lemon basil (bai menglak in Thai)

Lime wedges (preferably from Key limes)

MAKE THE CURRY

Combine the shallots, garlic, galangal, lemongrass, krachai, chiles, and shrimp paste in a small pot with 1 cup of water. Set it over high heat, bring the water to a simmer, cover, and decrease the heat to maintain a steady simmer. Cook, stirring occasionally, until all the ingredients, including the galangal and chiles, are tender, 20 to 25 minutes.

Meanwhile, preheat a grill pan or skillet over medium heat (or better yet, grill over a low charcoal fire). Put the gouramy fillets on a double-layer of aluminum foil (or banana leaf) and fold to make a

package. Add the foil package to the hot surface and cook, turning it over occasionally, until you can smell the floral funk of the gouramy, about 15 minutes. Open the gouramy package, discard any large bones and fins (don't try to remove the small bones), and transfer the gouramy to a granite mortar. Firmly pound it to a fine paste and until the bones have fully broken down, about 45 seconds. Once the krachai mixture is finished cooking, add 2 tablespoons of the gouramy paste, reserving any extra for another purpose.

Put the basa in a medium pot, pour in just enough water to cover the fish, stir in the salt, cover the pot, and set it over high heat. Bring the water to a boil, turn off the heat, and leave the pot covered until the fish is cooked through, about 2 minutes. Add the fish to a blender along with just enough of its cooking water (reserve the rest), to help it blend to a very thick puree. You might need to stir and prod the mixture occasionally.

Transfer the fish puree to a large pot. Add the cooked vegetable mixture, liquid included, to the blender, blend until very smooth, and add it to the pot with the fish puree. Measure 3 cups of the remaining fish-boiling liquid (or add enough fresh water to the liquid to make 3 cups); add to the blender, swish it around, and add it to the pot along with the coconut milk and fish sauce.

Set the pot over medium heat, bring the mixture to a rolling simmer, cover, and cook, stirring occasionally and adjusting the heat to maintain a steady simmer, until the mixture thickens slightly (it should still be soupy with a slightly grainy texture) and the flavors have had a chance to meld, about 15 minutes. Turn off the heat and let the curry cool to warm or, even better, just above room temperature. Taste and consider adding more fish sauce, keeping in mind that the curry is meant to be poured over bland noodles and should therefore be highly seasoned.

At this point, the curry will keep in the fridge for up to a few days. Before serving, gently reheat the curry.

ASSEMBLE THE THE DISH

Divide the noodles among 6 bowls, stir the curry well, then spoon a cup or so of the curry over each serving. Serve with the remaining ingredients alongside. Let everyone garnish and season the curry themselves.

Khanom Jiin Naam Ngiew

THAI RICE NOODLES WITH NORTHERN THAI CURRY

THE PLAN

- Up to 1 week in advance: Make the curry paste and toast the dried chiles

- A few hours in advance: Make the curry, prepare the rice noodles, and cook the eggs

SPECIAL EQUIPMENT

- A Thai granite mortar and pestle

SERVES 6 AS A ONE-PLATE MEAL

Exclusively from Northern Thailand, this brothy currylike dish features tomatoes, pork ribs, and chunks of steamed blood. My recipe contains more of this meat, by the way, than you'll likely see in markets or rural renditions. I make only one concession to convenience, leaving out the tough-to-find dried flower called *dawk ngiew* that gives renditions in Thailand a darker color and provides a little texture.

Flavor Profile MEATY AND UMAMI-RICH, SALTY, TART, SLIGHTLY SPICY

CURRY PASTE

7 grams stemmed dried Mexican puya chiles (about 4)

1/2 teaspoon kosher salt

6 grams cilantro roots, thinly sliced

7 grams thinly sliced lemongrass (tender parts only), from about 1 large stalk

9 grams peeled fresh or frozen (not defrosted) galangal, thinly sliced against grain

10 grams peeled fresh or frozen (not defrosted) yellow turmeric root, thinly sliced against grain

1 tablespoon plus 1 teaspoon Kapi Kung (Homemade shrimp paste), page 274

CURRY

1 pound pork spareribs, cut lengthwise across the bone into 2-inch-wide racks by your butcher (most Asian butchers sell them already cut), then cut into individual ribs, rinsed well

1 1/2 teaspoons kosher salt

4 1/2 cups water

12 ounces lean ground beef

1 1/2 tablespoons Thai fish sauce

1 1/2 teaspoons Thai thin soy sauce

1/2 teaspoon Thai yellow bean sauce

1 1/2 teaspoons granulated sugar

8 ounces cherry tomatoes (about 12), halved

4 ounces steamed blood, cut into 3/4-inch cubes

12 ounces Vietnamese or Thai dried rice vermicelli, prepared according to page 231

ACCOMPANIMENTS (PICK A FEW)

3 Khai Tom (Eight-minute eggs), page 270, quartered

Drained Thai pickled mustard greens, soaked in water for 10 minutes, drained again, then chopped into small bite-sized pieces

Bean sprouts, dunked in boiling water, shocked in ice water, and drained well

Finely shredded white cabbage

Dried Thai chiles, toasted (page 12)

MAKE THE PASTE

Combine the dried chiles in the mortar with the salt and pound firmly, scraping the mortar and stirring the mixture after about 3 minutes, until you have a fairly fine powder, about 5 minutes. Add the cilantro roots and pound, occasionally stopping to scrape down the sides of the mortar, until you have a fairly smooth, slightly fibrous paste, about 2 minutes. Do the same with the lemongrass, then the galangal, then the turmeric, fully pounding each ingredient before moving on to the next.

Pound in the shrimp paste until it's fully incorporated, about 1 minute.

You'll have about 1/4 cup of paste. You can use it right away or store it in the fridge for up to 1 week, or in the freezer for up to 6 months. You'll need all of this paste for 6 bowls.

COOK THE CURRY

Combine the pork and salt in a medium pot along with the 4 1/2 cups water. Set the pot over high heat, bring the

{continued}

{Thai rice noodles with Northern Thai curry, continued}

water to a simmer, then decrease the heat to maintain a steady simmer, skimming off any scum from the surface. After 30 minutes, stir in all of the curry paste, beef, fish sauce, soy sauce, yellow bean sauce, and sugar. Keep cooking until the pork is tender but still chewy (you'll be able to pull the meat from the bone with a fork but with some resistance), about 15 minutes more.

Add the tomatoes and blood cubes and cook until they're both hot through, about 5 minutes more. Turn off the heat and let the curry cool to warm or, even

better, just above room temperature. Taste and consider adding more fish sauce, keeping in mind that the dish is meant to be poured over bland noodles and should therefore be highly seasoned.

ASSEMBLE THE DISH

Divide the noodles among 6 bowls, then spoon a generous cup of broth and some of the meat, blood, and tomatoes over each one. Serve with the remaining ingredients alongside.

AJAAN SUNEE

A dirt lane brought me and a friend to a restaurant in Mae Rim built in someone's backyard. One of my favorite dishes on the table that day was *jin som*, sour fermented ground pork. It struck me as unusual that it was heated through but didn't have grill marks (the dish is often grilled) or come in a banana leaf (if it were grilled inside, that'd explain the lack of marks, though foods grilled in leaves are almost invariably served in them). This was typical, me setting upon some trivial wonder and feeling compelled to understand it.

Lucky for me I was with *Ajaan* Sunee. *Ajaan* is similar to the English title "professor" and a sign of respect when it precedes a name. Since well before we met in 1993, *Ajaan* Sunee has taught home economics at Chiang Mai University and earned a reputation as a great cook and a fine professor who inspires devotion in her students. A diminutive woman in teacherly spectacles, she often shows up to meet me for dinner with a homemade snack (last time she brought deep-fried, noodle-wrapped pork balls) and with (surprise!) five students in tow.

I met her through my friends Sunny and Lakhana, and she quickly became my *ajaan*. I'd come to her after wide-eyed trips to prepared-food markets, weighed down with mysterious soups, stews, and relishes in pudgy to-go bags, and ask, "Can you show me how to cook this?" Then she would.

She has a lot of knowledge to share. Like many of my Thai friends, she grew up just outside of Chiang Mai, thirty miles or so north in a village called Ban Chaw Lae. For a living, her parents grew potatoes and garlic on their twenty-seven-acre property, which included a large barn for drying the garlic. I get the sense that Sunee and her family lived comfortably. Still, they didn't buy much. She recalls picking vegetables that they'd planted between the rows of for-sale crops, foraging for wild herbs, and fishing in the irrigation ditches. Since she was a girl she has cooked local dishes with her mother, aunts, and grandmother.

Now she has a gig through the local government for which she travels to small villages, often those of indigenous groups, to learn about the food they cook and assess its healthfuless. I could listen for hours while she rattles off all the dishes she's come across—a *naam phrik* made from tiny eggplants and fried pork skins, soups made with the rodents that inhabit rice fields, and betel leaf packages enclosing the unusual combination of dried shrimp, ginger, toasted–sticky rice powder, and the liquid from fermented tea leaves. She has exponentially expanded my knowledge of Thai food.

In other words, if anyone was going to help me figure out how that sour sausage was made so hot and delicious without a grill, it was *Ajaan* Sunee. I took the lead and asked the vendor in Thai how she'd heated it. The woman answered, "*Sai wehb*." The first part, *sai*, I knew meant "in." The second, I didn't recognize. "In" what? Did I stumble upon a new (or at least, new-to-me) cooking technique? I wouldn't have been surprised. In the genre of grilling alone, I knew of five methods, each with a different name. This could have been number six.

I turned to Sunee, my face betraying my cluelessness. She and the vendor cracked up. "Wehb," said Sunee, between cackles, in her thickly accented English. "Like 'Microwehb.'" The woman had heated it up in a microwave. As much as I value having an *ajaan* in Sunee, sometimes all I need is a friend to laugh at my ignorance and then tell me the right answer.

Phat Khanom Jiin

STIR-FRIED THAI RICE NOODLES

SPECIAL EQUIPMENT

- **A wok and wok spatula**

Thais snack on this simple stir-fry made from leftover *khanom jiin* (page 231). It's meant for celebratory occasions—like a wedding or Thai New Year—because the long noodles represent long life and the golden color represents good fortune. In the US, we have to take the extra step of boiling dried rice noodles before they're ready for the hot wok, but it's well worth it.

Flavor Profile UMAMI-RICH, SWEET, AND SALTY

SERVES 1 AS A ONE-PLATE MEAL

4 ounces Vietnamese or Thai dried rice vermicelli	1¹/₂ teaspoons Thai thin soy sauce	2 tablespoons Hom Jiaw Daeng (Fried shallots), page 273
¹/₄ cup Naam Man Krathiem (Fried-garlic oil), page 272, or Naam Man Hom Daeng (Fried-shallot oil), page 273	1¹/₂ teaspoons Thai oyster sauce	A few dashes Thai fish sauce
	1 tablespoon granulated sugar	
1 tablespoon Thai black soy sauce	¹/₂ teaspoon kosher salt	

COOK THE NOODLES

Bring a large pot of water to a boil. Cook the noodles, stirring often, according to the package instructions. You do not want al dente noodles. They should be fully soft, but not cooked so long that they turn to mush.

Prepare a large bowl of cold water and ice cubes. Drain the noodles well in a colander, then rinse them well under lukewarm running water to wash off the starch. Shake the colander to drain the noodles well, then transfer it to the ice water, gently stirring the noodles with your hands. When the noodles have fully cooled, drain them well once more and let them sit in the colander, shaking it occasionally, for about 30 minutes.

STIR-FRY THE NOODLES

Toss the noodles well in a large bowl with 2 tablespoons of the oil. In a small bowl, stir together both soy sauces, the oyster sauce, the sugar, and the salt until the sugar and salt mostly dissolve. Add the mixture to the noodles and toss to coat well. (I like to use a handful of noodles to mop up any sauce stuck to the small bowl and return it to the bowl of noodles.) Let the noodles sit in the sauce for 10 minutes or so.

Heat a wok over very high heat, add the remaining 2 tablespoons of oil, and swirl it in the wok to coat the sides. When it begins to smoke lightly, add the noodles and 1 tablespoon of the fried shallots. Stir-fry (constantly stirring, scooping, and flipping the ingredients) until the noodles are hot through and have had a chance to absorb the sauce, 2 to 3 minutes. It's fine if the noodles break as you stir. Taste and gradually season with a little more sugar and some of the fish sauce, if you'd like.

SERVE THE NOODLES

Transfer the noodles to a plate, let them cool slightly, and sprinkle on the remaining tablespoon of fried shallots. Toss well before you eat it.

AAHAAN FARANG
Foreign food

There are several reasons why I don't like to call Pok Pok a Thai restaurant, the simplest of which is that not all the food we serve is Thai. Elsewhere in this book, you'll find recipes for foreign food so transformed by Thai cooks that the result becomes inextricably Thai. The dishes in this chapter have nothing to do with Thailand. They're just dishes I encountered and fell for during trips through Asia.

Stir-Fried Yunnan Ham with Chiles

SPECIAL EQUIPMENT

- A Thai granite mortar and pestle
- A wok and wok spatula

Years ago, as a hungry itinerant tourist in the southwestern Chinese province of Yunnan, I'm pretty sure I had this stir-fry every day. Among the ever-changing roster of vegetables, the constants were green chiles (chosen for flavor, not heat) and slivers of Yunnan's famous ham. Bracingly salty and smoky, the ham was used sparingly as a seasoning, just to suggest the flavor of meat throughout the dish.

While the stir-fry is thoroughly Chinese, I was already familiar with Yunnan ham from my travels in Chiang Mai, Thailand. At the Friday market called Kad Jin Haw, which draws Chinese Muslim and Shan vendors, you see it on offer. Many believe the people we now call Thai originally came from Yunnan.

After downing many versions, I hit upon a mixture of vegetables that I found especially compelling: mushrooms and corn, which is indeed popular in China (in Thailand, corn is mainly dessert fodder). The combination of sweet kernels, earthy mushrooms, and cured pork would be at home in a succotash pot in the American South, but it turns out to be equally awesome in a wok with ginger and soy sauce.

You can modify the ingredients as you wish—more mushrooms, less corn—and swap the hard-to-get Yunnan ham for a smoky country ham or even Spanish serrano.

Flavor Profile SWEET AND SALTY, UMAMI-RICH

Try It With Kaeng Jeut Wun Sen ("Bland soup" with glass noodles), page 149, or Plaa Neung Si Ew (Steamed whole fish with soy sauce, ginger, and vegetables), page 79, and Khao Hom Mali (Jasmine rice), page 31.

SERVES 2 TO 6 AS PART OF A MEAL

1/4 cup Sup Kraduuk Muu (Pork stock), page 268, or water	11/2 ounces large flavorful mild green chiles, such as Anaheim or Hungarian wax, seeded, halved lengthwise if large, and cut into 3/4-inch-wide bite-size pieces (about 1/2 cup)	1 cup raw corn kernels
Scant tablespoon Thai thin soy sauce		2 ounces oyster or mixed mushrooms, cut or torn into large bite-size pieces (about 1 cup)
1 teaspoon granulated sugar		
Pinch ground white pepper	1 (7-gram) piece peeled ginger, cut into long (2-inch), thin (1/8-inch) matchsticks (about 1 tablespoon)	2 ounces peeled yellow onion, thinly sliced with the grain (about 1/2 cup)
2 tablespoons vegetable oil		
1 (11/2-ounce) piece Yunnan ham, or smoky serrano or country ham, cut into 1/8-inch-thick bite-size slices	11 grams peeled garlic cloves, halved lengthwise and lightly crushed into small pieces in a mortar (about 1 tablespoon)	2 ounces peeled carrot, cut into 1/4-inch-thick bite-size slices (about 1/4 cup)
		14 grams green onions, cut into 2-inch lengths (about 1/4 cup)

Combine the stock, soy sauce, sugar, and white pepper in a small bowl and stir well. Then combine the ham, chiles, ginger, and garlic in one container, and the corn, mushrooms, onions, and carrot in another.

Heat a wok over very high heat, add the oil, and swirl it in the wok to coat the sides. When it begins to smoke lightly, take the wok off the heat, add the ham, chiles, ginger, and garlic, and stir-fry (constantly stirring, scooping, and flipping the ingredients) until the ginger and garlic are very fragrant but not browned, 30 to 45 seconds.

Put the wok back on the heat, add the corn, mushrooms, onion, and carrot, and stir-fry for another minute.

Add the stock mixture and stir-fry until the vegetables are just cooked through and the sauce has thickened slightly, another minute or so. Add the green onions, stir-fry for 10 seconds or so, transfer to a plate, and serve.

Chả cá Lã Vọng

VIETNAMESE TURMERIC-MARINATED CATFISH WITH NOODLES AND HERBS

THE PLAN

- **Up to a week in advance: Make the turmeric oil**

- **The night before: Marinate the fish**

- **A few hours in advance: Make the pineapple-fish sauce and prepare the noodles**

Before Pok Pok was up and running, I took an epic trip to Vietnam. Not for culinary inspiration so much, but because I knew I wouldn't be able to take another vacation for a long time.

After I'd had my fill of *phở* in Hanoi, the country's capital of the rightfully famous beef noodle soup, I set my sights on another of the city's iconic dishes. And there was no question about where I was going to eat it. Like many travelers before me, I hired a motorbike taxi and told the driver to take me to Chả cá Street, which is named for the dish I was after. I walked into Chả cá Lã Vọng, the restaurant that claims to have invented the namesake dish.

There's no menu. You don't order. The waitress appears with rice noodles, heaps of herbs, and a tabletop grill. On it, she sets a pan with lightly crisp chunks of fish, tinted orange-yellow and bubbling away in oil. The fish has this subtle, addictive, hard-to-pin-down sourness. *Mắm nêm*, a powerful condiment made from fermented fish and pineapple, contributes depth. And the handfuls of herbs you add to the pan before assembling your own bowl of noodles and fish bring a freshness and brightness common to so much Vietnamese food. I remember being pleasantly surprised that, besides cilantro and green onion, there was dill, which I was still too inexperienced to associate with the food of Laos, Southern China, Northern Thailand, and Vietnam.

I was immediately hooked and determined to put it on Pok Pok's menu. The only problem: although the dish seemed simple, with most of the ingredients parsed and sitting in front of me on the table, there were aspects of it I couldn't decipher. As I looked into it, the mythology that shrouds this renowned dish sent me on plenty of goose chases. I spent more time than I'd like to admit researching the extract of a certain beetle that the restaurant may or may not add to the dish. The recipe here reflects my best guesses, and I think turns out pretty damn close to the dish I remember. At Pok Pok, we serve the dish in individual portions, because there's not enough room on the tables to present the full DIY spread. But at home, that shouldn't be a problem.

Flavor Profile EARTHY, HERBACEOUS, RICH, AND TART, SWEET, AND FUNKY

{continued}

**SERVES 4 AS A
ONE-PLATE MEAL**

FISH

1¼ pounds basa fillets (also known as swai or pangasius), or other firm, mild white-fleshed freshwater fish fillets, cut into 2-inch pieces that are about ¹/₂ inch thick

2 tablespoons fermented sticky rice (also called fermented sweet rice, fermented sweet rice sauce, and khao mahk in Thai), jarred or homemade (see page 247)

1 tablespoon turmeric powder

1¹/₂ teaspoons kosher salt

PINEAPPLE-FISH SAUCE

3¹/₂ ounces peeled fresh pineapple (ripe and sweet), cut into small chunks (about ¹/₂ cup)

14 grams peeled garlic (about 4 medium cloves)

1¹/₂ tablespoons lime juice (preferably from Key limes or spiked with a small squeeze of Meyer lemon juice)

1¹/₂ tablespoons Vietnamese fish sauce

1¹/₂ tablespoons naam plaa raa (fermented fish sauce)

¹/₂ tablespoon granulated sugar

³/₄ teaspoon white vinegar, preferably a Thai brand

12 grams thinly sliced fresh red Thai chiles (about 2 generous tablespoons)

TURMERIC OIL

³/₄ cup vegetable oil

14 grams peeled fresh or frozen (not defrosted) yellow turmeric root, thinly sliced against the grain (about 1 tablespoon)

TO SERVE

8 ounces Vietnamese or Thai dried rice vermicelli

1 cup mint leaves (the smaller the better), very lightly packed

¹/₂ cup coarsely chopped cilantro (thin stems and leaves), very lightly packed

2¹/₂ cups green onions (thinly sliced on the diagonal into 1¹/₂-inch-long pieces), very lightly packed

2¹/₂ cups dill fronds (1- to 2-inch sprigs, without thick stems), very lightly packed

Heaping ¹/₄ cup coarsely chopped unsalted roasted peanuts

4 small lime wedges (preferably from Key limes)

MARINATE THE FISH

Put the fish in a medium mixing bowl, add the fermented rice, turmeric powder, and salt, and mix well to coat the fish. (Beware: turmeric stains skin and clothes.) Cover, put the bowl in the fridge, and marinate for at least 1 hour or as long as overnight.

MAKE THE PINEAPPLE-FISH SAUCE

Combine all the ingredients, except for the chiles, in the blender. Blend until smooth and let the foam subside. Pour the sauce into a bowl. You can keep the sauce at room temperature up to a few hours before you plan to serve it. Just before you do, stir in the chiles.

MAKE THE TURMERIC OIL

Combine the oil and turmeric in a small pot, set the pot over low heat, and wait for the oil to barely bubble. Cook for 5 minutes, then turn off the heat and cover the pot. Once the oil has cooled to room temperature, strain the oil, discarding the solids. You'll have 1 cup of turmeric-infused oil. (You can double or triple the amounts and

store the leftover turmeric oil in an airtight container at room temperature for up to a week.

MAKE THE DISH

Bring a large pot of water to a boil and cook the noodles, stirring often, until they're fully soft (you don't want al dente noodles), but not mushy. The amount of time depends on the noodle brand, so use the package instructions as guidance. Prepare a large bowl of cold water and ice cubes. Drain the noodles well in a large colander, then rinse them well under lukewarm running water to wash off the starch. Shake the colander to drain the noodles well, then transfer the colander with noodles to the ice water, gently stirring the noodles with your hands. Drain once more, shaking and tossing to drain the noodles very well, about 30 minutes.

Arrange the noodles in a low pile on a platter. On a plate, arrange the mint, cilantro, ¹/₂ cup of the green onions, ¹/₂ cup of the dill, peanuts, and lime wedges.

Heat the turmeric oil in a large frying pan over high heat until it smokes lightly. Add the fish (if necessary, work in two batches to avoid crowding the pan, then return all the fish to the pan once it's cooked), decrease the heat to maintain a loud sizzle, and cook, turning the pieces over once, until they're golden brown on both sides and fully cooked, about 5 minutes total. Turn off the heat, let the oil cool slightly, then add the 2 cups of green onions and 2 cups of dill and toss gently (to keep the fish pieces intact) just until the green onions and dill have wilted, about 15 seconds.

SERVE THE DISH

Bring the platter of noodles, plate of herbs, bowl of sauce, and frying pan to the table. Give your guests shallow bowls and let them assemble their own meals. My suggestion is to add about 6 ounces of noodles to each bowl. Spoon on some fish, along with a generous amount of the wilted herbs and oil. Add generous pinches of the raw herbs, a tablespoon or so of peanuts, a squeeze of lime, and about 2 tablespoons of the pineapple-fish sauce. Toss well before you dig in.

FERMENTED STICKY RICE

To make my recipe for Chả cá Lã Vọng, you'll need to seek out this product, which is creatively translated in many ways, including but not limited to "sweet rice," "fermented sweet rice," and "fermented sweet rice sauce." You'll find it in jars in the refrigerated section of Asian markets, particularly those with a Southeast Asian focus, and in some Vietnamese bakeries, where they make it themselves. If you can't find it (or you're inclined to make it yourself), have at it.

KHAO MAHK

6 ounces uncooked Thai sticky rice (also called "glutinous" or "sweet" rice), soaked overnight in enough water to cover by several inches, then drained

Scant 2 grams dried yeast ball (also called pang khao mahk), from one small ball

1 tablespoon plus 1 teaspoon granulated sugar

Wash, drain, and steam the rice in a sticky rice steamer pot as instructed on page 33. Meanwhile, prepare a large bowl of cool water.

Transfer the cooked rice to the cool water and use your hands to separate the clumps of sticky rice into more or less individual grains. When the rice has cooled to room temperature, drain the rice, leaving it slightly wet (figure about 2 tablespoons of water should still be hanging out with the grains).

Pound the yeast to a fine powder in a granite mortar, then add the sugar and mix well. Sprinkle the mixture on the rice and stir gently, trying your best to distribute the mixture evenly.

Transfer the rice mixture to a tall jar (the rice should come a little more than halfway to the top). Cover the rice with plastic wrap, gently pressing so it lays flat against the surface, and cover the opening of the jar with plastic wrap as well. Put it in a warm spot to ferment. Let the rice ferment, checking every few days and spooning the liquid that develops over the top to keep it from drying out, until the grains have broken down slightly and the mixture looks like coarse, thick rice porridge and smells winey, 8 to 12 days, depending on the temperature. To make sure the yeast is doing its thing, check the mixture after the first 3 days. You should notice bubbling.

Once it's ready, store it in an airtight container in the fridge for up to a few months.

Ike's Vietnamese Fish-Sauce Wings

THE PLAN

- **The night before:** Marinate the wings, fry the garlic, and make the pickled carrot and daikon

- **Up to an hour before:** Fry the wings

SPECIAL EQUIPMENT

- A fine-mesh strainer or cheesecloth

- A deep-fry thermometer

- A wok (nonstick strongly recommended)

I've spent the better part of the last twenty years roaming around Thailand, trying to figure out how to reproduce Thai food. To me, that's what Pok Pok is all about. Yet, the most popular item at Pok Pok isn't even Thai. I get a kick out of the irony.

These wings basically pay our mortgage. They allow me to take risks with the rest of the menu. Because even if you're apprehensive of the fire and funk of Isaan-style papaya salad or by shrimpy, sour *kaeng som*, you'll leave impressed by the thrill of these ridiculous umami bombs.

The wings happen to be a rather common dish in Vietnam called *gà chiên nước mắm*. Right before I opened Pok Pok, I tried to make a version I had eaten once in Saigon at a *bia hơi* stand. *Bia hơi* is often translated as "fresh beer" in Vietnamese, and little street-side stalls with comically low plastic tables and stools sell the watery, low-alcohol lager by the jug for cheap. You sit there, knees up around your ears, drinking the beer over ice and burning through delicious little snacks that help you pass the time required to get a buzz off *bia hơi*. By the time I'd sucked clean several orders of the wings, I knew I wanted them on the opening menu.

Back in Portland, I took a few swings and misses at the recipe before enlisting the help of Pok Pok's first employee, Ich Truong (who I nicknamed "Ike" because "Ich" is too hard for us honkies to pronounce). A recent arrival from Vietnam, Ike is an all-around handy guy who first joined my painting crew (when I was still working as a housepainter) and then joined me in the trenches to open the restaurant. (Literally, in the trenches. We once had to dig one so deep to find a drainpipe that he disappeared into it.) Not only did he help me build the restaurant, but he's also a good cook, and showed me a few tricks that helped the wings reach the level they're at now. We still work together today.

Making a home version requires some deviation from the method we use at the restaurant, where we have industrial deep-fryers and serious BTU fire power. Nevertheless, the result of this streamlined recipe comes pretty close to what you get at Pok Pok with about half the effort. If you're making the spicy version, open a window and turn on the stove's exhaust fan.

Flavor Profile INTENSELY SALTY AND SWEET, UMAMI-RICH

Try It With Chả cá Lã Vọng (Vietnamese turmeric-marinated catfish with noodles and herbs), page 245, or as a snack with plenty of beer.

{continued}

MAKES ABOUT ONE DOZEN WINGS, ENOUGH FOR 4 TO 8 AS PART OF A MEAL	SAUCE AND MARINADE	TO FRY AND FINISH THE WINGS	TO SERVE ALONGSIDE
	1 ounce peeled garlic (about 8 medium cloves)	**Vegetable oil for deep frying**	**Drained Cu Cai (Pickled carrot and daikon radish), page 284**
	1 teaspoon kosher salt	**1 cup white rice flour (*not* glutinous rice flour)**	**Several long spears Persian, English, or Japanese cucumbers (or any firm variety without large seeds and thick, bitter skin)**
	1/4 cup warm water	**1/4 cup tempura batter mix (preferably Gogi brand)**	
	1/2 cup Vietnamese fish sauce	**1/4 cup water**	
	1/2 cup superfine sugar	**1 to 2 teaspoons Naam Phrik Phao (Roasted chile paste), page 287 (optional)**	**Several sprigs of Vietnamese mint, cilantro, or Thai basil**
	2 pounds medium-size chicken wings (about 12), split at the joint		

MAKE THE SAUCE AND MARINATE THE WINGS

Very finely chop the garlic, sprinkle on the salt, then chop the two together for 15 seconds or so. Scrape the mixture into small bowl, add the 1/4 cup of warm water, and let it sit for a few minutes.

Set a fine-mesh strainer over another bowl, pour the garlic mixture into the strainer (or squeeze the mixture in cheesecloth over the bowl), and use the back of a spoon to stir and smoosh the garlic to extract as much liquid as you can. Reserve the garlic. Add the fish sauce and sugar to the bowl and stir until the sugar has fully dissolved. You should have 1 cup of liquid.

Put the chicken wings in a large mixing bowl, add 1/2 cup of the fish sauce mixture, reserving the rest, and toss well with your hands. Cover and refrigerate for at least 4 hours, or as long as overnight, tossing every hour or so.

FRY THE GARLIC

Meanwhile, pour enough oil into a small pan to reach a depth of 3/4 inch or so and set it over high heat until it shimmers. Set a fine-mesh strainer over a heatproof bowl. Test whether the oil is hot enough: as soon as a piece of garlic added to the oil bubbles right away, add the rest. Decrease the heat to medium-low (you don't want to rush the process with high heat), and stir once or twice. Cook the garlic just until it's evenly light golden brown, about 5 minutes. Strain the garlic, reserving the flavorful oil for another purpose. Gently shake the strainer, then transfer the garlic in more or less one layer to paper towels to drain and cool. You should have 2 tablespoons of fried garlic. It keeps in an airtight container at room temperature for a day or two.

FRY THE WINGS

Transfer the wings to a colander in the sink, shaking them occasionally, to let them drain well before you fry them, at least 15 minutes.

Pour enough of the oil into a wok, Dutch oven, or wide pot (even better, use a countertop deep fryer) to reach a depth that will completely submerge the wings, about 2 inches. Set the pot over medium-high heat, bring the oil to 350°F (use a deep-fry thermometer), carefully stirring the oil to maintain a consistent temperature, and adjust the heat to maintain the temperature.

In a large mixing bowl, stir together the rice flour and tempura batter.

Fry the wings in two batches. Toss half the wings in the flour mixture to coat them well and knock them against the edge of the bowl so any excess flour falls off before adding them to the hot oil. Add the first batch to the oil and cook, prodding the wings to move them around a bit after 4 minutes or so and then every few minutes, until they're evenly deep golden brown and completely cooked through, 6 to 8 minutes. Transfer them to paper towels to drain, let the oil come back to 350°F, and do the same with the next batch.

FINISH THE WINGS

Add the 1/4 cup of water to the remaining fish sauce mixture, stir well, and set it aside.

Work in two batches to finish the wings (if you have a very large wok, one batch will do). Combine 1/4 cup of the fish sauce mixture and half of the chile paste (if you're using it) in a nonstick wok, set it over high heat, and bring it to a boil. Cook until the mixture has reduced by about half, about 45 seconds. Add half of the chicken wings, and cook, using tongs, a wok spatula, or a deft flick of your wrist to toss the wings in the liquid every 15 seconds or so, until the liquid has become a sticky, caramel-colored glaze that coats the wings, about 1 minute. Add 1 tablespoon of the reserved fried garlic, toss well, and keep cooking, tossing constantly, until the glaze has turned a shade or two darker, about 30 seconds more.

Transfer the wings to a serving plate. The sticky coating seals in the heat, so this batch of wings should keep warm while you finish the next one. You can also keep the first batch in an oven set to warm.

Rinse and wipe out the wok, and repeat with another 1/4 cup of the liquid, the remaining chile paste, the remaining wings, and the remaining tablespoon of fried garlic.

Serve the wings with the pickled vegetables, cucumber spears, and herb sprigs.

KHONG WAAN

Sweets

At Pok Pok, the dishes in this chapter are served after meals, because American customers are used to seeing desserts on menus. In Thailand, however, the concept of dessert is a bit different. There, it is more of an anytime snack that just happens to be sweet.

Typically overlooked in the West in favor of bright, spicy salads and rich curries, Thai sweets have become one of my favorite aspects of the cuisine. They exist in breathtaking variety. There are little cakes made from coconut and rice flour steamed in banana leaf packets. There are golden sweets made from egg yolk and sugar (a confection derived from the Portuguese) formed into delicate threads or molded to resemble the seeds of jackfruit. There are icy mixtures topped with fruit and

beans and noodle-like things flavored with sugar syrup infused with smoke from special candles. Sometimes the flavors veer into the savory realm: sweet sticky rice filled with salty-sweet mung bean paste, and steamed tapioca cakes topped with fried shallots or even ground dried fish. But give them a chance. Once you get past how thoroughly these sweets defy your expectations, you'll be hooked.

Khanom Bataeng Laai

NORTHERN THAI MELON CUSTARD

SPECIAL EQUIPMENT

- **A wide aluminum Chinese steamer**
- **One large or two smaller heatproof bowls, pie plates, or round baking pans (to hold the mixture in an approximately 1-inch layer)**
- **A fine-mesh strainer**

My first trip to Chiang Mai to visit my friends Chris and Lakhana was one full of firsts—my Laap Meuang (page 106) virginity taken, my consciousness altered by a curry of wild mushrooms, and my notion of Thai sweets expanded beyond coconut ice cream and Khao Niaw Mamuang (Sticky rice with mango), page 257.

I was walking with Lakhana through the cafeteria at Chiang Mai University, where she worked, ogling colorful cubes of what she called *khanom*—basically, sweet snacks. These particular *khanom,* she explained, were a sort of steamed custard. I was intrigued by them all, the orange, the pale yellow, the lime green, and especially the midnight black.

What the hell was in it? I wondered, scrolling through the short list in my head of black foods. *It's definitely not made from squid ink,* I thought. *Was it licorice flavored?* Lakhana asked the vendor, and I remember my skepticism at the answer: charcoal. *Impossible translation,* I figured. *Happens all the time.* Still curious, I ordered some and took a bite. It tasted, sure enough, like charcoal, slightly sweet, bitter, and carbonic. To this day, I have no clue how they made it. I don't know whether I liked it. But the flavor is forever etched in my memory.

You're not likely to find charcoal-flavored sweets in the West, unless you're at a place with a ten-page wine list and a pastry chef with outsize ambition and a Pacojet. This speaks to the Thai palate for sweets, which doesn't always overlap with ours. Sometimes that means the use of ingredients like yellow beans, the starchy quality a bit too suggestive of sugary hummus for my taste. Other times that means sweetness and saltiness in almost equal amounts, something I've grown to love (and judging by the recent prevalence of desserts in the US featuring salted caramel and bacon chocolate, something Americans in general are warming to).

Sometimes Thai desserts hit the spot where just about all of our palates intersect. On that same trip, I traveled to Saluang Nai, the small village where Lakhana grew up. A woman came by selling *khanom bataeng laai,* hunks of custard named for an incredibly fragrant local melon. Against a backdrop of coconut milk and palm sugar, the fruit was on display, its aroma merged with the custard's flavor, sweet and perfumed but not too much so. Charcoal this was not, but the result was just as eye-opening.

Since the fruit doesn't exist on this side of the Pacific, I look to overripe cantaloupe or muskmelon.

Flavor Profile AROMATIC, SWEET, SLIGHTLY SALTY

{continued}

{Northern Thai melon custard, continued}

MAKES ABOUT 24 (1¹/₂-INCH) SQUARES (ENOUGH FOR 8 TO 10 PEOPLE, WITH LEFTOVERS)

1¹/₄ pounds peeled, seeded, coarsely chopped flesh from an overripe (very soft and fragrant) muskmelon or cantaloupe

1 cup unsweetened coconut cream (preferably boxed)

1¹/₄ cups white rice flour (*not* sticky rice flour)

¹/₂ cup tapioca starch

¹/₂ cup granulated sugar

1 teaspoon kosher salt

About 1 teaspoon vegetable oil, or cooking spray

Pour about 3 inches of water into a wide aluminum Chinese steamer (it should be wide enough to fit the bowl with a few inches to spare), insert the steamer layer, cover, and bring the water to a boil over high heat.

Put the flesh in the blender and blend the melon until it's fairly smooth, then add 3 cups of the puree to a large mixing bowl along with the coconut cream, rice flour, tapioca starch, sugar (if the melon is very sweet, add the sugar gradually; the mixture should taste sweet but not *very* sweet), and the salt. Whisk it well.

Rub the large heatproof bowl with just enough oil (or use spray) to coat the bottom and sides (if you're using two smaller bowls, you might have to cook in batches).

Strain the mixture through a fine-mesh strainer into another mixing bowl or container to remove any lumps.

Decrease the heat under the steamer slightly so the water is still boiling but not wildly. To make the transfer easy, put the bowl in the steamer first, then pour in enough of the mixture to reach a depth of approximately 1 inch. Cover the steamer and cook just until the khanom has set (a toothpick inserted into the center should come out clean; the khanom should jiggle when you gently shake the tray or bowl), about 45 minutes.

Let the khanom sit at room temperature until it's completely cool, then cut it into approximately 1¹/₂-inch squares. If you're planning to eat it that day, don't refrigerate it. You can refrigerate the khanom, covered, for up to one week. Let it come to room temperature before you serve it.

Khao Niaw Mamuang

STICKY RICE WITH MANGO AND SALTY-SWEET COCONUT CREAM

SPECIAL EQUIPMENT

- An inexpensive sticky rice steamer set (both the woven basket and pot-bellied pot)
- Cheesecloth or a clean mesh rice-steaming bag

There's a stand my friend Sunny refers to, in his lilting English, as "my temptation." The stand is on the side of the road, and we pass it whenever we drive to Chiang Mai from his home in the village of Ban Pa Du. When we're within a mile of My Temptation, I can almost see it in Sunny's posture, in the way he grips the wheel of his pickup. As often as not, Sunny surrenders to his temptation.

Neat stacks of mango serve as signage. Sunny pulls over so he's close enough to the corrugated steel structure that the woman in the pink apron can hand him a Styrofoam container. Inside is a mango that's been peeled, pitted, and carved into chunks—buttery flesh that's sweet and incredibly fragrant. Amazingly, this mango is not the best thing in the container. Instead, a clump of sticky rice steals the show.

Like most basic foodstuffs, sticky rice has echelons. Like sushi rice, it has its master practitioners. The woman in the pink apron has likely spent decades honing her skill at steaming. She likely seeks out a particular variety of sticky rice or an older crop, which are sought after in the same way as newer crops of jasmine rice are. She probably rinses the rice in water while scrubbing it with a large crystal of alum (aluminum sulfate) to wash away starch—a sort of early example of molecular gastronomy. The rice glistens with a coating of fresh coconut cream infused with pandan leaf, nearly as salty as it is sweet.

I'm no master practitioner, but as far as I can tell, this home version comes pretty damn close to Sunny's Temptation, even though I use typical sticky rice and boxed coconut cream. If you're dying to make this incredibly addictive sticky rice but can't find ripe Mexican Ataulfo mangoes, which are the tastiest, least fibrous option for our purposes, look to *sankhaya turian* (page 260) for your rice topper instead.

At Pok Pok, we serve this as dessert, but in Thailand, you eat it whenever the mood strikes. It's rich stuff, so if you're serving it after a meal, each plate will feed 2 to 4 people.

Flavor Profile SWEET AND SLIGHTLY TART, RICH AND SALTY

{continued}

SALTY-SWEET COCONUT CREAM	SWEET STICKY RICE	1 tablespoon kosher salt
2 cups unsweetened coconut cream (preferably boxed)	**2¹/₂ cups uncooked Thai sticky rice (also called "glutinous" or "sweet" rice), soaked for 2 hours in enough tepid water to cover**	**1 fresh or frozen pandan leaf, tied in a knot**
1¹/₂ tablespoons granulated sugar		DISH
1¹/₂ teaspoons kosher salt	**1 cup unsweetened coconut cream (preferably boxed)**	**3 large ripe Ataulfo mangoes, peeled**
1 fresh or frozen pandan leaf, tied in a knot	**¹/₂ cup granulated sugar**	**About 1 tablespoon toasted sesame seeds, optional**

SERVES 6 AS A HEFTY SNACK, AND 12 AS DESSERT

MAKE THE SALTY-SWEET COCONUT CREAM TOPPING

Combine the 2 cups of coconut cream, 1¹/₂ tablespoons of sugar, and 1¹/₂ teaspoons of salt in a small pot. Add the pandan leaf to the pot. It's fine if it isn't completely submerged. Set the pot over high heat, bring the mixture to a simmer (don't let it boil), then decrease the heat to low. Cover and cook until the cream has thickened slightly and is infused with pandan flavor, about 10 minutes. Remove and discard the pandan leaf. Covered, the cream keeps at room temperature for up to 2 hours.

MAKE THE SWEET STICKY RICE

Rinse and steam the sticky rice as instructed on page 33, but stop when the sticky rice is fully tender but slightly underdone, about 12 minutes rather than the typical 15 minutes.

Meanwhile, combine the 1 cup of coconut cream, ¹/₂ cup of sugar, and 1 tablespoon of salt in a medium pot. Add the pandan leaf, set the pot over high heat, and bring the mixture to a simmer (don't let it boil). Cook, stirring, just until the sugar has fully dissolved, about a minute. Turn off the heat, cover the pot, and let the mixture sit to infuse it with the flavor of pandan, about 5 minutes. Remove and discard the pandan leaf. Let this cream mixture cool just until it's warm but no longer hot.

Add the cooked sticky rice to the pot and gently stir and fold it until it's evenly coated in the cream mixture. Cover the pot and let it sit for 10 minutes. The rice will get more tender and absorb the coconut mixture.

The sticky rice mixture keeps covered in the fridge for up to a day. To reheat it, cover with plastic wrap and microwave on low just until the rice is warm (but not hot) through and serve it right away.

SERVE THE DISH

Cut each mango lengthwise on both sides of the pit to remove the flesh in two large pieces. Cut the pieces crosswise into approximately ¹/₂-inch-thick slices. Put ³/₄ to 1 cup of the sweet sticky rice on each of 6 plates, gently press it to make an even layer, then divide the mangoes evenly on top. Top each serving with about 2 tablespoons of the salty-sweet coconut cream topping and a sprinkle of the sesame seeds.

Khao Niaw Sankhaya Turian

STICKY RICE WITH DURIAN CUSTARD

SPECIAL EQUIPMENT

- **A wide aluminum Chinese steamer**
- **One large or two smaller heatproof bowls or round baking pans (to hold the mixture in an approximately 2-inch layer**
- **A fine-mesh strainer**

Durian has a powerful aroma. Westerners, who tend to shun the fruit, would probably choose a stronger term. In Southeast Asia, however, durian is considered the queen of fruit and it fetches a high price. Yet even where durian has fans, it's not always welcome. Cabs, trains, and hotels throughout Southeast Asia sport signs with a circle around the fruit's spiky silhouette and a line struck through it.

It took me a while to embrace the fruit, one of many products that remind me of the vast gulf between culinary cultures that prize fermented sea creatures and those dominated by olive oil and lemon. Now I'm a durian fan, for sure. And this custard was my gateway dish, a toe-dip alternative to jumping straight into the yellow lobes of unbelievably rich, almost creamy flesh offered by market vendors kind enough to have already extricated it from the mountains of thorny husks around them. You can eat the custard scooped onto sweet sticky rice, the fruit's texture and fragrance tempered by coconut milk, egg, and pandan leaf at morning markets. Some of these vendors top this custard with a blob of fresh durian before adding sweet-salty coconut cream.

Whether you're new to durian or an old hand, this custard is the ideal way to eat the fruit in the US, since the fresh fruit we get here tends not to be as tasty as the frozen kind. Any textural sacrifice from freezing is no big deal, since you'll be squishing and cooking it anyway. The custard isn't ultra smooth like a French *pot de crème* but more like a flan. Leftover custard and sticky rice make a great breakfast.

Flavor Profile SWEET, FUNKY, RICH, AND SLIGHTLY SALTY

SERVES 6 AS A HEFTY SNACK, AND 12 AS DESSERT

1¹⁄₂ pounds palm sugar	1 cup plus 2 tablespoons eggs (about 5 large)	2 fresh or frozen pandan leaves
3 tablespoons water	1 cup plus 1 tablespoon unsweetened coconut cream (preferably boxed)	¹⁄₂ teaspoon kosher salt
1¹⁄₂ teaspoons tapioca starch		Sweet Sticky Rice (see page 259), warm
4 ounces defrosted frozen durian flesh		

SOFTEN THE PALM SUGAR

Put the palm sugar in a large microwavable bowl, sprinkle on 2 tablespoons of the water, cover the bowl with plastic wrap, and microwave on low just until the sugar has softened (not liquefied), 10 to 30 seconds. Pound the mixture in a mortar (or mash it in the bowl) until you have a smooth paste. Covered, it will keep soft for up to 2 days at room temperature.

MAKE THE CUSTARD

Pour about 3 inches of water into a wide aluminum Chinese steamer, insert the steamer layer, cover, and bring the water to a boil over high heat.

In a small bowl, stir the tapioca starch with the remaining 1 tablespoon of water until it's smooth and lump free. In a large bowl, combine the durian, eggs, coconut cream, pandan leaves, 1¹⁄₂ cups of the softened palm sugar (reserving extra for another purpose, like papaya salad), salt, and the tapioca mixture.

{continued}

Use your hands to squeeze and firmly scrunch the ingredients together, especially the pandan, so its flavor infuses into the mixture, until there are no lumps of sugar or durian remaining, about 5 minutes.

Strain the mixture through a fine-mesh strainer into the large heatproof bowl or the two smaller bowls, stirring and smooshing to extract as much liquid as you can and discarding the remaining solids. The mixture should reach a depth of approximately 2 inches. If you're using two smaller bowls, you might have to cook in batches.

Decrease the heat under the steamer slightly so the water is still boiling but not wildly. Gently stir the mixture, then carefully add the bowl to the steamer basket. Cover the steamer and cook just until the custard has set (a toothpick inserted into the center should come out clean; the custard should jiggle when you gently shake the bowl), 45 minutes to 1 hour. You'll notice a few nooks and crannies on the surface. That's fine.

Use oven mitts or towel-wrapped hands to carefully remove the bowl from the steamer. Let the custard cool to room temperature. You can store the custard in the bowl, covered, or in an airtight container in the fridge for up to 5 days. I like to let it come to room temperature before serving, but it's also good slightly chilled.

SERVE THE DISH
Put about 1 cup of the sticky rice on each of 6 plates, gently press it to make an even layer, then top each with a scoop (about 1/2 cup, if you're counting) of the custard.

Khanom Pang Ai Tiim

{Pictured on page 264}

THAI-STYLE ICE CREAM SANDWICH

SPECIAL EQUIPMENT

- **A candy thermometer**
- **An ice cream maker with at least 1½-quart capacity**

When some people see that we serve an ice cream sandwich on a hot dog bun, they think we're being cheeky. Nope, this is more or less what you get in Thailand: a squishy, doughy white platform for ice cream (or "ai tiim," as it's pronounced there) drizzled with chocolate syrup and sweetened condensed milk and dusted with crushed peanuts. (I do, however, omit the more-common-than-you-might-imagine topping of corn kernels, though add some if you're up for it.) In this case, we're talking about ice cream made with jackfruit, which is popular in Thailand in both its unripe state (see Kaeng Khanun, page 166) as well as when the flesh is sweet and yellow-orange. You'll find ripe jackfruit flesh, conveniently removed from its massive shell (supposedly, it's the world's largest tree fruit), in the freezer section at many Asian supermarkets.

Try to find the split-top buns often used for lobster rolls or do as Thai vendors sometimes do: buy white bread and just fold it over.

Flavor Profile SWEET, RICH, NUTTY

COCONUT ICE CREAM WITH JACKFRUIT	SANDWICHES	Sweetened condensed milk, preferably Longevity or Black & White brand, for drizzling
1 cup granulated sugar	4 split-top hot dog buns, at room temperature	
½ cup water	Generous ½ cup Sweet Sticky Rice (see page 259), warm	About ¼ cup coarsely crushed unsalted roasted peanuts
4 cups unsweetened coconut cream (preferably boxed)		
8 ounces defrosted frozen mature or "yellow" (not "young" or "green"), ripe jackfruit flesh	Purchased chocolate syrup, for drizzling	

MAKES 4

MAKE THE ICE CREAM

Combine the sugar and the water in a small pot, set it over medium heat, and let it come to a simmer, stirring occasionally. Keep cooking until the sugar fully dissolves and the mixture registers 230°F to 235°F on a candy thermometer.

Take the pot off the heat and let the mixture come to room temperature. The mixture will harden slightly as it cools. Combine the mixture and the coconut cream in a mixing bowl. Cover and refrigerate the mixture, stirring occasionally, until it's fully chilled, at least 1 hour.

Meanwhile, cut the jackfruit flesh into approximately ¼-inch chunks. Once the mixture has fully chilled, stir in the jackfruit.

Pour the mixture into an ice cream maker and churn according to the manufacturer's instructions. (The specifics of the process vary from machine to machine.)

Transfer the mixture to containers and freeze until fully frozen, at least 4 hours; it will keep up to 1 week. You'll have about 1½ quarts.

ASSEMBLE THE SANDWICHES

Just before you plan to serve them, pull open the buns and spread a generous 2 tablespoons of the sticky rice on each one. Top each bun with 3 or 4 small scoops of the ice cream, then lightly drizzle the ice cream with chocolate syrup and condensed milk, then sprinkle on the peanuts. Don't be shy: pick it up and eat it like a sandwich.

Pok Pok Affogato

{Pictured on page 265}

I don't typically come up with dishes myself—I'm better qualified to play grateful imitator—but this one was almost a no-brainer. Just about anyone who has ever tried Vietnamese iced coffee gets hooked on the chicory-spiked blend sugared up with sweetened condensed milk. And just about any coffee lover fiends for *affogato*, the Italian dessert of ice cream drowned in hot espresso. A little tinkering and bingo, this mash-up was born: a shot of good espresso poured over two-ingredient condensed milk ice cream.

And because street vendors in Vietnam hawking coffee often sell deep-fried crullers (essentially a noncircular donut) with which I've begun many a morning in Thailand as well (there it's called *patanko*), I serve that alongside. Do yourself a favor and buy it from a Chinese market or bakery instead of attempting to make it at home.

SPECIAL EQUIPMENT

- An ice cream maker with at least 1½-quart capacity
- An espresso machine (or access to good espresso)

Flavor Profile SWEET, RICH, AROMATIC, SLIGHTLY BITTER

SERVES 4; THE RECIPE IS EASILY DOUBLED

CONDENSED MILK ICE CREAM

1 (14-ounce) can sweetened condensed milk, preferably Longevity or Black & White brand

2 cups heavy cream

FOR SERVING

12 small scoops condensed milk ice cream

4 shots espresso, freshly brewed

About 8 (4-inch-long) pieces purchased savory Chinese crullers, briefly deep-fried according to the package instructions (optional)

MAKE THE ICE CREAM

Combine the condensed milk and cream in a mixing bowl and stir gently until the two are very well combined. Don't whisk or beat or do anything else that creates bubbles. Cover and refrigerate the mixture, stirring occasionally, until it's fully chilled, at least 1 hour.

Pour the mixture into an ice cream maker and churn according to the manufacturer's instructions. (The specifics of the process vary from machine to machine.)

Transfer the mixture to a container and freeze until fully frozen, at least 4 hours; it will keep up to 1 week. You'll have about 1 quart.

SERVE THE DISH

Just before you're ready to serve it, brew the espresso (or buy it at a coffee shop and gently reheat it). Put 3 small scoops of ice cream in each of 4 small bowls and pour on the hot espresso. Serve with the crullers alongside.

SUNDRY ITEMS
STOCK, CONDIMENTS, AND PANTRY STAPLES

This chapter is a catchall where you'll find recipes for pork stock, tamarind water, and fried shallots, along with other items required to make many of the dishes in this book, plus a dozen or so dipping sauces and condiments. I hope all the page cross-references in the recipes don't make the instructions look too onerous, but they sure beat including the same instructions again and again for making stuff as simple as garlic oil and Thai chile powder.

Sup Kraduuk Muu

A cooking staple in Thailand, stock fortifies the flavor of many dishes, from soups to stir-fries. Pork stock is, in my experience, the most common version, though you do certainly see it made from beef, chicken, a mixture of pork or chicken, and of course, bouillon powder. If you want to cook from this book, I suggest making a batch straight away and freezing the stock in small portions. You'll use no more than 1/2 cup for stir-fries and steamed fish dishes. You'll use about 1 1/2 cups per portion for soups. I like to store some of the stock in ice cube molds and once the cubes are fully frozen, dump them into a freezer bag.

Like a good Westerner, I prefer my stock cooked a little more gently than the boiled stocks common in Thailand. A little cloudiness, however, certainly won't kill you. The first time you make it, use all the aromatics listed below so you understand how they play off each other to create a balanced stock. Soon, though, you'll be able to recreate a great stock with whatever scraps you have lying around from your other Thai cooking endeavors.

Flavor Profile **MEATY, UMAMI-RICH, AROMATIC**

MAKES 4 TO 5 QUARTS

5 pounds meaty pork neck bones, cut by the butcher, if necessary, so they can fit in your pot	**1 stalk lemongrass, outer layer removed, halved crosswise**	**3 or so cilantro sprigs (preferably leaves, stems, and well-washed roots)**
1 whole unpeeled head garlic	**About 6 ounces peeled daikon radish, cut crosswise into approximately 1-inch slices (about 2 cups)**	**3 or so leafy Chinese celery sprigs**
1 (approximately 1-ounce) piece unpeeled ginger		**1 teaspoon black or white peppercorns**
	3 or so green onions	

WASH THE BONES

Put the bones in a large pot, fill it with cold tap water, stir with your hands, and pour off the water. Add enough water to cover the bones by an inch or so, cover, and set the pot over high heat. Bring the water to a simmer, then turn off the heat. Skim any scum from the surface, then drain the bones and rinse them under running water. All this is to get any blood off the bones, which will give you a cleaner-tasting, clearer stock.

MAKE THE STOCK

Clean the pot, return the bones to the pot, and add enough water to cover the bones by 2 inches or so. Cover the pot, set it over high heat and bring the water to a bare simmer (do not let it boil), lightly stirring once and skimming off any surface scum. Uncover the pot,

decrease the heat to maintain a bare simmer and cook, skimming occasionally, until all the flavor has been cooked out of the meat on the bones, about 3 hours.

Working one at a time, use a pestle or heavy pan to lightly whack the garlic, ginger, and lemongrass a few times to bruise them. Add them to the pot along with the remaining ingredients and continue to simmer gently for 30 minutes more. Strain the stock into a large bowl or pot (don't press the solids), discarding what's left behind. Let the stock cool and skim off any fat from the surface. (This is even easier when the stock is chilled and the fat solidifies.)

The stock keeps in airtight containers in the fridge for up to 5 days and in the freezer for up to 6 months.

Muu Deng

BOUNCY PORK BALLS

Light, fluffy meatballs these are not. The goal, in fact, is just the opposite: these little orbs should have a slightly bouncy texture, with a little squeakiness when you bite into them, about halfway in between Italian meatballs and cooked hot dogs.

Flavor Profile MEATY, SALTY, PEPPERY

MAKES 30 TO 40 BALLS

14 grams peeled garlic cloves, halved lengthwise	¹/₄ teaspoon black peppercorns	8 ounces ground pork (not lean)
3 grams cilantro roots, thinly sliced	¹/₂ teaspoon kosher salt	2 teaspoons Thai fish sauce
	1 large egg white	

Bring a large pot of water to a simmer.

Combine the garlic, cilantro roots, peppercorns, and salt in a granite mortar and pound to a fairly smooth, slightly fibrous paste, about 1 minute.

Vigorously beat the egg white in a mixing bowl for about 45 seconds. It should be white, frothy, and nearly doubled in volume. You do *not*, however, want stiff peaks, soft peaks, or any peaks for that matter.

Add the pork, paste, and fish sauce to the bowl with the egg, and use your hand to stir and squish the mixture until it's all well combined. Then for the next 2 minutes or so, alternate between firmly mixing with your hand for 10 seconds or so and picking up the mixture, steadying the bowl with your free hand, and forcefully throwing the mixture into the bowl hard enough so you hear a good *thwack*. What you're doing is exactly what many meatball recipes tell you not to do: "overmixing" the meat until it's fairly sticky. When it's cooked, it'll have a dense, squeaky texture.

Transfer the mixture to a resealable plastic bag (or disposable piping bag, if you're fancy like that). Work the mixture toward a corner, twisting the bag to force the meat into the corner and firmly shaking to eliminate any air pockets. Use scissors to snip a 1- to 1¹/₂-inch-wide opening from the corner.

Hold the bag over the simmering water (as close as you can to avoid splashing) with one hand and hold the scissors or a small knife in the other. Squeeze the bag slightly to force out about 1 inch of the mixture and use the scissors or knife to coax it into the water. Don't worry that it's not a perfect ball. Keep this up until you've used a third or so of the meat mixture. Cook until the balls float to the surface and are just cooked through, about 1 to 2 minutes, using a slotted spoon to scoop the balls into a bowl as they're ready. Repeat in two more batches until you've used all of the meat mixture.

Keep the pork balls in an airtight container in the fridge for up to 5 days or in resealable plastic bags in the freezer for up to 6 months.

Khai Tom

A common accompaniment to curry-topped *khanom jiin* (page 231), these eggs are essentially hard-boiled but still have orange, slightly creamy (rather than chalky, powder yellow) yolks.

MAKES 1 TO 6 EGGS (FOR MORE, USE A LARGER POT)

1 to 6 large eggs, at room temperature

Bring a medium pot of water to a boil. Carefully add the eggs, cook them for 8 minutes (set a timer), and use a slotted spoon or spider skimmer to transfer them to a bowl of ice water. Peel the eggs once they've fully cooled.

Phrik Phon Khua

SPECIAL EQUIPMENT

- A Thai granite mortar and pestle or spice or meat grinder

Slowly toasted dried chiles—seeds and all—become a smoky, spicy ingredient that's essential to many recipes in this book. The key is to toast them over low heat until they're thoroughly dry and very dark, coaxing out a deep, tobacco-like flavor that has a bitter edge, but stopping before the pleasant bitterness turns acrid.

Flavor Profile SPICY, SLIGHTLY BITTER AND SMOKY

MAKES ABOUT 1/3 CUP

1 ounce stemmed dried Mexican puya chiles (about 15)

The goal here is to cook the chiles slowly so they get nice and dark but don't burn. Consider opening a window and turning on your stove's exhaust fan.

Put the chiles in a wok or pan, turn the heat to high to get the pan hot, then turn the heat down to medium-low to low.

Stir the chiles almost constantly, moving them around the wok and flipping them occasionally to make sure both sides of the chiles make contact with the hot pan. Keep at it until the chiles are very brittle and very dark brown (nearly black) all over, 15 to 20 minutes. Remove the chiles from the pan as they're finished. Discard any seeds that escape the chiles, because they'll be burnt and bitter.

Let the chiles cool. Pound them in a granite mortar to a coarse powder that's only slightly finer than store-bought red pepper flakes, or grind them in a spice grinder (or better yet, pass them twice through a meat grinder, first through a 1/4-inch die and then through an 1/8-inch die). Either way, take care to keep the powder coarse. Immediately put the chile powder in an airtight container or plastic bag.

The chile powder will keep for up to a few months in a sealed container kept in a cool, dry place (not in the fridge), though the flavor will begin to deteriorate after several weeks.

Khao Khua

TOASTED-STICKY RICE POWDER

This powder, made from toasted uncooked sticky rice, is used primarily in Northeastern food to add a toasty quality and subtle texture to salads, and occasionally in Northern food as a thickening agent. Its contribution is initially hard to pin down, but it's one you'd actively miss if it weren't there. Making it at home is beyond simple: it just takes patience and stirring. The only way to screw it up is to try to rush the process with high heat so the outside burns before inside fully toasts. The truly committed will toast over a low charcoal fire so the rice picks up a little smokiness.

Flavor Profile AROMATIC

MAKES ABOUT 1 CUP

1 cup uncooked Thai sticky rice (also called "glutinous" or "sweet" rice)

Put the rice in a bowl, add enough water to cover by an inch or so, and let the rice soak at room temperature for at least 4 hours or overnight. (If you're in a rush, you can soak the rice in hot tap water for as little as 2 hours.) Drain the rice very well, then lay the rice out on kitchen towels until it's dry to the touch.

Your goal is to toast the rice slowly so the grains toast all the way through before getting too dark on the outside, stirring constantly so the grains cook evenly. Put the rice in a large dry frying pan or wok and set the pan over medium-low to low heat.

Cook, stirring almost constantly, until the rice is evenly golden brown. After 15 minutes or so, you should see the grains begin to change color. After 30 minutes or so, the grains will have turned light golden brown. After 45 minutes to 1 hour, they will be golden brown, close to the color of peanut butter, and have a very toasty aroma. Ideally, every grain will be the same color, but you'll inevitably have some grains that are slightly darker or lighter.

Let the toasted rice cool slightly, then grind it in a spice grinder (or even better, in a burr grinder), in batches if necessary, until you have a powder with the texture of coarse sand or kosher salt.

The powder keeps for several months in an airtight container in a cool, dry place (not the fridge), though the flavor will begin to deteriorate after several weeks.

Krathiem Jiaw and Naam Man Krathiem

FRIED GARLIC AND GARLIC OIL

Common throughout Thailand, particularly in the north, fried garlic and shallots contribute texture, aroma, and flavor to salads and stir-fries, curries, soups, and noodles. The frying oil becomes a flavorful ingredient itself. The goal is low, steady heat—to draw out the water and to crisp the fibers before the sugars burn. For the crispiest result, palm oil is the ticket. For the most flavorful result, rendered pork fat is king. But soybean, rice bran, and vegetable oil work well, too.

Flavor Profile SLIGHTLY SWEET, AROMATIC, SLIGHTLY BITTER (FRIED GARLIC); AROMATIC, RICH (GARLIC OIL)

MAKES 5 TO 6 TABLESPOONS FRIED GARLIC AND ABOUT 2 CUPS OF OIL

3 ounces peeled garlic (about 30 cloves)

About 2 cups vegetable oil

Chop the garlic into approximately 1/8-inch pieces. Don't go nuts trying to get them all the same size.

Set a fine-mesh strainer over a heatproof container. Pour enough oil into a small pan to reach a depth of 3/4 inch or so. Set the pan over high heat and bring the oil to 275°F. (Or test whether the oil is hot enough: as soon as a piece of garlic added to the oil the piece bubbles right away, add the rest.) Add the garlic, then immediately turn the heat to low (don't be tempted to rush the process with high heat), and stir once or twice.

Cook, stirring and scraping the sides occasionally and adjusting the heat to maintain a gentle sizzle, until the garlic is light golden brown and completely crisp, 4 to 6 minutes. If the process takes less time, that means the oil is too hot and you risk a bitter result. You'll quickly get the hang of it.

Pour the pan's contents through the strainer, reserving the flavorful oil. Gently shake the strainer, then transfer the garlic in more or less one layer to paper towels to drain and cool. Because the garlic continues to cook after it leaves the oil, by this time it will have gone from light golden brown to golden brown.

The fried garlic will keep in an airtight container in a cool, dry place (not in the fridge) for up to 2 days. Any more and you risk losing crunch and flavor. The strained oil keeps in an airtight container for up to 2 weeks.

Hom Daeng Jiaw and Naam Man Hom Daeng

FRIED SHALLOTS AND SHALLOT OIL

SPECIAL EQUIPMENT

• A fine-mesh strainer

Same deal as fried garlic: A simple process leaves you with both a crisp garnish as well as a flavorful oil that you'll use to stir-fry and to season. Remember that the shallots will continue to cook after they leave the oil, so the key is to remove them when they're crisp and brown but not too dark.

Flavor Profile SLIGHTLY SWEET, AROMATIC, SLIGHTLY BITTER (FRIED SHALLOTS); AROMATIC, RICH (SHALLOT OIL)

MAKES 5 TO 6 TABLESPOONS FRIED SHALLOTS AND ABOUT 2 CUPS OF OIL

3 ounces peeled small shallots, preferably Asian (about 6)

About 2 cups vegetable oil

Halve the shallots lengthwise, remove the peel, and slice them against the grain as thinly as you can. (To do it especially quickly and accurately, use a mandoline.) You're shooting for slices that are all about 1/16-inch thick.

Set a fine-mesh strainer over a heatproof container. Pour enough oil into a small pan to reach a depth of 3/4 inch or so. Set the pan over high heat and bring the oil to 275°F. (Or test whether the oil is hot enough: as soon as a piece of shallot added to the oil bubbles right away, add the rest.) Add the shallots, then immediately turn the heat to low (don't be tempted to rush the process with high heat), and stir once or twice.

Cook, stirring and scraping the sides occasionally and adjusting the heat to maintain a gentle sizzle, until

the shallots are deep golden brown and completely crisp, 10 to 20 minutes. If the process takes less time, that means the oil is too hot and you risk a bitter result. You'll quickly get the hang of it.

Pour the pan's contents through the strainer, reserving the flavorful oil. Gently shake the strainer, then transfer the shallots to paper towels to drain and cool in more or less one layer. Because the shallots continue to cook after they leave the oil, by this time they will have gone from deep golden brown to deep brown.

The fried shallots will keep in an airtight container in a cool, dry place (not in the fridge) for up to 2 days. Any more and you risk losing crunch and flavor. The strained oil keeps in an airtight container for up to 2 weeks.

Kapi Kung

SPECIAL EQUIPMENT

- **Cheesecloth**
- **A Thai granite mortar and pestle**

My friends in Northern Thailand prefer a different shrimp paste than the kind we can easily get in jars here. It's called *kapi kung* and it's made from shrimp, unlike jarred *kapi*, which is made from another crustacean called *khoei*. If you find *kapi kung* in the US, please call me right away. Otherwise, you must recreate its distinctive flavor—salty and funky but decidedly more subtle than regular *kapi*, sort of like the difference between supermarket anchovies and the fancy Sicilian kind. The process is painless and the result keeps in the fridge for up to 6 months.

Flavor Profile **FUNKY, SALTY**

MAKES ABOUT 1 CUP

2 cups jarred Korean salted shrimp (look for the Choripdong brand in Korean grocery stores)

2 tablespoons Thai shrimp paste (called gapi or kapi)

Briefly rinse the salted shrimp, then put them in a double layer of cheesecloth and gently squeeze out most of the liquid.

Mix the salted shrimp and shrimp paste together in the mortar and pound, stirring occasionally with a spoon, until you have a coarse paste that's a more or less even light brown color, 3 to 5 minutes. It's fine if there are very small pieces of salted shrimp.

The paste keeps in an airtight container in the fridge for up to 6 months.

Naam Makham

SPECIAL EQUIPMENT

• A fine-mesh strainer

Tamarind pulp is a sticky, fibrous mass. Many of this book's recipes require turning it into a liquid extract. All you do is combine the pulp with boiling water, let it sit, mush it up, and strain the solids. Follow the recipe the first few times you do it (the ratio of water to pulp will give the liquid the proper intensity). Later you might be able to get away with eyeballing it.

Flavor Profile TART

MAKES ABOUT 3 CUPS

4 ounces seedless tamarind pulp (also called tamarind paste)

3 1/2 cups water

Combine the pulp and the water in a medium pot. Bring the water to a boil over high heat, breaking up the tamarind (preferably with a sturdy whisk) as it softens, then immediately turn off the heat, cover the pot, and let the mixture sit until the tamarind is very soft, about 30 minutes. There's no need to skim off the foam that may form on the surface.

Use a whisk or wooden spoon to mash and stir to break up any large clumps, then strain the mixture into a bowl through a mesh strainer, stirring, pressing, and smashing the solids to extract as much liquid as possible. There may be pulp clinging to the outside of the strainer. Add that to the bowl too. Discard the remaining solids. Stir well before each use.

The tamarind water keeps in the fridge for up to a week and in the freezer for up to 3 months. Freeze it in small portions, perhaps in ice cube trays (transferring the cubes to airtight containers once they're frozen).

Naam Cheuam Naam Taan Piip

Some recipes call for a dead-simple syrup made from palm sugar and water. You can easily double or quadruple the amounts.

Flavor Profile SWEET

MAKES ABOUT 1/2 CUP

2 1/2 ounces palm sugar, coarsely chopped

1/4 cup plus 1 tablespoon water

Combine the sugar and the water in a very small pot or pan. Set it over medium heat and cook, stirring and breaking up the sugar as it softens, just until the sugar has completely dissolved. If the water begins to bubble before the sugar has completely dissolved, turn off the heat and let it finish dissolving in the hot liquid.

Let it cool before storing. The syrup keeps in an airtight container in the fridge for up to 2 weeks.

Naam Jim Kai

SWEET CHILE DIPPING SAUCE

SPECIAL
EQUIPMENT

- A Thai granite mortar
and pestle or a
food processor

Most of us have had the sickly sweet jarred version of this Thai dipping sauce for fried and grilled foods. The real thing is in fact also quite sugary but balanced with acidity and heat. It's just the thing for Kai Yaang (Whole roasted young chicken), page 135.

Flavor Profile SWEET, SPICY, SLIGHTLY SOUR

MAKES ABOUT 1¼ CUPS

1 cup granulated sugar	½ cup water	1¼ ounces peeled garlic cloves, halved lengthwise
¼ cup plus 2 tablespoons distilled white vinegar, preferably a Thai brand	21 grams fresh or drained pickled red Thai chiles, coarsely sliced	1 teaspoon kosher salt

Combine the sugar, vinegar, and water in a medium pot set it over high heat, bring to a vigorous simmer, and cook for 10 minutes or so, whisking to help dissolve the sugar.

Meanwhile, pound the chiles, garlic, and salt in a granite mortar (or pulse in a food processor) to a very coarse paste. Stir the mixture into the pot.

Decrease the heat to maintain a steady simmer and cook until the liquid thickens slightly and becomes just slightly syrupy, 8 to 12 minutes. The sauce will thicken as it cools. Let it cool to room temperature.

Use right away or refrigerate in an airtight container for up to a few months.

Naam Jim Kai Yaang

Mr. Lit serves a particularly fine version of this tangy, spicy sauce with Kai Yaang (Whole roasted young chicken), page 135. This is a rustic dip, so there's no need to strain out any stray tamarind skin.

Flavor Profile SPICY, SOUR, FRUITY

MAKES ABOUT 1³/4 CUPS

4 ounces palm sugar, coarsely chopped

¹/4 cup Thai fish sauce

1 ounce seedless tamarind pulp (also called tamarind paste)

1¹/4 cups water

1 tablespoon Phrik Phon Khua (Toasted-chile powder), page 270, or more to taste

Combine the palm sugar, fish sauce, tamarind pulp, and water in a medium pot. Set the pot over high heat, bring the mixture to a boil, then immediately decrease the heat to maintain a simmer. Use a whisk or spoon to break up the palm sugar and tamarind pulp as they soften and cook just until the tamarind has fully softened and dissolved into the mixture, 5 to 8 minutes.

Stir in the chile powder, turn off the heat, and let the mixture sit, stirring occasionally, until it has cooled to room temperature. Use it right away or refrigerate in an airtight container for up to a week.

Jaew

SPECIAL EQUIPMENT

- A Thai granite mortar and pestle

Just about any grilled meat—Sii Khrong Muu Yaang (Thai-style pork ribs), page 128, in particular—benefits from a dunk in this fiery stuff. It's not all about the heat, though. There's plenty of umami from fish and soy sauces, tartness from lime, and aroma from toasted rice powder, stirred in just before serving.

Flavor Profile FIERY, TART, UMAMI-RICH, AROMATIC

MAKES A GENEROUS 1/2 CUP (THE RECIPE IS EASILY DOUBLED)

SAUCE

10 grams thinly sliced lemongrass (tender parts only), from about 2 large stalks

2 tablespoons Thai fish sauce

1 1/2 tablespoons Thai thin soy sauce

3/4 teaspoon Thai seasoning sauce

3 1/2 tablespoons lime juice (preferably from Key limes or spiked with a small squeeze of Meyer lemon juice)

1 1/2 tablespoons Naam Cheuam Naam Taan Piip (Palm sugar simple syrup), page 275

1 1/2 tablespoons Phrik Phon Khua (Toasted-chile powder), page 270

TO FINISH THE SAUCE

1 tablespoon Khao Khua (Toasted–sticky rice powder), page 271

1 tablespoon coarsely chopped cilantro (thin stems and leaves), lightly packed

Pound the lemongrass in a granite mortar until you have a coarse, fibrous paste, about 45 seconds. Scrape the paste into a medium bowl or container and stir in the fish sauce, thin soy sauce, seasoning sauce, lime juice, simple syrup, and chile powder. Let it sit at room temperature for at least 1 hour (it'll get even better) or in the fridge for up to 2 days.

Right before you serve it, let it come to room temperature, then stir in the toasted-rice powder and cilantro.

Phrik Naam Som

SPECIAL EQUIPMENT

• **A Thai granite mortar and pestle**

A welcome sight beside Kuaytiaw Pet Tuun (Stewed duck noodle soup), page 200, or Khao Kha Muu (Pork shank stewed with five spice), page 185, this yellow sauce provides bracing acidity from vinegar and a flavorful punch from chiles. This is not meant to be a spicy condiment, so make sure to use fairly mild chiles. The sauce will range in color from the yellow-orange (pictured on page 202) to yellowish green, depending on the chiles.

Flavor Profile SOUR, SLIGHTLY AROMATIC, AND BARELY SPICY

MAKES ABOUT 1 1/2 CUPS

3 1/2 ounces fairly mild, not particularly sweet yellow or yellowish green chiles, such as Fresnos, Anaheim, gueros, or Hungarian wax, seeded and cut into approximately 1/4-inch slices

7 grams cilantro roots, thinly sliced

1 1/2 teaspoons kosher salt

1 ounce peeled garlic cloves, halved lengthwise

1 cup white vinegar, preferably a Thai brand

2 tablespoons granulated sugar

Bring a medium pot of water to a boil, add the chiles, and cook just until the chiles have lost their raw texture and flavor, about 45 seconds. Drain them well.

Pound the cilantro roots and salt in a granite mortar to a coarse, slightly fibrous paste, about 15 seconds.

Pound in the garlic until it's fully broken down, then add the chiles and pound until you have a coarse paste, about 1 minute. Stir in the vinegar and sugar until the sugar fully dissolves. Serve right away or store in the fridge in an airtight container for up to 3 days.

Naam Jim Seafood

SPICY, TART DIPPING SAUCE FOR SEAFOOD

It's funny, but this tart, spicy *naam jim* (dipping sauce) is known in Thailand as "naam jim seafood." You'd expect the Thai word *thaleh* to finish the phrase instead of its English equivalent. Perhaps the use of English began as an attempt to communicate to foreigners how much they'll love this stuff with grilled shrimp, squid, and fish.

That said, despite its title, the sauce eats well with grilled protein of virtually any sort. At Pok Pok, we often serve it alongside Kha Muu Thawt (Deep-fried stewed pork shank), page 187, as well as beside Plaa Thawt (Deep-fried whole fish), page 83, and Kung Op Wun Sen (Shrimp and glass noodles baked in a clay pot), page 210.

It will keep several days in the fridge, though it tastes best just after you make it.

Flavor Profile SPICY, SOUR, SWEET

SPECIAL EQUIPMENT

- A charcoal grill (highly recommended), grates oiled
- 1 or 2 wood skewers (but only if you're grilling), soaked in tepid water for 30 minutes
- A Thai granite mortar and pestle

MAKES ABOUT 1 CUP

21 grams fresh green Thai (about 14) or serrano (about 3) chiles

7 grams cilantro roots, thinly sliced

1/2 teaspoon kosher salt

21 grams peeled garlic cloves, halved lengthwise

6 tablespoons lime juice (preferably from Key limes or spiked with a small squeeze of Meyer lemon juice)

1/4 cup Thai fish sauce

1 tablespoon plus 2 teaspoons granulated sugar

2 tablespoons coarsely chopped cilantro (thin stems and leaves), lightly packed

Prepare a grill, preferably charcoal, to cook over high heat (see page 124), or preheat a grill pan or skillet over high heat. If you're grilling, skewer the chiles through the sides.

Cook the chiles, turning them over once or twice, until both sides are completely blistered and almost completely blackened and the flesh is completely cooked, 8 to 10 minutes, depending on the size of the chiles. Remove the chiles from the skewers and use your fingers or a small knife to peel them. You don't have to remove every last bit of skin. In fact, you want to see bits of char in the finished sauce.

Combine the cilantro roots and salt in a granite mortar and pound to a fairly smooth, slightly fibrous paste, about 30 seconds. Pound in the garlic until it's fully incorporated, about 1 to 2 minutes. Add the chiles and pound them until you have a fairly smooth paste (the seeds will still be visible), about 1 minute more.

Scrape the paste into a bowl or other container, then add the lime juice, fish sauce, and sugar, and stir well. Let the sauce sit for an hour or two before you serve it. It'll taste even better after it does. Right before you serve it, stir in the cilantro.

Naam Jim Sateh

To appease the peanut sauce brigade, and because the stuff is labor intensive to make, here's a recipe for close to a quart. Some peanut sauce has just one dimension: sweetness. This one is sweet, sure, but it's complex and herbal, too. The dose of lemongrass, turmeric, and galangal sees to that. The sauce is a dip for *sateh*. The typical Thai name for it (which essentially translates as "sauce for *sateh*") underscores this point and hints at its foreign origin (that is, people don't call it *naam jim thua lisong*, "peanut sauce"). I do not recommend just dumping it on rice, as do many American diners, though if you do, well, no one will know but you.

Flavor Profile SWEET, RICH, AND SLIGHTLY EARTHY

MAKES ABOUT 3 1/2 CUPS

PASTE

4 grams puya chiles (about 2), stemmed but not seeded

2 teaspoons kosher salt

1 ounce thinly sliced lemongrass (tender parts only)

1 (21-gram) piece peeled fresh or frozen (not defrosted) galangal, thinly sliced against the grain

1 (21-gram) piece peeled fresh or frozen (not defrosted) yellow turmeric root, thinly sliced against the grain

1 ounce peeled garlic cloves, halved lengthwise

1 1/4 ounces peeled Asian shallots, thinly sliced against the grain

SAUCE

1 cup coarsely chopped unsalted roasted peanuts

1 1/2 cups unsweetened coconut cream (preferably boxed)

3 ounces palm sugar, coarsely chopped

1 1/2 cups unsweetened coconut milk (preferably boxed)

5 tablespoons Naam Makham (Tamarind water), page 275

Kosher salt

MAKE THE PASTE

Combine the dried chiles and salt in the mortar and pound firmly, scraping the mortar and stirring the mixture occasionally, until you have a fairly fine powder, about 3 minutes. Add the lemongrass and pound, occasionally stopping to scrape down the sides of the mortar, until you have a fairly smooth, slightly fibrous paste, about 2 minutes. Do the same with the galangal, then the turmeric, then the garlic, and then the shallots, fully pounding each ingredient before moving on to the next.

You'll have about 1/2 cup of paste. You can use it right away, or store it in an airtight container in the fridge for up to 1 week or in the freezer for up to 6 months. You'll need 6 tablespoons of the paste for 3 1/2 cups of peanut sauce (you can freeze the leftover paste for a mini-batch of peanut sauce).

MAKE THE SAUCE

Process the peanuts in a food processor (or pound in a mortar) until they look like very chunky, slightly dry peanut butter.

Pour 1/2 cup of the coconut cream in a medium pot or a wok and set it over high heat. Bring the cream to a boil, stirring often, then decrease the heat to maintain a steady simmer. Cook, stirring occasionally, until the cream has reduced by about half and "breaks"—it'll look like curdled milk—anywhere from 3 to 10 minutes, depending on the brand of coconut cream. What

{continued}

{Peanut Sauce, continued}

you're doing as you simmer is cooking off the water in the cream so you're left with some white-ish solids but primarily the translucent fat, which you'll use to fry the curry paste. Patience is essential here. (If for some reason it doesn't crack after 10 minutes, add a tablespoon of vegetable oil, but know that the sauce will be oilier than it should be.)

Decrease the heat to medium-low, add 6 tablespoons of the paste, and cook, breaking it up a bit at first, then stirring often, until it's very fragrant and the garlic and shallots in the paste no longer smell raw, about 3 minutes. Add the palm sugar and cook, breaking up the palm sugar and stirring often, until the palm sugar is completely melted, about 2 minutes. Add the remaining coconut cream and the coconut milk, increase the heat to medium-high, and let the mixture come to a simmer. Add the peanuts and tamarind water, adjust the heat to maintain a gentle simmer (don't let it boil), and cook until the sauce has thickened slightly and the flavor has concentrated, about 8 minutes. Turn off the heat and let the sauce sit until it has cooled to room temperature. It'll thicken further as it cools. Season to taste with salt.

Use it right away and store any extra in an airtight container in the fridge for up to a week.

Yam Makheua Thet

FISH SAUCE-SOAKED TOMATOES

This simple concoction eats especially well with Laap Meuang (Northern Thai minced pork salad), page 106, but it also goes great with anything that deserves a little extra salt, funk, and heat. In a rare departure from the way they do it in Thailand, I use sweet, ripe summer tomatoes here instead of the crunchy and tart ones you'd see there.

Flavor Profile SALTY, SPICY, SLIGHTLY SWEET AND TART

MAKES ABOUT 1½ CUPS

1½ tablespoons Thai fish sauce

1½ tablespoons water

Scant ½ teaspoon granulated sugar

1 pound ripe tomatoes, cut into bite-size wedges (about 1½ cups)

6 grams fresh Thai chiles (about 4), preferably green, thinly sliced

1 tablespoon coarsely chopped cilantro (thin stems and leaves), lightly packed

Combine the fish sauce, water, and sugar in a serving bowl and stir well to dissolve the sugar. Add the tomatoes and chiles, stir well, and just before you serve it, add the cilantro.

Ajaat

As instrumental to the *sateh* experience as peanut sauce, this spicy, sweet-tart, crunchy relish is just what your palate needs in between bites of smoky meat and rich sauce. That said, any grilled meat would benefit from this stuff.

Flavor Profile TART, SWEET, SPICY

MAKES ABOUT 2¼ CUPS

8 ounces medium, crisp, thin-skinned cucumbers, quartered lengthwise and cut into ¼-inch-thick triangular slices (about 1½ cups)

3 ounces peeled small shallots, preferably Asian, cut into pieces about the same size as the cucumbers (about ¾ cup)

6 grams fresh red Thai chiles (about 4), thinly sliced

6 tablespoons white vinegar, preferably a Thai brand

6 tablespoons granulated sugar

¼ teaspoon kosher salt

½ cup water

A generous ¼ cup cilantro leaves, lightly packed

Combine the cucumbers, shallots, and chiles in a serving bowl. In a separate bowl, whisk together the vinegar, sugar, salt, and water until the sugar has completely dissolved. Pour enough of this mixture into the bowl with the cucumbers to cover them and stir well.

The relish will be ready to eat after just a few minutes. You can also cover and store it in the fridge for up to 1 day. Sprinkle with the cilantro leaves right before serving.

Cu Cai

PICKLED CARROT AND DAIKON RADISH

I'm still shocked, even after all these years, that most customers pound our Vietnamese chicken wings (page 249) and leave the vegetation I serve with them on the plate. Shocked, because these dead-simple pickles—sweet, tart, and crunchy—are just the thing, along with fresh cucumber and herbs, to eat between bites of those intensely flavored wings.

Flavor Profile SWEET, TART

SERVES 8 AS A SNACK OR PARTNER TO A MEAL

1/2 cup granulated sugar

6 tablespoons white vinegar, preferably a Thai brand

1 teaspoon kosher salt

1 cup water

About 8 ounces peeled carrots, cut into approximately 5-inch-long, 1/2-inch-thick sticks

About 8 ounces peeled daikon radish, cut into approximately 5-inch-long, 1/2-inch-thick sticks

Mix the sugar, vinegar, salt, and water in a large, preferably straight-sided container until the sugar has fully dissolved. Mix the carrot and daikon together and add them to the container, gently pushing them down so they're more or less submerged.

Cover the container and store in the fridge for at least 4 hours or up to 1 day.

Phrik Tam Naam Som

GRILLED-CHILE VINEGAR

SPECIAL EQUIPMENT

- **A charcoal grill (highly recommended), grates oiled**
- **1 or 2 wood skewers (but only if you're grilling), soaked in tepid water for 30 minutes**
- **A Thai granite mortar and pestle**

MAKES ABOUT ½ CUP

Two noodle dishes in this book—Kuaytiaw Reua (Boat noodles), page 204, and Ba Mii Tom Yam Muu Haeng (Spicy, sweet, tart noodles with pork, peanuts, and herbs), page 207—require this simple concoction, but the spicy, acidic liquid, aromatic from grilled fresh green chiles, makes a great condiment for any dish that needs a spark.

Flavor Profile TART, SPICY, AROMATIC

1 ounce stemmed fresh green Thai (about 16) or serrano (about 4) chiles	**6 tablespoons white vinegar, preferably a Thai brand**

Prepare a grill, preferably charcoal, to cook over high heat (see page 124), or preheat a grill pan or skillet over high heat. If you're grilling, skewer the chiles through the sides. Cook the chiles, frequently turning them over and occasionally pressing on them to help them cook evenly, until both sides are completely blistered and almost completely blackened and the flesh is fully soft, about 5 minutes total for the Thai chiles and about 10 for the serrano chiles.

Take the chiles off the skewers and roughly slice them (nope, don't peel them). Pound the chiles in a granite mortar to a very chunky paste, about 30 seconds, then stir in the vinegar.

This chile vinegar keeps in an airtight container in the fridge for up to 5 days.

Phrik Naam Plaa

FISH SAUCE-SOAKED CHILES

This two-ingredient condiment barely deserves a recipe: you just pour fish sauce over thinly sliced Thai chiles—but these proportions make a good guideline. It's on the table whenever I make dishes like Kai Kaphrao Khai Dao (Stir-fried chicken with hot basil), page 189, Khao Phat Muu (Thai-style fried rice with pork), page 191, Phat Phak Ruam Mit (Stir-fried mixed vegetables), page 98, or even a plate of jasmine rice topped with a fried egg—anything that benefits from a little extra salt, umami, and heat.

Flavor Profile SALTY, FUNKY, SPICY, AROMATIC

MAKES A GENEROUS 1/2 CUP	21 grams fresh Thai chiles (about 14), preferably green, thinly sliced	About 1/2 cup Thai fish sauce About 2 tablespoons thinly sliced garlic (optional)

Combine the ingredients in a bowl or container and stir.
Covered, it keeps for only two or so days in the fridge.

Phrik Naam Som

VINEGAR-SOAKED CHILES

Another recipe-in-name-only, the combination of vinegar and chiles makes a classic member of the *khruang phrung* ("four flavors") on tables at noodle shops.

Flavor Profile TART, MODERATELY SPICY, AROMATIC

MAKES ABOUT 3/4 CUP	21 grams fresh serrano chiles (about 3), thinly sliced	1/2 cup white vinegar, preferably a Thai brand

Combine the ingredients in a bowl or container and stir.
Covered, it keeps for 4 to 5 days in the fridge.

Naam Phrik Phao

ROASTED CHILE PASTE

Khao soi always comes with this dark, oily chile paste alongside for you to season your bowl. It adds smoky depth and welcome heat (though keep in mind that *khao soi* isn't meant to be super spicy). At Pok Pok, we use the same paste to make the spicy version of Ike's Vietnamese Fish-Sauce Wings (page 249).

Flavor Profile FIERY AND SLIGHTLY BITTER

MAKES A GENEROUS ¼ CUP

¼ cup vegetable oil

1 ounce dried Thai chiles (about 1 cup)

A very small drizzle of Asian sesame oil (look for brands that are 100 percent sesame oil)

Heat the oil in a wok or frying pan over low heat until it shimmers. Add the chiles and cook, stirring frequently, until they're evenly dark brown but not black, 10 to 15 minutes. Ideally every chile will be the same color, but you'll inevitably have some that are lighter than others.

Use a slotted spoon to transfer the chiles to a food processor, reserving the oil, and let them cool. Process to a coarse paste. (Alternatively, you can pound them in a granite mortar.) Stir in just enough of the reserved oil to saturate the paste but not so much that it's swimming in oil. (The consistency should be like that of chunky peanut butter.) Stir in the sesame oil.

You can store the paste in an airtight container at room temperature for up to 6 months.

acknowledgments

This book is dedicated to the cooks of Thailand, in homes and at restaurants, food carts, and market stalls. *Pok Pok* is a celebration of what you make, which deserves much more recognition than it gets.

No one is more important to my journey of learning than my dear friend, teacher, and kitchen compatriot Sunny Chailert. Thank you for your patience, your generosity, your selfless sharing of knowledge, and your prejudice for the *chao wang*. And please don't hesitate to smack me on the back with a vegetable if I'm not living up to your standards.

I would never have started down this path in the first place were it not for Chris and Lakhana Ward. Thank you for introducing me to my future those twenty-odd years ago. I hope that we will all be together again soon, cooking in your kitchen in Mu Baan Saluang Nai—where it all began.

And to Lakhana's family—Da Chom, Chai Cha Tri, and all the brothers, sisters, cousins, sons, daughters, nephews, nieces, and in-laws from the Doomkham clan—thank you for the years of hospitality, wisdom, and kindness. I will always return to Chiang Mai.

To Ajaan Suneemas Noree, thank you for your early teachings, your kindness and humor over the years, and your friendship. Okay, go!

To chef David Thompson, for being first an inspiration, then a hero, and finally a dear friend, trusted advisor, and relentlessly bad influence. Am I still banned?

Mr. Lit, thank you for being open to this curious *farang*, for helping me buy and modify my first rotisserie, and becoming a good friend who I look forward to seeing every year. Keep on writing and enjoy your

retirement—your daughter is carrying the torch forward perfectly!

To all the cooks that I have learned from and continue to learn from, especially to those in Chiang Mai and Northern Thailand: Thank you for your generosity and for sharing with me what you know. I hope I have conveyed how incredible and delicious the food you produce every day for your customers, families, and friends truly is.

To all the employees of Pok Pok enterprises, for your hard work! You all share in the accomplishment of bringing this book to fruition.

To the amazing team at Ten Speed—especially my editors, Jenny Wapner and Emily Timberlake, and the book's designer, Toni Tajima—for making this first outing as painless as you could and for helping me create a book I'm incredibly proud of. Aaron Wehner, great team you have there. Thank you for the guidance and for bringing this to fruition.

To Kimberly Witherspoon, my terrifyingly skillful and elegant agent. I don't know how you decided that I was worthy of a place in your incredible stable but I'm grateful you took me on.

To JJ "Hap-pee" Goode: Thank you for putting up with a grump and his bombast, for the extracurricular recipe testing and your OCD, for knowing what to do and when to do it, and for the endless "*laap, laap, laap, laap*." I do not envy your job and am amazed by the skill and grace with which you navigate the process. BTW, your wife is a saint for putting up with the endless "*laap, laap, laap, laap.*"

To Austin "How the fuck do you eat and drink so much and stay so skinny" Bush, for working your ass off on the incredible photos, for sharing your encyclopedic knowledge of Thai food, language and culture, for your translation and guide skills, and for introducing me to so much great food over the years. And for introducing me to Megachef and MegaPaul (holler)!

To my best friend and de facto brother Adam Levey, thank you for always believing in me, no matter how crazy I seem to be going, and for using your unparalleled skill in making this book even more beautiful. Love you, man.

To Andrea Slonecker, thank you for making your house smell like fish sauce for a month while testing these recipes.

Special shout out to Ba Daa, our kitchen assistant in Saluang Nai!

To the city of Portland and its denizens: I love you and miss you when I'm not home. Thank you for making Pok Pok, and hence this book, possible.

And thank you coffee, for without you we would never have made the deadlines. I am worthless without a good cup of coffee.

Khop khun maak khrap thuk khon!

index

Library of Congress Cataloging-in-Publication Data
Ricker, Andy.
   Pok Pok : food and stories from the streets, homes,
and roadside restaurants of Thailand / Andy Ricker
with JJ Goode : [foreword by] David Thompson.
      pages cm
1. Cooking, Thai. I. Goode, JJ II. Title.
   TX724.5.T5R53 2013
   641.9593—dc23
                  2013012451

Hardcover ISBN: 978-1-60774-288-3
eBook ISBN: 978-1-60774-289-0

Printed in China

Design by Toni Tajima
Photo look and color by Adam Levey

10 9 8 7 6

First Edition